Hogs, Blogs,
Leathers and Lattes

# Hogs, Blogs, Leathers and Lattes

*The Sociology of Modern American Motorcycling*

WILLIAM E. THOMPSON

McFarland & Company, Inc., Publishers
*Jefferson, North Carolina, and London*

LIBRARY OF CONGRESS CATALOGUING-IN-PUBLICATION DATA

Thompson, William E. (William Edwin), 1950–
    Hogs, blogs, leathers and lattes : the sociology of modern
American motorcycling / William E. Thompson.
        p.      cm.
    Includes bibliographical references and index.

    ISBN 978-0-7864-6859-1
    softcover : acid free paper ∞

    1. Motorcycling — Social aspects.   I. Title.
GV1059.5.T56  2012
796.7'5 — dc23                                    2012032916

BRITISH LIBRARY CATALOGUING DATA ARE AVAILABLE

Cover art: Marilyn R. Thompson, *Bikes, Books, Bill
and Bruno,* oil on canvas, 40" × 30", 2011

Manufactured in the United States of America

*McFarland & Company, Inc., Publishers
    Box 611, Jefferson, North Carolina 28640
    www.mcfarlandpub.com*

For Leah and Jaxon

# Contents

# Preface

Although I purchased my first motorcycle, a 1964 Honda Sport 50, and began riding almost daily at age 14, my love for motorcycles and riding began much earlier. When I was approximately five years old, my neighbor across the street rode an old BSA motorcycle to and from work. Each evening around five o'clock, I waited outside on the front porch until I heard the "roar" of his pipes (his BSA didn't really roar; in fact, it was barely audible more than a block away) as he turned the corner onto our street. I leapt from the porch and ran down the street as fast as I could, usually meeting him about 100 to 200 yards from our house. He stopped, reached down, lifted me up onto the passenger's pillion and I wrapped my arms around him as we sped (about 20–25 mph) to his driveway. As soon as he parked the bike under his carport, I leapt from the motorcycle, thanked him for the ride, and raced home before my father returned home from work or my mother realized what had taken place. Later, I discovered my neighbor had permission from my mother to give me that 30-second ride, but at the time he allowed me to think that we were doing something clandestine. On weekends I crossed the street to sit on the motorcycle, where I spent hours revving the engine and squealing the brakes until my voice became hoarse. I leaned into the curves and dodged imaginary obstacles as I dreamed of motorcycle adventures yet to come.

This book is *not* about motorcycle gangs, outlaw bikers, or riders committed to the biker lifestyle. In fact, it's not about *hardcore bikers* at all, except to compare and contrast them to modern-day motorcyclists. It's about women and men like my neighbor across the street who owned his own home (or at least was purchasing it), worked a 40-hour-per-week job, was raising a family, and drove a car as his primary means of transportation, but rode a motorcycle to and from work because it saved a few dollars, and more importantly, rode as often as possible because he loved to ride motorcycles. It's about people like me, a college professor who owns three automobiles, but would rather travel on two-wheeled vehicles whenever the opportunity arises. In short, this book is about motorcycle enthusiasts and what I call the *motorcyclist sub-culture*.

You may be asking about the difference between a "biker" and a "motor-cyclist." That is a valid question, and not as easily answered as a simple dichotomy might suggest. As with any categorization of people, the "catego-rizer" soon learns that because riders are people, very few of them fit neatly into any niche, and categories are rarely mutually exclusive or exhaustive. Nevertheless, my 45 plus years of riding experience combined with more than 5 years of sociological research on the topic reveal that there are a few simi-larities but a wide range of differences between *bikers* and *motorcyclists*. The obvious common denominator is a love of motorcycles and riding. Beyond that, however, in many ways the two categories (and subcategories within each) of riders and their social worlds could not be more different. This book is an attempt to clarify those distinctions and to focus on the growing sub-culture of motorcyclists in the United States, comparing and contrasting the two different worlds of riders, while avoiding oversimplifications, misleading stereotypes, and value judgments about either group.

Because I am a sociologist and for the most part reject biological deter-minism, I refuse to believe that some people are "born to ride" while others are not (although experience with my grandson's seemingly innate love of motorcycles has raised questions). I am thoroughly convinced, however, that there are those among us who, whether we ride or not, are almost mystically attracted to motorcycles. We are the people who always turn and look when we hear the roar of a V-twin engine and cannot walk past a parked motorcycle, regardless of make, model, or color, without stopping to take a closer look while others never even notice. This book is written for the former and will be of little or no interest to the latter, unless they live with, know, or want to better understand those who are inexplicably drawn to life on two wheels.

Data for this book are primarily the result of more than five years of participant observation at motorcycle shows, rallies, and other motorcycling events including extensive ethnographic interviews with more than two hun-dred (224 exactly) fellow riders. Moreover, these research data are described, analyzed, and interpreted within the context of more than four decades of motorcycle riding experience.

Each chapter of this book begins with an opening vignette introducing the topic covered in that chapter. Most of these vignettes are actual accounts, either experienced or witnessed by me or told to me by one of the riders I interviewed. In some cases, the vignettes are composites of anecdotes related to me by more than one interviewee, and in one case (chapter 4), the vignette comes directly from another rider's personal experience that is well docu-mented in the bibliography. Nevertheless, pains were taken to keep all of these vignettes as accurate as possible and to insure that they reflect real-life experiences of motorcyclists in this study. Throughout the remainder of the manuscript, all direct quotes, statistics, and other data came directly from personal observations, interviews, or the source cited.

Unlike most scholarly works, this book is written in the first person. That is because it is highly personal. Nevertheless, great pains were taken to follow the rigorous requirements of qualitative social science field research design and data collection. Moreover, in the sociological tradition of Max Weber, analyses and interpretations are couched within the framework of *verstehen* and, while not totally value-free, are attempted to be as objective and accurate as humanly possible.

As with any book, there are a number of people who helped make this finished product possible. Special thanks go to my wife, Marilyn, who indulges my boyhood fantasies and "mid-life" crises, not only supporting me in my quest for expensive toys, but also understanding my need for adventure and thrills that sometimes flirt with danger and put both of us in harm's way. She also has become an accomplished ethnographic interviewer over the years, accompanying me to motorcycle rallies and shows, and gaining information and insight into the world of women riders that I otherwise would never have been able to obtain. My daughter, Mica, who rides her own motorcycle, has also been a great companion on rides and has been helpful in providing both a female and younger perspective on observations, interviews, events, and activities, not to mention how helpful she has been in reviewing and critiquing manuscript drafts. Her sociological insight was also very helpful throughout the book and especially in chapter 10.

Louis White, a lifelong motorcycle enthusiast as well as a long-time friend and riding companion, provided many valuable insights as we discussed motorcycling in general, and my research in particular, during long conversations over campfires, in tents, and in motel rooms on the road. His casual comment, "You know I've always loved and ridden motorcycles, but I never considered myself a biker," helped crystallize the framework for this book when my sociologically trained mind was overcomplicating the obvious. Special thanks go to Alan Buttell, a former student and longtime friend who has ridden motorcycles all his life. Alan helped with some of the photographs, reviewed the manuscript, and introduced me to Ron "the King" Loomis, another lifelong enthusiast whose riding experiences are worthy of a book in and of themselves. I also want to extend thanks to Jack Harred for reading earlier drafts of the manuscript and providing helpful suggestions regarding research methods, theoretical framework, and data analysis. He also introduced me to a group of "stunters," a segment of the riding population that otherwise might have gone ignored in my research.

A hearty thank you is extended to the thousands of men and women motorcyclists who are the subjects of this book. Their openness, friendliness, candor, camaraderie, and willingness to talk and share are the glue that holds the motorcycling "brotherhood" together. Also, thanks to the hardcore bikers out there who share the road with motorcyclists, tolerate our periodic intrusions into their world, and for the most part practice a spirit of détente and peaceful coexistence. Finally, a sincere thank you is in order to the car and truck drivers who do not pull out in front of motorcyclists, try to share our lane, left turn in front of us, or slam on their brakes unexpectedly while talking or texting on their cell phones. To those who do those things, my fellow riders and I would like to say ... never mind, I cannot put that in print, and they are probably unlikely to be reading this book anyway.

# Introduction

"Nobody — except another cyclist — likes a man on a motorcycle," proclaimed Hal Burton (1954) in a *Saturday Evening Post* article just one year after the premier of *The Wild One* (1953), starring a young Marlon Brando and an equally young Lee Marvin. That movie, destined to become a classic, was very loosely based on alleged events that took place one weekend in Hollister, California, when a band of motorcyclists invaded a small town, terrorized its citizens, paralyzed its police force, and created an indelible image of outlaw bikers that would last for decades, perhaps even to this day. Actually, the movie was based on a short story, "The Cyclists' Raid," by Frank Rooney published in the January 1951 issue of *Harper's* magazine that was itself derived from an article published in the July 21, 1947, issue of *Life* magazine, replete with exaggerated tales of the so-called "Hollister riot" and staged photographs of male and female models hired to pose as if intoxicated on motorcycles surrounded by broken beer bottles. Other accounts of bikers also relied on highly selective facts as well as pure fiction to reinforce the perception that people who rode motorcycles were notoriously rebellious, lawless, and predatory. Gonzo-journalist Hunter S. Thompson (1967), for example, rode with the Hell's Angels and wrote of their notorious exploits including illegal drugs, guns, fights, and general mayhem. Hell's Angels founder Sonny Barger (2001, 2005) confirmed most of these dangerous and criminal activities in his autobiographical accounts of the motorcycle club he helped establish. Numerous other articles have appeared in scholarly journals and books that document the violent and criminal nature of hardcore motorcycle clubs and gangs, widely referred to as one-percenters[1] (e.g., Montgomery, 1976, 1977; Watson, 1980; Hopper and Moore, 1990; Quinn, 1987, 2001; Quinn and Koch, 2003; Barker, 2007).

Where the literature and media documentaries are sparse, and where media portrayals and public perceptions of bikers differ markedly from social reality, is in the area of the other 99 percent of motorcycle riders. This is most notably the case regarding the millions of Baby Boomers and other working-middle- and upper-middle-class people who ride motorcycles. These riders tend to be married, hold full-time jobs, have mortgages, pay their bills and taxes on time, obey the laws, drive automobiles as their primary means of transportation, and happen to enjoy riding motorcycles, mostly for leisure activities and recreational purposes. These millions of riders—truck drivers, plumbers, construction workers, and other blue-collar workers along with college students, doctors, lawyers, college professors, nurses, and other white-collar professionals—comprise the American motorcycle subculture and are the subjects of this book.

Chapter 1 compares and contrasts *bikers* with *motorcyclists,* creating and describing a typology of motorcycle riders with subcategories ranging from hardcore one-percenters and today's "new bikers" to Baby Boomer motorcycle enthusiasts, "Rolex Riders," "crotch rocketeers" and "stunters." Each of these categories and subcategories is worthy of a book in themselves, but the focus of this book is motorcyclists in general rather than any specialty group.

Chapter 2 provides a theoretical framework for the research in this study, drawing heavily from the rich sociological tradition of symbolic interaction and dramaturgical analysis merged with theories surrounding *edgework* and risk-taking behavior. The qualitative social science field research methods of participant observation and ethnographic interviewing are explained and the demographic characteristics of the 224 motorcyclists interviewed for this project are presented and summarized.

Members of one-percenter motorcycle clubs often wear a "1%er" diamond-shaped patch on their vests or jackets. This has led some motorcyclists to sport a similarly shaped "99%er" patch on their vests or jackets, declaring that they are not members of a one-percenter club.

In Chapter 3, values, attitudes, and beliefs of bikers and motorcyclists are explained, compared, and contrasted. Striking similarities yet important distinctions between bikers and motorcyclists are explored and presented in an overview of meaningful symbols for both groups.

The informal "biker brotherhood" that is well known among motorcycle riders in both fact and fiction is described and analyzed in Chapter 4 along with a brief list and description of formal organizations created by and for motorcyclists. The role of women in this "brotherhood" is introduced at the end of Chapter 4, and then much further developed in Chapter 5, which is about women and the motorcycling "sisterhood." Women have a long and rich tradition of riding motorcycles that is often overlooked and overshadowed by stereotypical roles assigned to them by hardcore bikers, various forms of media, and the general public. A typology of roles filled by women in today's motorcycle subculture is described, as is how women deal with the sexism of such a macho-driven environment and the techniques women riders use to attempt to feminize such a heavily male-dominated activity.

Chapter 6 looks at motorcycle shows and provides observational accounts of major biker rallies such as Laconia Motorcycle Week, Daytona Bike Week, and the Bikes, Blues and BBQ festival held in Fayetteville, Arkansas each year. Then, attention is turned to perhaps one of the most famous motorcycle rallies in the world: Sturgis, South Dakota. These rallies provide some of the rare times when hardcore bikers and motorcyclists come face-to-face and members of the two subcultures briefly intermingle.

Chapter 7 focuses on motorcycles and motorcyclists in motion pictures. We take a much more detailed look at the influence of what is often considered the first biker movie, *The Wild One* (1953); a sociological content analysis of it, along with two other popular biker movies, *Easy Rider* (1969) and *Wild Hogs* (2007), reveals a number of common and recurrent themes in the three films. Several other so-called "biker" movies are described and analyzed, and the chapter culminates with a discussion of the hypothesis that bikers and motorcyclists in movies are somewhat characterized as modern-day versions of the cowboys of yesteryear.

Chapter 8 continues a media theme, looking at the portrayal of motorcycles and motorcyclists on the small screen. Several popular television series have featured motorcyclists, as have a number of so-called "reality shows." Advertisers have not been unaware of the resurgence of interest in motorcycling and have capitalized on its renewed popularity in a wide variety of television commercials—some perpetuating popular stereotypes while others debunk and satirize them.

The Baby Boomers along with other middle- and upper-middle-class riders have not only contributed to increased sales of motorcycles and changing images of those who ride them, but their interest in technology and demand for creature comforts have led to a major transformation in motorcycles and motorcycling. No longer basically a bicycle with a motor, motorcycles now come equipped with cruise control, heated seats and grips, back-rests, floorboards, dashboards, antilock brakes, AM/FM satellite radios, MP3 players, GPS navigational systems, intercoms, and even airbags. All of these technological innovations, as well as mobile phones and computers, along with their impact on motorcycling, are discussed in Chapter 9.

The final chapter attempts to answer the question of why motorcyclists ride. Along with the obvious and most often cited factors of fun, excitement, exhilaration, and freedom, more complex sociological explanations are postulated, including a trend toward the "vulgarization" of the middle class, mid-life crises, and Baby Boomers[2] facing their mortality. Finally, the growing social and cultural phenomenon of risk-taking, or what some call living "on the edge," is suggested as a general social psychological framework for understanding the growing popularity of motorcycling in American society.

# CHAPTER 1

# *Bikers* and *Motorcyclists*

Dogs bark, a car alarm sounds, and some residents look up in disgust or fear, while others ignore the deafening sound of the pipes, as dozens of high-powered motorcycles roar into the small community, down the main street of town, and park in front of a small diner. Like a scene out of the classic Marlon Brando movie, *The Wild One,* the leather-clad riders dismount, shake the road dust and bug carcasses from their clothes and hair, and descend on the only establishment in town that sells both food and beer. Most of the men have moustaches or beards, some sport an earring in the left earlobe, and a few of them have colorful tattoos on their biceps, forearms, or shoulders. Almost all appear to be wearing the traditional biker "uniform" of leather boots, leather gloves, blue jeans or leather pants, and t-shirts or sleeveless shirts with motorcycle-related words or drawings peeking out from under black leather vests, many of which are covered with pins and colorful patches. Most wear helmets while a few sport either a black or colorful skullcap. Others wear bandanas with symbols of motorcycles, skulls, flames, and other colorful or fearsome decorations. One wears a baseball cap turned backwards on his head. Women who accompany some of the riders or ride their own bikes are clad in similar attire. Apparently, town residents have much to fear as it seems an outlaw biker gang has arrived to take over their town, and drinking, wild partying, fighting, and other forms of chaos, crime and deviance will ensue [Thompson, 2011: 164–65].

Actually, this is an example of "the first wisdom of sociology — things are not what they seem" (Berger, 1963: 23). The new arrivals are not gang members or part of an outlaw biker club. In fact, it could be argued that they are not even "bikers" at all. Rather, they are part of today's growing motorcycle subculture which is dominated by millions of Baby Boomer doctors, dentists, lawyers, corporate executives, and college professors, and comprised of other middle and upper-middle-class professionals as well as a host of blue collar workers of all races, ages, and sexes. By *subculture,* I mean a group that shares many elements of mainstream culture but maintains their own distinctive customs, values, norms, beliefs, traditions, and lifestyles (Thompson and Hickey, 2011). Who are these motorcyclists? How do they compare and contrast to the hardcore "biker" subculture comprised mainly of outlaw club members and one-percenters committed to the biker lifestyle? What differentiates them from so-called "real bikers" and the alleged "pseudo-bikers," "posers," and "wannabes" discussed in biker literature? What are the identifiable elements of their subculture that bind them in terms of attitudes, values, beliefs, norms, and meaningful symbols? And, most importantly, what motivates these middle- and upper-middle-class Baby Boomers to buy expensive motorcycles that cost more than some automobiles and spend thousands more on equipment and attire that may contribute to them being labeled as deviant or might even get them killed? These questions, along with my long-held interest and experience in motorcycling, prompted me to study what I call the American "motorcyclist" subculture.

Although the focus of this book is on motorcyclists, it is necessary to briefly describe the characteristics of hardcore and new bikers as compared to motorcycling enthusiasts in order to contrast the distinct subcultures. These depictions are meant to be generally descriptive and analytical while attempting to avoid stereotypes, and are not considered to be exhaustive or mutually exclusive. No doubt, some motorcycle riders could fit into both categories while others may not fit either. Nevertheless, these typologies provide insight into at least two distinctive subcultures that exist in the world of motorcycle riders: bikers and motorcyclists. In this chapter, I will establish a classification scheme of motorcycle riders and attempt to delineate some of the differences between "bikers" and "motorcyclists," admittedly a distinction that is somewhat blurred, and far from universally agreed upon in the motorcycle world.

## Establishing a Classification Scheme

Most accounts of bikers, whether based on fact or fiction, divide motorcycle riders into two distinct camps: *authentic* (or *real*) *bikers* and *posers* (or *wannabes*) (e.g., Barbieri, 2007). As with most dichotomies, dividing motorcycle riders into these two categories is overly simplistic and, for the most part, an inaccurate and misleading endeavor. Researchers tend to differentiate between "authentic" bikers— one-percenters and hardcore riders either affiliated or unaffiliated with clubs, but committed to the "biker lifestyle"— and "posers" or "wannabes"— basically everybody else who rides a cruiser or touring-style motorcycle. As best I can tell, this dichotomy originated with the one-percenters and hardcore bikers who believe they are the only *real* bikers. Nevertheless, there always have been and still are a wide variety of motorcycle riders who are neither one-percenters nor hardcore bikers, but also are not "posing" as them and they most certainly do not "wanna be" one of them.

This over-simplified dichotomy has led to many misunderstandings about bikers and motorcyclists and, in some cases, may have added to strained relations and even outright hostility between the two groups.

Some efforts have been made to more accurately divide the motorcycling world into two basic categories: bikers and motorcyclists. *Motorcycle News* columnist Fred Rau (2010a: 47), somewhat tongue-in-cheek and yet to some extent seriously, suggested that there are some subtle and not so subtle clues as to whether a rider is a "biker" or a "motorcyclist." At the risk of oversimplification and perpetuating stereotypes, I offer his paraphrased and heavily supplemented list of generalizations to help distinguish bikers and motorcyclists.

| *Bikers are more likely to* | *Motorcyclists are more likely to* |
|---|---|
| ride only Harley-Davidsons | own more than one motorcycle and ride a wide variety of brands and types of motorcycles |
| learn to ride by trial and error | take an MSF safety course |
| wear a beanie-type novelty helmet, do-rag, or skull cap | wear a DOT-approved full-face or modular helmet |
| wear all black riding gear (usually leather) | select riding gear for safety and maximum visibility |
| wear leather jackets with more than three zippers | wear brightly colored jackets with Kevlar or other types of protective padding or plates |
| purchase and install aftermarket pipes because they are loud and intimidating | purchase and have installed aftermarket pipes because they enhance performance and fuel efficiency, and perhaps safety |
| go to Sturgis as often as possible because it's a great party | go to Sturgis once because it seems interesting and all the new motorcycles are on display |
| occasionally read biker magazines containing photos of half-naked women, choppers and customized bikes on the cover and inside | subscribe to one or more motorcycle magazines which feature reviews of motorcycles and motorcycling equipment |

Although interesting and perhaps more accurate, this dichotomy is also oversimplified and more than a little bit stereotypical. It is always risky to create taxonomies or typologies that involve human beings because people rarely fit into the neat categories that researchers and others create to identify them. Trying to distinguish between "bikers" and "motorcyclists" is no exception, and as previously mentioned, like most typologies, the categories are neither exhaustive nor mutually exclusive. To complicate matters, if indeed there exists two broad categories of motorcycle riders, *bikers* and *motorcyclists*, then within each of those categories there are at least two or three subcategories, and perhaps even more. *Bikers* can probably be subdivided into at least three subcategories: (1) one-percenters; (2) hardcore bikers; (3) blue-collar bikers often referred to as *posers* or *wannabes* (a category I prefer to call "neo-bikers" or "new bikers"). Because this last subcategory, "neo-bikers," is so highly visible and is part of today's motorcycling subculture, I consider them to be almost a distinct third category somewhere between one-percenters/hardcore bikers and motorcyclists. Motorcyclists are an even more diverse group that can be subdivided into at least four subcategories: (1) "Rolex Riders" or "Rich Urban Bikers (RUBS);" (2) Motorcycle Enthusiasts; (3) "Crotch Rocketeers" "Stunters" and Racers; and (4) Dirt Bike and Off-Road Riders.

## "Bikers"

Since the end of World War II, or at least the 1950s, the public's image of motorcycle riders has been shaped largely by the exploits of the Hell's Angels and other "one-percenter" outlaw motorcycle gangs or, more likely, by media portrayals of them. Renegade bikers such as characters played by Marlon Brando, Lee Marvin, and James Dean dominated media images and public perceptions (although Dean never rode a motorcycle in a movie, he did in real life and his character in *Rebel Without a Cause* represented the rebellious, disenfranchised feelings that many young people related to riding motorcycles). These real-life people and make-believe characters are generally referred to as *bikers.* These rebellious bikers wore denim vests or leather jackets, boots and bandanas, displayed skulls and cross bones, sported tattoos, drank heavily, cursed, and brawled with rival gangs, law enforcement, or anybody else who got in their way. Whether portrayed accurately or not, their macho image and demeanor helped redefine masculinity and shaped public perception of bikers for decades (Willett, 2009).

Although these stereotypical images of bikers were not an accurate portrayal of all, or even most, motorcycle riders, there was an element of truth behind the stereotypes, especially for those bikers that later took the moniker "one-percenters" or "outlaw"[1] bikers." One-percenters of the 1950s tended to be World War II veterans who returned home from combat armed with little formal education, no jobs, and a fatalistic attitude fueled by the fact that they had seen dozens, if not hundreds, of their fellow soldiers' lives snuffed out at the age of 19 or 20 (Barger, et al., 2001). With very little fear, and an almost insatiable need for thrills and excitement, the motorcycle somewhat filled that need while simultaneously providing cheap and easy-to-fix transportation. Having just fought a war against Germany and Japan, these young bikers were not about to ride "kraut" or "jap" bikes, so the American-made Harley-Davidson became the motorcycle of choice.[2] Accustomed to the camaraderie provided by the military, some of these men formed motorcycle clubs, developed both informal and formal rules for membership, and developed a hierarchical system somewhat similar to rank in the service.

Whether because of its association with a deviant biker lifestyle, or a variety of other factors, American-made motorcycle sales slumped during the 1960s and 1970s, and the only remaining American manufacturer, Harley-Davidson, struggled to maintain solvency. Just prior to and during that time frame, Japanese manufacturers flooded the American market with less expensive, faster, sleeker, and quieter motorcycles that appealed to less rebellious types, and offered alternative transportation for working and middle-class people to and from work, or for weekend outings. Hardcore and one-percenter motorcyclists remained loyal to Harley-Davidson, but they comprised a very small part of the motorcycle market, most of whom were not purchasing new bikes. Meanwhile, Honda launched an advertising campaign in the mid-sixties with the slogan, "You meet the nicest people on a Honda," attempting to change the popular image of motorcycle riders from that of rebellious teenagers, hoodlums, and outlaws, to Mom, Dad, and the children out for a Sunday afternoon ride. These developments contributed to the emergence of today's motorcyclists, and as Jay Barbieri (2007: 17) quips in his *Biker's Handbook,* "defined the two sides of the American motorcycle culture.... The American-made motorcycle rider was an outlaw. The Japanese motorcycle rider was a well-respected, clean-cut, law-abiding citizen."

Similarly, in a more serious vein, Glynn Kerr (2011: 38) contends that motorcyclists and bikers wear "uniforms" that help distinguish them:

> As motorcyclists, both our bikes and our gear give out visual signals that identify us as a particular type of rider, and pre-supposes attitudes and behavior which accompany that group. The image projected by a mature BMW rider in a Gore-Tex suit couldn't be more at odds with a leather-clad outlaw with tattoos and a rat-bike.

More about these "uniforms" (motorcycling attire) and other meaningful symbols is discussed in chapter 3. Despite these oversimplifications, both Barbieri's and Kerr's analyses hold some elements of truth and help explain at least one of the differences between bikers and motorcyclists. An illustration of this distinction can be found in a post on the Road Runner Motorcycle Touring and Travel website from a rider who asked:

> Hello all. Im a newbie to riding, took my safety class this past june and picked up my new sportster in july. Sometimes I feel like a round peg in a square hole.

I enjoy the look and styling of the bike I bought, the size is matched well for my riding ability (883). Here is my thing, I dont fit the harley type stereotype. Im not into the group riding thing, I like to wear safety gear, Im clean cut and not into wearing t-shirts. I guess im looking for some feed back on what you think makes a motorcyclist or a biker. Does what someone drives matter either way. Thanks.

Numerous responses came in from the magazine's readers indicating that many of them also felt that they occupied a somewhat nebulous or marginalized status somewhere between that of being a "biker" or a "motorcyclist." Hence, the need for a "middle" category: "Neo-bikers"—riders who may emulate the hardcore biker lifestyle, but are not part of it. One-percenters and hardcore bikers are committed to a lifestyle (Hayes, 2010). Although my guess is that there always will be some ambiguity along these lines, despite the fact that neo-bikers are often mistaken for one-percenters and hardcore bikers, they know they are not really members of that tiny minority. In this case, looking like a duck, walking like a duck, and quacking like a duck does not make you a duck—especially to real ducks. These riders tend to have more in common with motorcyclists than they do with one-percenters or hardcore bikers, but they do not fit neatly into that broad category either. I think there is much credence to those who responded to the above query with "If you ride a motorcycle and enjoy it, who cares whether you are called a biker or a motorcyclist?" Nevertheless, I also know that labels are important. With apologies to Shakespeare, sociologically speaking, "a rose by any other name might *not* smell as sweet." As discussed in chapter 2, this book is couched within a symbolic interaction framework, focusing not only on the activities and behaviors of motorcyclists, but also on a wide array of meaningful symbols, one of the most important of which is language.

In order to set the stage for analysis of motorcyclists and who they are, it is important to first take a brief look at who and what they are *not*. Let's begin with a brief overview of the one-percenters and hardcore bikers and then look at the "neo-bikers" before turning our attention to the main focus of this book, motorcyclists and the motorcycle subculture.

## *"One-Percenters"*

Volumes have been written about bikers. As noted in the introduction to this book, most of these works focus on the activities and exploits of motorcycle clubs known as "one-percenters" ranging from the first-hand accounts of Gonzo-journalist Hunter S. Thompson (1967) who rode with the Hell's Angels, and Sonny Barger (2001, 2005), Hell's Angel's founder, to first-rate scholarly journal articles and books (e.g., Montgomery, 1976, 1977; Watson, 1980; Hopper and Moore, 1990; Quinn, 1987, 2001; Quinn and Koch, 2003;

Many motorcycle riders do not fit neatly into any particular category. These riders, for example, are decked out in leather and two of them have jackets with insignias indicating they are members of a motorcycle club. Members of the public might assume that they are hardcore bikers or one-percenters, or at least neo-bikers imitating that lifestyle. In reality, these middle-aged, middle-class riders can best be classified as motorcyclists who on this particular weekend were participating in a ride to help raise funds for the local high school booster club.

Barker, 2007). Other accounts abound; some based on fact and others solely based on fiction. Even more fictionalized and sensational accounts of bikers can be found in the American cinema ranging from the 1953 Marlon Brando classic *The Wild One* and the cult classic *Easy Rider* (1969), to the comedic adventures of *Wild Hogs* (2006). On the small screen, the FX television series *Sons of Anarchy* became an immediate hit with both the riding and non-riding public, and perpetuated the commonly perceived image of bikers. Chapters 7 and 8 take more in-depth looks at media portrayals of bikers and motorcyclists in motion pictures and on television.

Today's one-percenters trace their lineage back to those World War II veterans who formed some of the original "big four"[3] motorcycle clubs that later became dubbed as one-percenters. Consequently, their motorcycles,

attire, demeanor, and behaviors are not noticeably different from their predecessors. One-percenters almost exclusively ride Harley-Davidson motorcycles, although some may ride modified versions of older model Triumphs
and a few ride the American-made Victory motorcycle manufactured by
Polaris Industries. Research on these groups suggests that they are more identified with organized criminal activities than they are with riding motorcycles
(Barker, 2007; Queen, 2007). "Turf" battles among rival clubs are probably
more related to controlling the distribution of illegal drugs and weapons than
pride over colors or the defense of riding territory. Although one-percenters
wear the patch and rockers[4] and proudly call themselves one-percenters, they
probably comprise much less than one percent of all motorcycle riders today.

### Hardcore Bikers

A somewhat larger segment, but still a numerical minority of the riding
population, who are often mistaken for one-percenters are those I categorize
as "hardcore bikers." The riders I call hardcore bikers have much in common
with the one-percenters, with the exception of being affiliated with a recognized motorcycle club.[5] A few are peripherally affiliated with a nationally recognized club, but more of them are members of locally recognized motorcycle
clubs if affiliated with any organization. Many more of these riders are not
affiliated with any type of club or formal organization, but are at least somewhat committed to the biker lifestyle. They tend to come from lower- and
working-class backgrounds, often do not have full-time employment, or may
work in bars, garages, or shops often related to motorcycles. They almost
exclusively ride Harley-Davidsons and usually work on their own and each
other's bikes. From a distance, or even up close, it is difficult to distinguish
a hardcore biker from a club-affiliated one-percenter, although one-percenters
have little problem making the distinction, which to them is significant.

# Neo-Bikers: Betwixt and Between

Much larger than both one-percenters and hardcore bikers are those
who the one-percenters and hardcore bikers call "posers" or "wannabes," the
category I prefer to call "neo-bikers." The riders in this category probably
consider themselves to be bikers, but may in fact have more in common with
riders I classify as motorcyclists. They tend to be predominantly working-
class blue-collar workers, often with Southern roots, who take some pride in
being referred to as "rednecks." They almost exclusively ride Harley-
Davidsons or some customized version of the Harley-Davidson often adorned
with Confederate flags, iron crosses, skulls and crossbones, or similar accou-

trements. Few of them are affiliated with any club, but tend to imitate the look and lifestyle of those who are. These riders are the "bikers" that the non-riding public are most likely to encounter and assume to be representative of motorcyclists in general, and bikers in particular. They attend Sturgis and other rallies in droves (often hauling their bikes there on trailers), congregate in "biker" bars, and are probably the riders most likely to get into arguments or even fights over brands or types of motorcycles. Ironically, they are the riders most likely to accuse other motorcyclists of being *posers*. I encountered numerous "neo-bikers" during my research and interviewed several of them because they are a highly visible element of today's motorcycling world. One encounter with a "neo-biker" at a rally in Arkansas magnifies the distinction between riders in this category and those in the other two. As I parked and dismounted my bike, a man who appeared to be in his early 40s wearing a leather skullcap, decked out in black t-shirt and leather from head to toe, approached me and stated, "You posers need to park over there," pointing toward a row of mostly European and Japanese motorcycles. "This area's for *real* bikers." The woman with him rolled her eyes and said, "Excuse Mr. Badass biker here, but he's had a few too many beers." Then she continued, "Tomorrow he will wake up and go back to being his old self—a laid-off bricklayer, but a decent guy—he gets like this the five or six times a year he rides his motorcycle and drinks a little too much." The man glared at her but put up no argument or defense. Conversely, at rallies and organized rides across the country, I have encountered hundreds if not thousands and interviewed several "good ol' boy" neo-bikers who looked terribly intimidating but turned out to be fairly friendly and informative. They all considered themselves to be bikers but distanced themselves from the one-percenters and hardcore bikers that attended those same rallies. Or perhaps more accurately, the one-percenters and hardcore bikers distanced themselves from them, and everybody else.

## Motorcyclists

In contrast, at that same Arkansas rally I interviewed a rider I had seen and spoken to a couple of times and asked him whether he considered himself to be a biker, motorcyclist, or something else. He gave the following response:

> I really get tired of being called a poser. I don't consider myself a biker, and never have. To me bikers are guys like Sonny Barger, and members of the one-percent clubs.... Now, to me those guys are *real* bikers. I don't strut around trying to make people think I'm some bad biker dude like these good ol' boys who strip down their Harleys, wear their do-rags and vests, go to Lynyrd Skynyrd concerts, and badmouth guys like me who ride for pleasure. To me, they are the *posers*.

> Me, I'm just a guy who loves to ride motorcycles. Always have. I've ridden almost every type of motorcycle made — cruisers, crotch rockets, dirt bikes, and touring bikes — Harleys, Yamahas, BMWs, and the rest. If that makes me a poser, then so be it, but I don't think so.

That rider represents thousands, if not millions, of others like him, who in my view are most aptly referred to as motorcyclists or motorcycle enthusiasts and are the primary subjects of this book. They are less concerned with looking like a biker or fitting any stereotypical model and much more interested in riding motorcycles for fun and pleasure. They comprise the vast majority of today's growing motorcycle subculture and are the primary focus of this research.

Since the invention of the motorcycle around the turn of the 20th century there have been people who see motorcycles as viable alternatives or even preferable to the four-wheeled mode of transportation of cars or trucks. Others simply ride motorcycles for fun and enjoyment. They love to ride motorcycles, but these people were not and are not *bikers*. They also are neither *posers* nor *wannabes*. These riders are more aptly *motorcyclists* than *bikers*. A lot of today's motorcyclists are Baby Boomers (those born roughly between 1946 and 1964) who began riding in the 1960s. In the mid–1980s, motorcycle riding and sales experienced a large increase in volume, with motorcycle registrations reaching over 5.4 million in 1985, fueled largely by middle-class Baby Boomers who accounted for the huge increase in sales (NTSA, 1995; National Safety Council, 2007). Ninety percent of these motorcyclists were male, roughly 75 percent were between the ages of 31 and 60, and the vast majority were white. Today's motorcycle purchasers and riders have similar characteristics (see Table 1.1 for demographics of motorcyclists nationwide).

As with almost every other element of American society, the Baby Boomers — some 70+ million strong, and the single largest age cohort in the United States — redefined what it meant to be a motorcycle rider. These motorcyclists took to two wheels and along with stimulating the housing and automobile markets, revived the sagging motorcycle industry. As wealthier buyers emerged, motorcycle prices rose dramatically (Packer and Coffey, 2004). Through engineering and manufacturing changes, limited production, brilliant marketing, and massive advertising campaigns, Harley-Davidson, once on the verge of bankruptcy, gained such popularity that dealers had difficulty filling orders and developed waiting lists for new bikes — something that made them even more desirable to consumer-oriented Boomers. While maintaining their popularity with one-percenters and hardcore bikers, the average prices of their new models rivaled or exceeded those of compact cars, and fulfilled the wants and needs of this new breed of motorcyclists that included a large number of doctors, lawyers, dentists, college professors, and other professional people. Packer and Coffey (2004: 661) noted, "The demo-

| Table 1.1—General Demographics of Motorcycle Riders in the U.S. | | | |
|---|---|---|---|
| **Age** | | **Sex** | |
| 20 years and younger | 1% | Male | 90% |
| 21–25 | 7% | Female | 10% |
| 26–30 | 9% | | |
| 31–40 | 22% | **Marital Status** | |
| 41–50 | 30% | Married | 65% |
| 51–60 | 23% | Single (never married) | 17% |
| 61–70 | 7% | Widowed | 2% |
| 71 and older | 1% | Divorced/separated | 16% |

SOURCE: Knol. 2010. "The U.S. Motorcycle Market." http://knol.google.com/k/the-u-s-motorcycle-market# and "An in-depth study on the new bike buyer," Power-sports Business, *Market Data Book 2010,* p. 38.

graphics have shifted upscale and the typical Harley buyer of the new millennium is, at least according to HD, as likely to be a professor, lawyer, doctor or investment broker as he is a classic rock-listening factory worker."

Polaris Industries began manufacturing Victory Motorcycles as American companions to Harley-Davidson, and talk of a rebirth of the famous Indian motorcycle flooded the motorcycle subculture, with new Indian prototypes being produced almost annually. In 2011, Polaris Industries purchased all the rights to Indian and promised mass production of a new line of Indian motorcycles. Years prior, Japanese manufacturers, quick to realize the resurgence of Harley-Davidson, and the marketing potential offered by the Baby Boomer consumers, began making Harley "clones"—larger and louder bikes that were difficult to distinguish from the well-known popular "hog." Harley-Davidson even attempted to trademark the sound of its V-twin engine to keep Japanese and German manufacturers from copying or imitating it. By 2007, motorcycle registrations reached an all-time high of over 6 million, with middle-class men aged 35 to 50 accounting for the largest number of sales, followed closely by middle-class women in the same age categories (National Safety Council, 2007; Box, 2007). According to the Motorcycle Industry Council, motorcycle sales in the United States declined in 2009 and again in 2010, but despite the sagging economy, were still just below one-half million (Madson, 2011).

## *"Rolex Riders" and "Rich Urban Bikers" (RUBS)*

For some, expensive motorcycles became a status symbol and a new category of motorcyclist emerged which popular culturists refer to as "Rolex Riders" or "RUBS" (rich urban bikers). A motorcyclist does not necessarily have to wear a Rolex watch or be rich to fit into this category, but as one journalist noted, "With price tags ranging from $7,000 to $30,000 for a fully loaded motorcycle, the hobby has become attractive to 'yuppie' or 'Rolex' riders who have the extra money to spend" (Person, 1996). Rolex Riders or RUBS usually purchase brand-new motorcycles off the dealer's showroom floor at the sticker price along with several hundred or even thousands of dollars of riding gear and apparel. After completing a motorcycle safety course (sometimes offered by the dealer), they typically put 2,000 to 5,000 miles on a bike before they grow tired of it, or, more often than not, have a close encounter or minor accident that vividly reminds them of the inherent dangers associated with riding a motorcycle. Often, they sell the motorcycle and move on to some less dangerous but equally expensive hobby or pastime. An Aspen real estate agent who has ridden for over 40 years commented that Rolex riders are often derided for "compulsive cleanliness of the bikes and the riders; carefully coordinated clothes and accessories; low-mileage use of their hogs coupled with a habit of trailering their bikes over long distances, flying in to pick them up, and then riding them around whatever town they're in" (Colson, 2005). Every blue-collar neo-biker and all the Baby Boomer motorcyclists and enthusiasts know that some of the best bargains in used motorcycles are the low-mileage super-clean bikes sold back to dealers, put up on auction on eBay, or placed on Craig's List by terrified Rolex Riders or RUBs who learned first-hand that riding motorcycles is not for everybody — or at least not for them.

## *Motorcycle Enthusiasts*

Motorcycle enthusiasts can be members of either sex, any age, from any social class, and any race or ethnicity, but this category is primarily comprised of middle- and upper-middle-class white male professionals. Like me, most motorcycle enthusiasts have loved motorcycles for as long as they can remember. These riders include large numbers of baby boomers, many of whom started riding in their childhood or early teens, then took a hiatus to marry, raise families, develop careers, and later in mid-life took up motorcycling again. Others started riding in their early teens or even younger, became addicted, and have ridden motorcycles ever since. The common characteristic of all the men and women in this category is that they *love* motorcycles. They ride Harley-Davidsons, Victorys, Hondas, Kawasakis, Suzukis, BMWs, Buells, touring bikes, sport bikes, dirt bikes, and almost any other brand or type of motorcycle. If it has two wheels, they want to ride it. This category includes women who either ride two-up on the back of motorcycles or ride their own bikes and are described in more detail in chapter 5 which deals with women motorcyclists and depicts how they are distinctively different from "biker chicks" and the women that populate the hardcore "biker" subculture both past and present. These categories of motorcycle enthusiasts comprise a sub-

Motorcycle enthusiast Ron "the King" Loomis first began riding motorcycles in his early teens. Since that time he has ridden almost every make and model of motorcycle ever made and has won numerous on-road and off-road racing titles. In his mid–70s, Ron is owner and CEO of Loomis Racing in Las Vegas and rides one of his many bikes almost every single day.

stantial portion of the men and women interviewed for this study and along with the other categories of motorcyclists will be described in greater detail in subsequent chapters.

Although devoted to motorcycle riding, and often decked out in leather so-called "biker" gear, these people do not emulate the biker lifestyle. Most ride motorcycles as often as possible primarily for fun, recreation, and leisure. Some of these motorcyclists, like me, own more than one bike, usually at least one of which is a sport bike designed primarily for high performance and speed which many people refer to as "crotch rockets," and at least one that is a cruiser or touring bike designed for long rides and comfort. These riders have grown in numbers to the point that they have given rise to the manufacture and sale of a new classification of motorcycle known as the "sport touring" bike. These motorcycles, primarily produced by Japanese and German manufacturers, combine large high-performance fuel-injected engines and sport-bike nimbleness and control with features such as cruise control, thick padded seats, radios, removable saddlebags, and retractable windshields.

These "crossover" bikes are particularly popular with the over-50 riders who still enjoy speed and performance, but also demand a certain amount of creature comfort—the same crowd who gave rise to the "crossover" vehicle in automobiles.

Motorcycle enthusiasts usually subscribe to several motorcycle magazines and like to keep abreast of new makes and models, especially reading reviews and comparisons of various motorcycles, gathering facts and data that will influence their next purchase. On rainy or inclement days when they cannot ride (although they tend to ride year-round in all types of weather) motorcycle enthusiasts often haunt motorcycle dealerships or peruse the Internet looking for "good deals" on bikes, equipment, clothing, or other motorcycle paraphernalia. They turn to look when they hear or see a motorcycle go by and they find it almost impossible to walk past a parked motorcycle without walking over to it and taking a closer look. Their daily conversations are often punctuated with motorcycle stories and experiences, and if not riding, they are often talking about or planning their next ride. Motorcycle enthusiasts often attend motorcycle shows and love to look at antique or classic motorcycles. They also attend rallies, but more often than not, they enjoy the ride to and from these events more than the events themselves. As one of these enthusiasts shared with me,

> I went to Sturgis one time just to see all the bikes and what all the hubbub was about. Spent three days riding up there, two days riding in the Black Hills, and three days riding back. All total, I was probably actually in the town of Sturgis at the rally less than three or four hours. I think if I were to go back to that area, I'd prefer to go during some other time when it would be less crowded. It's the riding that I enjoy, not the rallies, per se.

Needless to say, motorcycle enthusiasts do not trailer their bikes to events. In fact, many of them do not own a trailer, and must borrow one or have their motorcycle towed if it breaks down or must be taken to a shop for repairs. To enthusiasts, it is all about the machine and the ride.

## "Crotch Rocketeers," "Stunters," and Racers

In addition to the motorcycle enthusiasts who often ride high-performance sport bikes (often called "crotch rockets") on the streets preferring their light weight and responsive handling to their cruisers or touring bikes, there also are a large number of motorcyclists who ride sport bikes exclusively, often treating the streets and highways as race tracks and stunt venues. I have coined the term "crotch rocketeers" for these riders because they are often looked down upon by other motorcyclists who view them as reckless and needless risk takers who give motorcycling a bad name. Riding at dangerously high speeds, crotch rocketeers often speed down the center stripe on one wheel dodging in and out of traffic, terrifying automobile drivers and other motorcyclists alike. Even stunters and racers who may restrict their riding to parking lots, racetracks or other locations for performing stunts or competitive racing do not appreciate the tactics of the crotch rocketeers. Because they ride the same types of motorcycles and share many common characteristics, I have lumped these three types of riders together, but it could be argued that these are three separate categories of motorcyclists, each deserving a book about them alone. There are important distinctions between street sport bike riders and stunters, the latter of whom often reserve their risk-

taking stunts for more controlled environments such as parking lots or closed off areas. Some even compete in organized stunting shows or competitions.

There are even more differences between these two groups and racers who do most of their riding in organized competitive events. Motorcycle racing could be further divided into several subcategories (motocross, track, enduro, etc.), and entire books could be (and have been) written about each. Still, members of these three groups often share many commonalities and there is probably more crossover among these three types of riders than the other categories described. These riders tend to be younger and much more daring than the aforementioned Rolex riders, RUBS, and enthusiasts. There is an old saying that "there are *old* riders and there are *bold* riders but there are no *old bold* riders."

Stunters are a special category of motorcyclists who meet in parking lots and other non-street venues to do tricks and shows on their specially modified sport bikes. Although stunters also ride sport bikes on the streets, they tend to separate themselves from the "crotch rocketeers" who ride at high speeds sometimes on one wheel in traffic and on highways, endangering themselves and the public.

That said, I did meet and interview at least one old and bold rider, a 54-year-old "stunter," who, despite a few minor injuries, had ridden almost all his life and "stunted" for the past 10 years. The owner of eight sport motorcycles (crotch rockets), he indicated that he seldom drives a car, much preferring to ride one of his bikes wherever he goes. In his words, "I'd give up my car long before I would go without a motorcycle." For the most part, however, crotch rocket riders tend to be young and bold—very bold. Much like their Japanese counterparts, the *bosozuku,* many of them engage in high-speed urban motorcycle riding, dodging in and out of traffic, performing stunts and taking unbelievable risks (Sato, 1998). They can often be seen tearing down the highway at speeds in excess of 100 miles per hour; sometimes on only one wheel. A few may actually be involved in street racing, others in trick riding or stunting, and although some occasionally attend motorcycle rallies, they rarely participate in the motorcyclist subculture.

Each of these subcategories could and perhaps should be considered a separate category. Although I have had numerous encounters with crotch rocketeers, and a few with stunt riders and racers, members of this subcategory comprise a very small part of this research study (eight male stunt riders and two male racers). Perhaps more on these categories of riders at another time. For purposes of this study, they all are collapsed under the general moniker of "motorcyclists."

## *Dirt Bike and Off-Road Riders*

Two other subcategories, worthy of mention but not interviewed for this study unless they also rode street bikes, are the numerous dirt bike riders and off-road riders, many of whom never get motorcycle licenses or ever take a motorcycle onto a paved surface. These riders range in age from pre-schoolers (some of the Japanese manufacturers make dirt bikes with small engines replete with training wheels) to post-retirement, but generally include young males in their teens, twenties, and early to mid-thirties. They ride specially designed dirt or off-road motorcycles with special frames and suspensions designed for the rough and tumble riding in dirt, sand, rocks, and almost any other terrain imaginable. Dirt bike and off-road riders primarily ride for fun and recreation, most often on private property or open lands, and they often mingle with riders of four-wheelers and other all-terrain vehicles. Some take dirt-biking much more seriously and participate in organized competitive motocross racing, trial racing, enduro, or other dirt-bike or off-road events. Some of these events are officially sanctioned by various riding organizations while others are unofficially organized by local groups and others who enjoy the sport. Off-road and dirt-bike riders rarely participate in motorcycle shows or rallies unless they also own and ride a cruiser or some other street-legal bike, although some dirt bike riders engage in a popular recreational activity known as "dual sport" motorcycling which involves riding motorcycles built to be ridden both on and off-road (Adams, 2008). Only two professional off-road racers are included in this study and both of them also ride street bikes, but several other motorcyclists interviewed indicated they had ridden a dirt bike at one time or another.

## Why Study Motorcyclists?

Why study motorcyclists? There are several reasons. Less than 7 percent of Americans ride motorcycles (American Motorcyclists Association, 2011). If nothing else, motorcyclists are a statistical minority and by some definitions, that makes them a deviant group. That alone makes them sociologically interesting and worthy of study. Nevertheless, motorcycle riders encompass a substantial number of people. There are some six and a half million motorcycles registered in the United States and motorcycling is one of the fastest growing phenomena in North America with close to a million new motorcycles being sold each year (see Table 1.2). Those facts alone also make studying motorcyclists sociologically worthwhile. It is not the number of motorcycle riders, however small or large, that make them interesting and worthy (or unworthy) of study. Rather, it is the social and cultural misconceptions and stereotypes about motorcyclists— their values, dress, demeanor, camaraderie, and risk-taking behavior — along with various media portrayals of bikers and motorcyclists that captivate the attention and spur the imagination of the non-riding public. Few American pastimes are so simultaneously attractive and repulsive.

Deviance has long been of interest to sociologists, but as Goode and Vail (2008: xi) noted, the bulk of research on deviance in the United States "centers on the 'big five' subjects, the meat-and-potatoes, nuts-and-bolts of deviance: crime; alcoholism; illicit drug use; mental disorder; and sexual deviance." The hardcore biker subculture includes aspects of all five of those topics, but that is not the subject of this research. Bikers, especially one-percenters and hardcore motorcycle clubs, have been thoroughly studied, written about, and to some extent, immortalized. So, the potential contribution of research on motorcyclists to the literature on deviance is worthy of attention itself.

There are other aspects of motorcycling, however, that are more attractive to sociologists and of interest to the public. Erving Goffman (1963) noted that most people labeled as deviant experience *stigma,* a trait that disqualifies them from full social acceptance. Hardcore motorcyclists and the so-called "one-percenters" thrive on this deviant persona. Numerous magazine articles, books, movies, and television programs based on both fact and fiction have focused attention on these renegade bikers and have created and perpetuated a cultural stereotype of them that often extends to all motorcycle riders. If

## Table 1.2 — 2010 Motorcycle Sales in U.S.

| | |
|---|---|
| Dual Sport | 42,250 |
| Off Road | 46,779 |
| Street Bikes | 611,133 |
| Scooters | 76,748 |
| Totals | 776,910 |

SOURCE: Adapted from various sources, edited by webBikeWorld and Motorcycle USA.com, 2011. <http://www.webbikeworld.com/motorcycle-news/statistics/motor cycle-sales-statistics.htm> <http://www.motorcycle-usa.com/2/5588/Motorcycle-Article/Motorcycle-Sales-Down-40–8 — Says-MIC.aspx>

"outlaw" bikers comprise only one percent of motorcycle riders, however, who makes up the other 99 percent? Even if you add in other hardcore bikers who may or may not be affiliated with one of the "big four" or other high-profile 1 percent motorcycle clubs, you still are talking about probably far less than 20 percent (maybe less than 10 percent) of all motorcycle riders. So, what about the other 80 to 90 percent? What about those who I have categorized as neo-bikers and the even larger number of motorcyclists? What do we know about them? Who are they? Why do they ride?

Given the negative social consequences of stigma, most people do everything in their power to avoid being stigmatized or discredited, often employing a variety of information control techniques such as concealment of stigma symbols, passing, dividing the social world, mutual aid, covering, and disclosure (Goffman, 1963). This offers the question of why well-educated, middle-class, professionals[6] would not only intentionally, but proudly, display many of the stigma symbols associated with the hardcore motorcycle subculture, albeit temporarily, subjecting themselves to being labeled as deviant Moreover, why would these same people, with mortgages, spouses, children, careers, two or more cars, savings accounts, and 401Ks, engage in risk-taking behavior that not only threatens their reputations, livelihood, and security, but literally their lives? Now, those questions are worthy of investigation.

Over the past five-plus years of research, I have counted no fewer than a dozen different occasions when some rider has commented to me either seriously or somewhat in jest, "Somebody ought to study this." My typical response: "My thoughts exactly." To the question, "Why study motorcyclists?" my first response would be: "Why not?" Hopefully, the rest of this book will answer that question much more substantially. Chapter 2 describes the theoretical framework and research methods used to study motorcycling and motorcyclists and provides more details about the thousands of motorcyclists observed and the more than 200 riders interviewed for this research.

# CHAPTER 2

# Studying Motorcyclists

A riding buddy and I had been on our motorcycles for about four hours and had covered parts of two states when we pulled into the roped-off parking area designated as "Bikes Only." We had never even heard of, much less ever attended, this particular motorcycle show and rally. A motorcycle show combined with an annual watermelon fest and "hillbilly horseshoe" throwing contest sounded like an interesting combination of fun, entertainment, and competition. As we dismounted, we were greeted by a man who appeared to be in his early 60s accompanied by a woman about the same age who had just gotten off a two- to three-year-old Electra Glide Ultra Classic. "Where y'all from?" asked the man. I responded, "Texas," as my riding partner took off his helmet and began looking through his saddlebag for a baseball cap he usually donned after a ride. "Meet a lot of Texans at this event — we're from northwest Louisiana," he rejoined. I chatted with the man, who I learned was 62 years old and had been riding since he was 15. His wife, who turned out to be a year younger, had taken up riding on the back of motorcycles when she married, but at age 50 decided to take a motorcycle safety course and purchase her own bike. She said she usually rode her own bike to rallies, but she had decided to go two-up with her husband on this particular trip because her bike was in the shop getting new tires, and it had been quite some time since they had ridden double for any distance. Plus, she wanted to see if the new touring bike was "all that it was cracked up to be." After approximately 20–25 minutes of non-stop visiting, I noticed that my riding companion seemed bored and obviously wanted to move on. I began the disengagement process and the couple and I said our farewells with the typical admonition to "ride safe" and the assurance that we hoped to see each other again some time. As we turned to walk away, my friend, who knew I was conducting research on motorcyclists, said, "They were awfully friendly; you ought to interview them for your book." My response: "I just did."

The *science* of ethnographic interviewing is mostly the *art* of conversing. A good interview should be like receiving an injection from a very skilled nurse — painless, and after it's over, the patient (interviewee) should not even be aware that it took place. Social scientists sometimes debate whether good qualitative research skills come naturally, can be taught, or if they must be learned through a long apprenticeship (Hammersley, 2004). In my case, I had the benefit of all three. Although my mother only had a seventh-grade education, she was naturally inquisitive, could talk to any- and every-one, and always took everything anybody told her with a grain of salt. I shared those traits and throughout my childhood developed a precocious and easygoing inquisitive nature that many people found disarming, and no doubt, some found annoying. My wife and several of my friends are fond of saying, "Bill never met a stranger"—a trait that comes in handy when interviewing people I am meeting for the first time. Throughout my elementary, junior high, and senior high school years, I developed an intellectual curiosity that later in college and as a teacher I learned was referred to as "critical thinking." I always wanted to know the answers to questions, but I also always questioned answers. Moreover, I was particularly interested in people, especially what they do and why. I was a sophomore in college before I discovered the discipline of sociology and realized that people could actually make a career out of doing the things I had been doing most of my life — observing people, asking questions, and analyzing human behavior. During my doctoral program I took the only graduate course offered on qualitative research methods (in addition to the three required quantitative methods courses and two statistics classes) and I gravitated toward the faculty members and other graduate students who favored qualitative field research over the more common quantitative survey methods and statistical analyses that dominated sociology at that time. I learned that conducting surveys, crunching numbers, and generating mounds of statistical data were relatively quick and easy, but not very satisfying for answering the types of research questions that most interested me. I devoured everything I could get my hands on related to qualitative research and read and reread classic studies by William Foote Whyte, Margaret Mead, Elliott Liebow, Erving Goffman, and Howard Becker. When I took my first teaching job, I teamed up with an established colleague who was a cultural anthropologist by training. He and I embarked on qualitative research studies that resulted in more than three decades of participant observation and ethnographic research on topics as diverse as American cowboys, Bokkos Fulani, Santa Claus and the Easter Bunny at shopping malls, assembly line work on the kill floor of a beef packing plant, morticians and funeral directors, topless dancers, and motorcyclists. Soon, I was teaching courses in qualitative methods, and today participant observation and ethnographic interviewing come as naturally to me as simply watching people and talking to them. These research techniques are explained more thoroughly later in this chapter, but first, should be put in a theoretical context in order to understand why they are most appropriate for this particular study.

# Theoretical Orientation

Three overriding theoretical perspectives guide this descriptive analysis of today's American motorcyclists. First, Symbolic Interaction offers a partial explanation for motorcyclists' willingness to voluntarily enter the world of deviance, stigma, and risk-taking through *definition of the situation*, the insistence that as people interact, they continually define and redefine social situations and social reality (Thomas, 1931; Mead, 1934; Lemert, 1967; Blumer, 1969). Herman and Miall (1990:264) noted, "The possession of a discrediting attribute can be a positive experience dependent on actor definitions and actions." In other words, deviance and stigma, like beauty, are in the eye of the beholder. Similarly, Gramling and Forsyth (1987) described how people can exploit stigma to their benefit in some social situations and under certain social conditions. Consequently, members of today's motorcyclist subculture redefine old stigma symbols transforming them into new status symbols. Harley-Davidsons and other loud V-twin motorcycles are no longer defined as anti-establishment, but are redefined as luxury items along with BMWs (both cars and motorcycles), Rolex watches, high-powered ski boats, sailboats, and summer houses. Leather, once linked to toughness, rebellion, and debauchery, is redefined as stylish and expensive, as well as practical and safe. Tattoos, facial hair, and body piercings, once signs of youthful angst and rebellion, become visible symbols of free-thinking, hipness, and fashionable chic. Motorcycle shows, biker rallies, and organized rides are now weekend getaways, reunions, and charitable events for those who can afford both the time and expense of participation. Thus, today's motorcyclists are not engaging in deviance at all, but are conforming to many middle- and upper-middle-class values and expectations. Consequently, they experience relatively little stigma if any, and even then, only for a brief period of time.

Motorcyclists might be mistaken by the general public for rebels challenging the norms and values of middle-class America, but they are actually conforming to and promoting norms and values related to capitalism, consumerism, freedom, charity, and individuality. If the classic scene from *Easy Rider* when Peter Fonda's character removed his Rolex watch and tossed it away to symbolize his newfound freedom were replayed in real life today, dozens of motorcyclists would scramble from their bikes to recover such a valuable possession. Because a substantial number of motorcyclists are not RUBs (rich urban bikers), however, but are hardworking blue-collar motorcyclists, they might just as well be called "Timex riders." Still others, like me, are neither rich nor blue-collar and do not even wear wrist watches, but have small clocks mounted on our handlebars so that we always know the time and can terminate rides in time to go to work, attend a meeting, or ensure that we do not miss dinner or our favorite television program. Moreover,

This new BMW luxury sport-touring motorcycle equipped with cruise control, navigational system, detachable hard luggage, satellite radio, intercom system, heated seats, heated grips, ABS, and other amenities retails for just under $35,000. These types of motorcycles transform what once might have been considered a "stigma symbol" into status symbol.

most of us carry mobile phones, so we rarely escape the invisible bonds related to time and our non-riding commitments and responsibilities.

## Symbolic Interaction

Symbolic interaction provides a pragmatic theoretical framework for observing, participating in, and analyzing the American motorcycle subculture. Tamotsu Shibutani (1955) contended that human beings interact with and within a wide variety of reference groups—groups that help individuals understand their social world. These various societies, "social worlds," or what many refer to as *subcultures*, are held together through shared values, communication, and social interaction. From a symbolic interactionist perspective, meaning arises through social interaction (Blumer, 1969). Consequently, to understand the world of motorcycle riders, it is imperative that we not be "slavishly bound by standard scientific research protocols." Rather, as the symbolic interactionist perspective insists, "the empirical social world consists of ongoing group life and one has to get close to this life to know what is going on in it" (Blumer, 1969:38).

Within the context of symbolic interaction, this research also applies Walter Miller's (1958) theory of lower-class focal concerns as a generating milieu for delinquency to the motorcyclist subculture (see chapter 3). J. Mark Watson (1980) concluded that "outlaw motorcyclists" were an outgrowth of lower class cultural concerns identified by Miller (1958): *trouble, toughness, smartness, excitement, fate*, and *autonomy*. Symbolic interaction and this study poses the questions: to what extent do members of today's predominantly middle-class motorcyclist subculture define, redefine, embrace, express, or reject those same values? Or, is their riding simply a reflection of the so-called trend of the *vulgarization* of the middle class whereby highly educated middle-class Americans increasingly participate in so-called unsophisticated activities that used to be primarily the domain of the working or lower classes, such as boxing, hockey, NASCAR, professional wrestling, and perhaps riding motor-cycles? Since those activities, once inexpensive and requiring little formal education or training, have increasingly become more expensive and more technological, an equally valid question might be, if they are now more appeal-ing to educated members of the middle and upper-middle-classes.

Much of the previous research on bikers implies that middle- and upper-middle-class motorcycle riders are merely posers or wannabes, pretending to be bikers on weekends, holidays, and special occasions, but as illustrated in chapter 1, my research indicates that explanation is far too simplistic, and for the most part, inaccurate. As revealed in subsequent chapters, the vast major-ity of motorcyclists are neither pretending to be outlaws, nor do they "wanna be" outlaws. Not only do motorcyclists include all types of both blue-collar workers and white-collar professionals, but a fairly sizable contingency of motorcyclists are police officers, attorneys, probation and parole officers, and judges. These people not only do not "wannabe" outlaws, but they do not even want to be mistaken for them. They simply enjoy riding motorcycles, and like most active people prefer to engage in motorcycling with others who have similar backgrounds and interests as themselves. Again, consistent with the symbolic interaction perspective, the focus of this study is on how motor-cyclists define and redefine activities and meaningful symbols previously asso-ciated with hardcore bikers and one-percenters in such a way as to make them more consistent with middle- and upper-middle-class values and lifestyles. Probably one of the few things that both bikers and motorcyclists might agree upon is that posers are "those that dress and act as if they are motorcycle riders or 'bikers' while actually riding very few miles and pos-sessing questionable [if any] riding skills" (Austin, 2009:85). This hardly fits the description of most motorcyclists in this study.

## *Dramaturgical Analysis*

Within symbolic interaction is a more specialized theoretical framework that views social life as analogous to theater (Goffman, 1959). Consistent with Shakespeare's famous quote in *As You Like it*, this perspective contends "all the world's a stage, and all the men and women merely players." This does not mean that people are merely pretending to be things that they are not. Rather, sociologically speaking, it means that we all occupy a wide variety of social *statuses*, or positions in society, that require us to fulfill an equally wide variety of *roles*. For example, I am a male, a husband, a father, a grandfather, a university professor, and a motorcycle rider, to name but a few of my statuses. Each of these positions is accompanied by a *role*, or a set of behavioral expectations for that particular status. As with theater, each role includes wardrobe, script, and the necessity to stay in character (fulfill our role expectations) when interacting with others as they in turn carry out their role expectations. Throughout the course of a lifetime (and even a single day), people move in and out of multiple statuses, carry out multiple roles, and present to others a multitude of *situated selves*—the social self that emerges

Long-time friend and lifelong motorcycle enthusiast Louis White (on right) and I are probably never going to be mistaken for one-percenters or hardcore bikers, but we typify many of the motorcyclists in this study who are married, middle-aged, middle-class baby boomers who love to ride and manage to put 10,000 to 15,000 miles per year on our motorcycles.

in a particular situation (Thompson and Hickey, 2011). Thus, a person's social behavior is predicated on time, place, situation, and who is witnessing the interaction (an audience). The motorcyclists in this study occupy numerous other social statuses, and perform vastly different roles when at home, at work, at church, or in other social settings. Although various aspects of the lives of those observed and interviewed for this research undoubtedly have impact on the descriptions and analyses, this study focuses almost exclusively on their status and role as motorcyclists.

## Edgework and Risk-Taking Behavior

Another, and perhaps most useful, theoretical orientation for explaining why motorcyclists ride can be found in the literature on *edgework* — engagement in risk-taking behaviors such as skydiving, scuba diving, mountain climbing, and other extreme sports, which can be expanded to include motorcycle riding (Lyng, 2005). Edgework essentially means "skirting the edge between safety and danger" (Cockerham, 2006:11). Lyng (2005:5) suggests that "risk-taking experience can be understood as a radical form of escape from the institutional routines of contemporary life." As illustrated in the demographics of the riders in this study, today's motorcyclist subculture is comprised largely of middle-aged men and some women who have conformed to virtually all of the values, norms, and demands of their middle-class Baby Boomer lifestyles. Education, careers, families, civic clubs, little league, soccer, PTA, and dance classes — they have raised children, cared for elderly parents, put kids through college, and provided financial security for grandchildren — most of them have done it all. So, it is not difficult to understand why when the weekend rolls around, they don their leather vests, chaps, gloves, and boots, straddle their ten-thousand-plus-dollar motorcycles, and take to the roads to hang out at motorcycle-friendly bars, attend motorcycle shows and rallies, or to just experience the freedom and relaxation that is a significant part of their subculture. These Baby Boomers and other motorcyclists work hard, play hard, and take recreation seriously. They do not embrace the biker lifestyle, but ride on weekends, holidays, and whenever else their busy schedules allow — a phenomenon that has sometimes earned them the nickname of "weekend warriors" — a reference analogous to military reservists who carry out civilian activities throughout their everyday lives, but one weekend a month fulfill their military obligations as soldiers. According to "the 'weekend warrior' thesis ... participants in [risk-taking] activities are seen as seeking a temporary escape from the stultifying conditions of work life and bureaucratic institutions" (Lyng 2005:6). This is especially true of the types of activities that can be the most consequential — those involving "the line between life and death" (Lyng, 2005:4). Motorcycling is one such activity.

## Research Methods and Data

As indicated in the preface, I have loved motorcycles all my life and have owned and ridden motorcycles since the age of 14. More accurately, I rode almost daily between the ages of 14 and 18, and then less frequently up to age 21. Like many Baby Boomers, when I married and later had children, I took an approximately 30-year hiatus from motorcycle ownership and only rode occasionally, borrowing bikes from friends. During that time, I continued to yearn for the two-wheeled life, but with the exception of visiting motorcycle dealerships, perusing motorcycle magazines, and taking a few sporadic rides, I squashed the "motorcycle bug." After my children were grown and out on their own, and after suffering a major heart attack while sitting in the living room watching television (usually not considered risk-taking behavior), I decided my love of motorcycles and riding had been put on hold for long enough. I purchased a new motorcycle, completed a motorcycle safety training course to brush up on my riding skills, and joined the ranks of the American motorcyclist subculture. I place myself squarely in the motorcycle enthusiast category of riders. Data and other information for this book are derived from approximately 45 years of various experiences with motorcycles and motor-cyclists, but rely most heavily on approximately five years of participant obser-vation that includes riding in groups, attending major motorcycle rallies (including Sturgis, Fayetteville, Austin, Hot Springs, and a host of others), and going to bike shows, as well as communicating with motorcycle riders through chat rooms, websites, and other media forums.

## Participant Observation

This participant observation research method is what Adler and Adler (1987:67) describe as the "opportunistic complete membership researcher who examines people and social settings in which he/she is already a member." Or, as sociologists often call it, *full participation*, where the researcher becomes actively and completely involved in the behavior or activity being studied (Spradley, 1980; Thompson and Hickey, 2011). Herbert Blumer (1969:38) con-tends, "The empirical social world consists of ongoing group life and one has to get close to this life to know what is going on in it." In sum, you cannot get close to the motorcycling subculture without immersing yourself in it. These data include observation, interaction, and casual conversations with literally thousands of bikers and motorcyclists from all parts of the United States, and even a few other countries.[1]

Anthropologist James Spradley (1980:53–54) differentiates between the "ordinary participant" and the "participant observer":

> The ordinary participant comes to a social situation with only one purpose: to engage in appropriate activities. The participant observer comes to a social sit-

uation with two purposes: (1) to engage in activities appropriate to the situation and (2) to observe activities, people, and physical aspects of the situation.

Explaining further, participant observers practice what researchers characterize as "explicit awareness," becoming aware of those actions, events, and behaviors that often go overlooked or unnoticed in everyday activities (Spradley, 1980:55). Consequently, participant observers simultaneously experience what they are researching as an "insider" (a subjective understanding of who and what they are studying because they are one of them) and an "outsider" (an objective view of who and what they are studying because they are a social scientist trained to observe others with a sense of detachment and objectivity (Spradley, 1980:56–57).

In the course of this research, I was repeatedly aware of this insider/outsider experience. When you are riding a motorcycle, all of your senses and attention must be focused on riding. Every rider knows that "where you look is where you go" on a bike. More than occasional glances at other riders, scenery, or anything but the road ahead of you can often spell misfortune for a motorcyclist. Also, motorcycle riding has a transcendental effect that tends to lull the rider into almost a trance. This is part of the attraction of motorcycling, in that it is relaxing, relieves stress, and creates an almost euphoric state. I have heard countless riders refer to this as "being in the zone," and I have used that phrase numerous times myself to describe the pleasure of riding. Unfortunately, this aspect of riding is one of the contributors to the danger of motorcycling. Just about the time a rider gets "in the zone," which might just as readily be described as a "dulling of the senses," a car pulls out from a side road, or a squirrel runs across the road (better a squirrel than a dog or a deer), or some other unexpected obstacle appears in the rider's path that requires quick thinking and even quicker reflexes resulting in evasive action. Momentary lapses in attention while driving an automobile can have disastrous results, but more often than not, have minimal or no consequences. Those same lapses on a motorcycle can be and often are deadly. Consequently, participant observation on a motorcycle can be doubly dangerous and must be kept to a minimum and done with utmost caution. Conversely, once stopped, *being* a motorcyclist put me in the perfect position to become the "outside" observer from within. Researchers must always be aware of the potential "Hawthorne effect" on their subjects, that is, if people are aware that they are being observed or studied, that awareness may in fact alter their behavior.[2] As a fellow rider interacting with and informally chatting with other riders, chances of the "Hawthorne effect" coming into play were remote to non-existent. Motorcycle shows and rallies are a "people watcher's" paradise, as almost everybody is watching everybody else. Consequently, they are excellent venues for participant observation research. As the Hall of Fame catcher and great philosopher Yogi Berra once said, "You can observe an awful lot just by watching." To really find out what people are doing and why they are doing it, however, you need to talk to them. So I did.

## Ethnographic Interviews

Ethnography is the work of describing a *culture* or *subculture*— a set of beliefs, values, norms, and material goods shared by members of a group (Thompson and Hickey, 2011:58). "Rather than *studying people*, ethnography means *learning from people* [italics in the original] (Spradley, 1979:3). An ethnographic interview shares many common elements with a casual conversation. As Spradley (1979:58–59) notes:

> skilled ethnographers often gather most of their data through participant observation and many casual, friendly conversations. They may interview people without their awareness, merely carrying on a friendly conversation while identifying a few ethnographic questions.... Think of ethnographic interviews as casual conversations with explicit purpose.

I am continually amazed at how much people are willing to tell total strangers. You see and hear this in supermarkets, on airplanes, and just about anywhere people meet and interact. If you include the social media such as *Facebook* and *Twitter*, you know that most people share way too much information. We even have a texting shorthand for it: TMI. Standing in line at the supermarket, I have overheard conversations between customers and clerks about emergency appendectomies, extramarital affairs, and numerous other personal issues. One of my favorites was when an elderly woman was checking out at a major discount store with items that included a tube of hemorrhoid cream and a young male clerk aged about 18 picked up the tube and asked, "Does this stuff really work?" The dumbfounded woman turned red, and then instead of storming out or slapping his face as I thought she might, she responded, "Not as well as they claim in the commercials, but it does help quite a bit." Note to researchers: people will tell you almost anything if you ask them nicely. Given that, imagine asking people questions about something for which they have great passion, especially when they assume (correctly) by your actions and questions that you share that same passion. Pet owners love to talk about their animals, gun collectors about their guns, and motorcyclists can go on forever about their bikes and riding. The biggest problem I faced as a researcher interviewing motorcyclists was not getting them to provide the information I wanted, but trying to politely keep them focused on the topic at hand, and then disengaging them when I had obtained all the relevant information so that I could move on to the next interviewee.

An interview schedule was developed and followed as a general guideline (see Appendix A), but all interviews were conducted through casual conversations, and like any meaningful ethnographic study, questions were added, modified, and/or deleted as individual circumstances dictated. Sometimes only one question needed to be asked, and 30 minutes to an hour later, I would have answers to all the questions I had intended to ask along with answers to many other questions that had not occurred to me. Consequently, while the questions included on the interview schedule provided some consistency and a degree of uniformity to the interviews, in actuality, no two interviews were conducted exactly the same, except for occasions when two or more people were interviewed at the same time (this occurred fairly frequently especially when people were riding two-up or in small groups traveling together). Interviews usually ranged in time from a little over fifteen minutes to an hour with some lasting as much as two to three hours or more. In some cases, interviews were briefly interrupted and then continued at a later time, sometimes over the course of two or three days. As illustrated in the opening vignette to this chapter, most interviewees were not aware that they were part of a research study.

No participants in the study were subjected to any harm, and all data have been aggregated to assure anonymity. In fact, no actual names or any other identifying personal information about participants were ever recorded. Although many of my fellow riders knew or discovered that I was a sociology professor, less than a half dozen specifically asked if I was "conducting research." A few even remarked, "You know, this [riding motorcycles and attending rallies] would make an interesting study." In each case, when asked if I was doing research, I responded in the affirmative, and each of the subjects agreed to participate fully. When taking photographs of people who could be recognized, signed release forms were obtained. Otherwise, I adopted the "don't ask, don't tell" approach, simply riding, observing, talking, and interacting with other riders, while carefully noting meaningful symbols and patterns of behaviors, and being sure to ask questions pertinent to the research objectives. Nevertheless, there was never an attempt to deceive research participants and all aspects of data collection adhered to the guidelines of research protocol outlined in the American Sociological Association's Code of Ethics (ASA, 2001) and to the widely accepted research protocol established for social scientists employed by universities.[3] Sociologists and other social scientists have long grappled with the ethical question: "Do social scientists have the right to study people who do not know they are being studied?" The American Sociological Association addressed this issue head-on with a resounding "Yes!" as long as researchers abide by the following guidelines:

1. Maintain objectivity, integrity, confidentiality, and social responsibility in research.
2. Respect and protect the privacy, dignity, and safety of research subjects.

3. Do not discriminate or misuse or abuse the research role.
4. Disclose all assistance and support.
5. Disassociate from any research that violates the ASA Code
    of Ethics (ASA, 2001).

All of these criteria were met. Moreover, I am confident that participant observation and ethnographic interviewing were the most appropriate methods for this particular type of research. It would be not only impractical but ridiculous to ask motorcycle riders in the course of riding activities to fill out questionnaires or other types of survey instruments. And one can hardly imagine what might transpire if I had wandered around Sturgis during Bike Week asking the approximately one-half to one million participants to sign release forms so that their activities and behaviors could be observed.

I carried a small spiral notebook and pen or pencil with me at all times, and when alone or unobserved by other riders made as detailed notes as possible. On longer rides, I kept a journal making brief entries during breaks in riding sessions and longer, more detailed entries each night. In line with classic qualitative fieldwork methods, no tape recorders or other obtrusive electronic devices were used (Webb et al., 1966). I took copious field notes, and admittedly relied on memory for parts of conversations and direct quotes, but tried to be as true to the words of the riders as possible. On several occasions, my wife and/or daughter served as research team members and asked questions and helped me remember specific responses (especially with women riders).[4] If we remembered a conversation or interpreted it differently, we either came to a general consensus or threw it out. Additional selected information has been gleaned from online postings and polls of well over a 1,000 motorcyclists on motorcycle message boards.[5] When these data are cited, the fact that they came from online sources is duly noted, but no information is provided that might threaten participants' anonymity, privacy, dignity, or safety.

Because the focus of this research is on motorcyclists, no attempt was made to participate with or interview any one-percenters, known outlaw club members, or other hardcore bikers committed to the biker lifestyle, although during the course of this research it was inevitable that riders from those categories were encountered, observed, and even very briefly engaged in conversation. In virtually all cases, these encounters were brief and non-noteworthy. The only motorcycle club members included in this research are some members of a local chapter of Honda Goldwing owners, which is not actually a motorcycle club; some members of a local chapter of Blue Knights, an organization of law enforcement officers and firefighters who ride motorcycles; a few BMW owners who belonged to an organization for BMW riders and a few women who belonged to motorcycle organizations listed in chapter 4.

Numerous other riders were "members" of organizations for riders of their particular make or model of motorcycle, but in most cases buying the motorcycle or subscribing to a particular magazine or newsletter constituted the extent of their involvement with the group. In all cases, these riders were interviewed as individual motorcyclists and not as representatives of any organization. A few other riders who rode with friends or family sometimes called themselves a "club," but they had no official organizational status, did not wear "colors," and in no way pretended to be hardcore bikers or "recognized" motorcycle club members. At large rallies such as Sturgis, one-percenters and hardcore bikers were present, but in almost all cases, they tended to hang around with each other and avoid motorcyclists as much as possible. Generally, with rare exceptions, motorcyclists were smart enough to return the favor. On the very rare occasions when I encountered a hardcore biker or one-percenter, we both practiced what Goffman (1967:83) calls "civil inattention," the process whereby individuals who are in the same physical setting of interaction demonstrate to one another that they are aware of one another, but without being either threatening or over-friendly, basically ignoring one another while showing a modicum of dignity and respect. Even though the focus of this research is on motorcyclists and not bikers, some riders who I would categorize as "new bikers" are included in this research because despite their physical appearances, these riders who look and sometimes act like hardcore bikers are not affiliated with biker clubs, are not committed to the biker lifestyle, and seem to have more in common with the riders I categorize as motorcyclists than they do their "outlaw" counterparts. Table 2.1 shows a tentative breakdown of new bikers and motorcyclists interviewed for this research by each category.

Although one-percenters, outlaw motorcyclists, or hardcore bikers committed to the biker lifestyle probably comprise more than one percent of the

| Table 2.1—Types of Riders Interviewed by Category | |
|---|---|
| **Bikers** | **Motorcyclists** |
| One-Percenters = 0 (0.0%) | "Rolex Riders"/RUBS = 47 (21.0%) |
| Hardcore Bikers = 0 (0.0%) | Motorcycle Enthusiasts = 134 (59.9%) |
| | Crotch Rocketeers/Stunters/Racers =13 (5.8%) |
| **Neo-Bikers** | Dirt Bike/Off-Road Riders = 2 (0.1%) |
| Blue-Collar/Neo-Bikers = 28 (12.5%) | |
| (Percentages may not add to 100 due to rounding) | |

6 million plus motorcyclists in the United States, they still represent a fairly small minority of motorcyclists. Yet, very little serious attention has been paid to the majority of today's motorcyclists who ride primarily for fun and recreation and enjoy taking to the road on two wheels (and sometimes three), participating in what I call the *motorcyclist subculture*. This book is about them.

Years ago, Harley-Davidson commissioned two marketing professors to study the consumer patterns and habits of Harley riders in order to develop specific marketing strategies to create and sell more motorcycle-related products, especially clothing and accessories, and to enhance brand loyalty (Schouten and McAlexander, 1995). Although their research, which involved approximately three years of observing, photographing, and talking to motorcyclists, sheds light on the motorcyclist subculture, neither of them had previous interest or experience in riding motorcycles, and in their words, they "tiptoed through [their] fieldwork as naïve nonparticipant observers ... 'passing' as bikers and making a conscious effort to maintain a scholarly distance from the phenomena [they] were constantly experiencing and observing" (Schouten and McAlexander, 1995:45). They conceded, "What was missing methodologically, was an empathetic sense of a biker's identity, psyche, and social interactions in the context of everyday life" (Schouten and McAlexander, 1995:46). Moreover, they limited their operational definition of "new bikers" to "owners of Harley-Davidson motorcycles who do not belong to known outlaw organizations" (Schouten and McAlexander, 1995:44). While that made sense for their marketing research commissioned by Harley-Davidson, it severely limits the concept of motorcycle riding subculture as it leaves out an enormous number of motorcyclists. Data indicate that although Harley-Davidson represents the lion's share of the 20-billion-plus-dollar-motorcycle market (28 percent), it is followed closely by Honda (25 percent), and then, Yamaha (17 percent), Suzuki (13 percent), and Kawasaki (13 percent) all of whom make high-powered V-twin motorcycles, sometimes referred to as "Harley clones," that are very popular with motorcyclists (Knol, 2010). While the marketing prospects alone make the study of motorcyclists worthwhile, a better understanding of a subculture that includes millions of ordinary, hardworking, law-abiding people, who voluntarily participate in a potentially stigmatizing and dangerous subculture that from time to time may even involve brief encounters and interaction with hardcore outlaw bikers, offers much more.

This research addresses both of the aforementioned weaknesses. Despite a protracted hiatus from routine riding, I think I can make a strong case for having "an empathetic sense of a biker's [motorcyclist's] identity, psyche, and social interactions in the context of everyday life." And, as previously noted, I observed and interviewed riders of motorcycles made by almost every manufacturer on the planet.

## Content Analysis

Chapter 7 employs an additional social scientific research method: content analysis. Content analysis is designed to study communication in the form of movies, television, books, newspapers, magazines, websites, and other formats (Babbie, 2013). Through the use of an online poll motorcyclists were asked to indicate three motorcycling movies that they considered to be the most popular depictions of motorcycle riders. Although numerous films were listed, the three most common were *The Wild One* (1953), *Easy Rider* (1969), and *Wild Hogs* (2006). Four independent raters (three other people and me) viewed each of the three movies and identified common themes throughout the four films. The specific details of this content analysis are described and analyzed in chapter 7.

# Motorcyclist Demographics

I spoke with several hundred, if not thousands of, riders, but detailed data were collected from ethnographic interviews with slightly over 200 (224) motorcycle riders, both male (N=193; 86.2 percent) and female (N=31; 13.8 percent) ranging in ages from 16 to 93, with the majority (72.8 percent) of the riders being between 31 and 60 years old (N=163). An additional 24 women who do not ride solo, but ride on the backs of motorcycles as passengers, were also interviewed. Although they are an important part of today's motorcycling subculture, they are not included in the demographics or analyses of motorcycle *riders*. Some of their

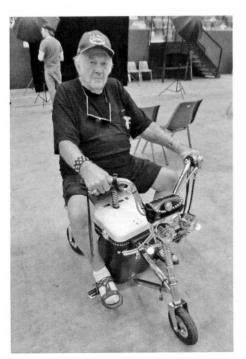

Ninety-three-year-old World War II veteran Shelby Highsmith was the oldest motorcyclist interviewed in this study. He actively rode motorcycles up until the age of 89 when he suffered an accident and his daughter decided that he should stop actively riding. Today, he still attends bike shows and motorcycle rallies and rides on his customized 5-hp motorized "trike" replete with throttle, hand brakes, and an ice chest/seat combination that allows him to travel with his favorite liquid refreshment.

comments and responses are included in chapter 5, which focuses on women in the motorcycling subculture. I rarely asked any of the riders their age directly; many of them volunteered the information. Older male riders seemed almost proud to tell me how old they were and how long they had been riding. By asking how long a rider had been riding, and then later asking when he or she had begun riding, simple math induced his or her age. In some cases, especially among females but also with some males, the rider's age had to be approximated as they would answer more vaguely with statements such as "I guess I've been riding for about 20 years" or "I began riding back when I was a kid" or "since I was in high school" or "I bought my first motorcycle when I got out of the service."

The vast majority of the riders were white (193 or 86.2 percent); 9 were black (4.0 percent), 6 (2.7 percent) Native American (although several of the whites had some Native American ancestry), 11 were Hispanic (4.9 percent), one of which described herself as "Texican," and 5 (2.2 percent) were Asian (See Table 2.2). The majority of interviewees were married (151 or 67.4 percent) with 13 married couples included among the interviewees. Forty-six were divorced (20.5 percent); 24 were single (10.7 percent); and 3 (1.3 percent) were widowed; one woman avoided answering the question although all indications were that she was either single or divorced. As Table 1.1 in the previous

---

### Table 2.2 — Demographics of Motorcycle Riders Interviewed for This Research (N=224)

| Age | Sex |
|---|---|
| 20 years and younger = 3 (1.3%) | Male = 193 (86.2%) |
| 21–25 = 14 (6.3%) | Female = 31 (13.8%) |
| 26–30 =19 (8.5%) | |
| 31–40 = 39 (17.4%) | |
| 41–50 = 61 (27.2%) | |
| 51–60 = 63 (28.1%) | |
| 61–70 = 21 (9.4 %) | |
| 71 and older = 4 (1.8%) | |
| **Marital Status** | **Race/Ethnicity** |
| Married = 151 (67.4%) | White = 193 (86.2%) |
| Divorced = 46 (20.5%) | Black = 9 (4.0%) |
| Single/Never Married = 24 (10.7%) | Hispanic = 11 (4.9%) |
| Widowed = 3 (1.3%) | Native American = 6 (2.7%) |
| | Asian = 5 (2.2%) |

Percentages may not = 100 due to rounding

chapter indicated, these sex, age, and marital categories are fairly consistent with the demographics of today's motorcycle riders which is estimated to be approximately 88 percent male and 12 percent female, and dominated by white men ranging in age between 30 and 60 years old (Box, 2007).

Data gleaned from the remainder of the interview schedule are shared throughout the book where appropriate. Whenever possible and relevant, direct quotes are used, as I prefer to allow riders to tell their stories in their own words. In other cases, where I either could not remember direct quotes, or when I consistently heard similar answers indicating particular patterns or trends, I have tried to paraphrase or summarize the data as accurately as possible. It is probably fair to say that there is no "typical," much less stereotypical, motorcyclist. If hard-pressed to give a "composite" demographic description of today's motorcycle rider, he or she would most typically be a white male, married, in his mid 40s to early 60s, who began riding in his mid- to late teens and then took a break from motorcycle ownership and riding until children were grown and out of the house and then resumed riding sometime within the last two decades (although many have ridden consistently since beginning). He would be a member of the working middle or upper middle class who rides motorcycles for fun, recreation, and excitement. In chapter 3, we explore the values, attitudes, beliefs, and meaningful symbols that exemplify the motorcycle subculture in the United States.

# CHAPTER 3

# Biker and Motorcyclist Values, Old and New

A half-dozen riders stand next to their high-powered motorcycles and go through their pre-ride ritual. Full tank of gas? Check. Oil level okay? Check. Correct tire pressure? Check. Turn signals work? Check. Brakes functioning properly? Check. Clutch cable tight enough? Check. Headlight working? Check. Taillight? Check. Turn signals? Check. Plenty of sunscreen; fresh bottle of water; cell phones, GPS? Check, check, check, and check. They put on helmets, sunglasses, and perhaps a touch of lip balm to prevent chapping. Zip their leather jackets, don pairs of matching leather gloves, mount the motorcycles, and they are ready to go. Obviously, this is not a local chapter of some one-percenter motorcycle club or a group of hardcore bikers out to wreak havoc on the highways. Rather, these five men and one woman represent a growing phenomenon in the United States—the motorcyclist subculture.

Every subculture shares a set of values, attitudes, beliefs, norms, and behaviors that unite them. Many Americans are members of racial or ethnic subcultures, others are part of a religious subculture, and many adults participate in some type of occupational subculture. Musicians tend to hang around with other musicians, teachers associate with other teachers, and police officers with other cops. Similarly, recreational subcultures abound. Common interests reflect values, attitudes, and beliefs that create a strong social bond. Common activities create a sense of community and belonging. When danger is involved, as in police work, mountain climbing, or skydiving, the bond seems to be even stronger. Such is the case with motorcyclists.

## Traditional "Biker" Values

Chapter 1 briefly looked at the emergence of neo-bikers and motorcyclists and contrasted them with hardcore bikers and one-percenters. J. Mark Watson (1980) concluded that "outlaw bikers" reflected what criminologist

Walter B. Miller (1958) had earlier identified as "lower class cultural concerns": trouble, toughness, smartness, excitement, fate, and autonomy. Watson takes each of these "lower-class cultural concerns" or *values*,[1] and illustrates how they are manifested in the hardcore biker lifestyle.

Bikers and trouble go hand in hand — trouble with the law, trouble with each other, and especially trouble between one biker club and another. A biker who is not in trouble or causing trouble is probably not being a biker. I asked a tavern owner in Sturgis about a sign at the front entrance that indicated people wearing club "colors" would not be admitted, and he remarked, "We get a lot of one-percenters in here from time to time, and usually there's no problem, but if even one of 'em comes in wearing his colors, there is always trouble." At the Republic of Texas (ROT) Rally one year a hardcore biker who stood about 6 feet 5 inches and easily weighed 300 pounds sported a sleeveless t-shirt that read: "You lookin' for trouble?" on the front and the words "You found it!" on the back were accompanied by a drawing of a one-percenter on a chopper with his middle finger stuck high in the air. At the same rally a much smaller but equally intimidating-looking hardcore biker wore a t-shirt that simply said "Badass" on it. I did not see anybody challenge either of these biker's assertions.

Toughness needs little explanation and the word is almost synonymous with biker when talking about hardcore bikers and one-percenters. Old Harley-Davidson motorcycles used to be referred to as "hard tails" because they did not have any rear shock absorbers. Some riders found it necessary to wear a kidney belt or some other form of protection when riding long distances just to keep their internal organs intact. Some one-percenters still ride those old Harleys and take great pride in being tough enough to take the beatings those old bikes can deliver. Of course being tough enough to ride is only one aspect of biker toughness, and most biker beatings do not come from a motorcycle. Early biker clubs routinely engaged in fistfights that as often as not would include brass knuckles, motorcycle chains, knives, or even guns. Today's bikers take great pride in their toughness and often carry or have access to semi-automatic and fully automatic weapons that can bring down even the toughest adversary. It is tough to get into a biker club and even tougher to get out of one. Probably few traits are valued more than toughness in the hardcore biker world.

Although bikers may not place a lot of value on smartness in terms of formal education, they do place extreme importance on "street smarts." A biker who is not street savvy will not last long, and a naive or gullible biker suffers a lot of humiliation from other bikers who will con him out of money and possessions and make him the butt of numerous practical jokes. A new type of smartness is probably more important to modern-day one-percenters as many of those clubs are allegedly involved in the trafficking of illegal drugs and weapons as well as laundering money. Most clubs run different types of legitimate businesses to account for earned income and bikers with accounting skills and legal knowledge who can fight the Internal Revenue Service and state and federal prosecutors are as valuable to a club as those who can fight rival club members.

Motorcycles and excitement are virtually inseparable. Add to the sheer exhilaration of riding at high speeds on the open roads on two wheels the excitement of doing it under the influence of alcohol and other drugs, and "keeping the shiny side up" takes on a whole new meaning. Sprinkle in wild parties, occasional barroom brawls, periodic gang fights, and confrontations with the police, and there is rarely a dull moment in the biker world.

Bikers tend to be fatalists. They usually do not wear protective helmets or any other safety equipment. Most bikers smoke heavily, drink and ride, and engage in numerous other high-risk activities, usually under the mantra of "when your time is up, your time is up"—leaving their life chances in the hands of fate. Their good fortune is usually viewed as a result of being in the right place at the right time, or simply good luck, and their misfortunes are the polar opposites. Again, a t-shirt worn by a biker at Sturgis comes to mind. On the front was a picture of a scantily clad woman on a customized motorcycle. On the back, the slogan: "Don't ever fuck with lady luck."

Finally, no one word epitomizes the biker lifestyle more than "freedom"—their word for autonomy. They tattoo it on their bodies, paint it on their bikes, sew it on their vests, and exhibit their version of it in everything they do—freedom from laws, from legal and social obligations, from "cages,"[2] and essentially freedom from any/all of the constraints of "straight" society. Freedom Rides and Freedom Runs are mainstays at many biker rallies, and American flags, freedom flags, and freedom-related pins, decals, and patches abound in the biker subculture.

Although rebellion was not listed as one of the values linked to Miller's theory or Watson's research, no list of traditional biker values would be complete without it. Non-riders, once referred to as "squares" or "straights" are more often referred to as "citizens" by bikers today, and essentially, bikers rebel against virtually everything that squares, straights, or citizens stand for: values, norms, laws, cars, and most everything else associated with the non-biker world. That rebellion and contempt is also directed toward neo-bikers and motorcyclists.

## Biker Values Revisited — Motorcyclist Style

Bikers might be surprised at the extent to which members of the motorcyclist subculture, comprised primarily of well-educated, middle-class professionals and working-class Baby Boomers, also embrace some of these so-called "lower-class focal concerns." They express them in far different ways, however, more reflective of their social class, educational levels, and commitment to social values and norms. Nevertheless, although motorcyclists are rarely classified as "rebels," they do violate many of the normative expectations for people of their social status and both intentionally and subconsciously exhibit many of the values that Watson linked to hardcore bikers.

## Trouble

One would think that the last thing a middle-class motorcyclist would want is trouble, and to some extent, that would be correct. Unlike the hardcore bikers or the "one-percenters," today's motorcyclists do not go on the lookout for trouble. Nevertheless, trouble often finds the motorcycle rider, and despite generally being law-abiding citizens, some motorcyclists violate mandatory helmet laws and quite a few ride their motorcycles after consuming alcoholic beverages. I am constantly amazed that some motorcyclists do not have a motorcycle endorsement on their license, fail to have up-to-date registrations or bike inspections, and do not carry even the state-mandated liability insurance. Interviews with over 200 motorcyclists indicated that approximately 13 percent (29) did not have up-to-date motorcycle inspections and/or registrations; almost 11 percent (24) did not have proper motorcycle licenses or endorsements; and 8 percent (18) carried no liability insurance other than what was issued for their automobile. Most of those committing these infractions were among the neo-bikers and blue-collar/working-class motorcyclists, but some upper-middle-class professionals also committed them. I spoke with one woman who had just completed a motorcycle safety course and gotten her motorcycle license, who said, "My husband and I ride with 3 other couples all the time, and we decided that one of us should get a motorcycle license, so if we ever get stopped, at least one of us would be legal." Almost all of the upper-middle-class professionals interviewed met the minimum legal requirements, and the majority of them (roughly two-thirds or 66%) had completed a motorcycle safety course. Nevertheless, on one occasion when riding with two other riders (another college professor and an attorney), I noticed that one of them (the attorney) had an expired safety inspection sticker on his motorcycle. When I commented on it, he replied, "Oh, I don't waste my time or money on getting my bike inspected anymore." He went on to indicate that he had been stopped by police officers on at least three or four occasions, showed his license and proof of insurance, and the expired safety inspection was either never noticed or never mentioned. He concluded, "I figure if anybody ever makes a big deal out of it, they'll just write me a warning, and I'll run down and get a new sticker." A 31-year-old rider who also had an expired safety inspection sticker on his bike told me, "I get my

This photo taken in 1965 of high school buddy Danny McHenry (on back) and me on a Honda 150 reveals that we were anything but "bikers" in those days. Nevertheless, it doesn't take a lot of imagination to envision how two 15-year-olds could manage to get into trouble and experience a little excitement on this two-wheeled "beast."

car inspected every year. I'm not paying the same amount for a guy to hear me honk the horn and flash the turn signals on my bike."

It is rare to find a bike show or motorcycle rally where there are not some infractions of open container laws, marijuana possession statutes, nudity laws, or other violations of state and local laws and ordinances. Bikers and neo-bikers are most likely to participate in these activities. Although motorcyclists may only be on the fringes of these law-violating behaviors mostly as spectators, they participate in some of them, and almost never report any of them — in many cases, a legal violation in itself. Trash talking and gang fights are uncommon at motorcycle shows and rallies, but they do occur at some of the larger rallies such as Laconia, Sturgis and Daytona (usually at campgrounds or on the outskirts of the actual event) and they abound on Internet blogs, message boards, in chat rooms, and other cyberspace venues. This allows even motorcyclists to create or maintain the "tough" image associated with those who ride motorcycles.

A very large percentage (just under 80 percent) of the riders I interviewed responded that they had consumed at least one beer and ridden their motorcycles, a figure that was more than substantiated by personal observations. Poker runs and other organized motorcycle rides often use bars or restaurants that serve alcohol as stops along the way. Although some riders, myself included, make it a habit to only consume water or soft drinks while riding, the beverage of choice among motorcyclists seems to be beer. Needless to say, five or more stops on a ride would more than put almost any rider over the legal limit.

Unlike their hardcore biker counterparts, motorcyclists attempt to avoid trouble with other riders if at all possible. Most view the motorcycle subculture as a "brotherhood" (see chapter 4), and they do not want any trouble with their "brothers." Nevertheless, riders are an independent lot, and they tend to resent others who attempt to infringe upon their rights or freedoms. A subject that appears on many blogs and in several chat rooms is the topic of wearing logos and insignias on jackets or vests— something that can arouse the ire of hardcore bikers and one-percenters if interpreted as being disrespectful of their colors or invasion of their turf. Many riders make statements like, "Nobody can tell me what to wear when I ride my bike." Other riders usually point out, however, that if you want to avoid trouble, it is wise to not wear anything that might alienate fellow riders, especially those from the hardcore biker and one-percenter ranks.

A colleague with whom I ride fairly regularly often does not wear a helmet despite the law requiring a helmet unless the rider is over 21 years of age (he is) and has completed a motorcycle safety course (he has not). His view: "It's my head and my life, so it's none of the government's business— plus, since I'm obviously over 21 and over half the riders in the state don't have to

wear helmets, I can't imagine that any cop's going to pull me over for it."
When I pointed out that he was probably correct about not getting stopped
for it, but if he gets pulled over for speeding or some other violation, that he
most likely will also be hit with the non-helmet violation, his response was,
"I'd rather pay the fine once or twice than sacrifice the great feeling of riding
without a helmet."

## Toughness

It is difficult to think of doctors, dentists, lawyers, college professors,
and other white-collar professionals who comprise a large segment of the
motorcycle subculture as tough, but a certain amount of toughness is required
to ride a motorcycle, and is highly valued by almost all motorcyclists.
Although motorcycles have come a long way in terms of creature comforts,
most riders find that more than a couple of hours or a hundred miles or so
before stopping can be taxing on the body. The *Iron Butt Association* calls
itself the "World's Toughest Motorcycle Association" and prides itself on long
distance rides, such as the SaddleSore 1000 (1000 miles in 24 hours), Bun-
Burner 1500 (1500 miles in 24 or 36 hours), and the 50cc Quest which goes
coast to coast in 50 hours (IBA, 2007). Anybody who has ridden a motorcycle
knows how tough an individual has to be to complete such long-distance
rides in such short periods of time. One-percenters and hardcore bikers have
probably accomplished such feats numerous times, but you will not find an
"Iron Butt" patch on a biker's vest or jacket. Such accoutrements are strictly
for neo-bikers and/or motorcyclists. Although many motorcyclists have never
accomplished any of those achievements, they are the types of riders that are
most likely to participate in such events or seek such recognition.

The inherent risks and dangers in motorcycle riding demand a certain
amount of physical and mental toughness. Despite university degrees and
social status, if a motorcyclist is involved in an accident and goes sliding
across the pavement, the dangers and the pain are just as real as they are for
hardcore bikers and one-percenters. While middle- and upper-middle-class
motorcyclists may be more likely to wear helmets, body armor, leathers, and
other protective apparel, the risks associated with riding are very real. I am
reminded of this every time I ride, but had it verbally driven home when I
pulled into a filling station and encountered the driver of an 18-wheeler who
was re-filling the underground gasoline tanks from his truck. He looked at
me and my motorcycle and said, "Damn, you gotta be tough to ride one of
those things." This coming from a man who drives an 18-wheeler loaded with
several thousand gallons of highly explosive fuel for a living!

No doubt much of the "tough" image of bikers and motorcyclists comes
from movies and television (see chapters 7 and 8), but in real life, riders find

that their toughest challenges usually come from braving the elements, dealing with flying objects, and trying to guess what drivers of automobiles and trucks are going to do, rather than from battling with law enforcement or rival biker clubs. On one occasion after purchasing a new motorcycle without a windshield, I was out riding at about sunset when I was suddenly struck in the chest hard enough to temporarily knock the wind out of me. My first reaction was to slow down and see if I could find the sniper who had evidently taken a shot at me and hit me dead center. Instead, I glanced down to see the partial remains of a June bug on my t-shirt. Although it seems exaggerated, any motorcyclist can attest to the pain inflicted by stinging rain, flying bugs, rocks, and other debris at speeds of even 40 or 50 miles per hour, much less speeds in excess of 70. Other times, I have ridden through 40- and 50-mile-an-hour winds, torrential rains, and temperatures ranging from the low teens to the hundred and teens. These are the minor tests of toughness associated with riding. The major tests involve the inevitable — taking a spill on a motorcycle.

There is an old expression among motorcyclists that there are two kinds of riders: "Those who have, and those who will." This, of course, refers to having some type of accident, and probably is the most accurate of any attempt at categorizing motorcycle riders. Like most people who have ridden as long as I have, I fit into the "have" group. My first "spill" experience came at age 15 riding a 50cc motorcycle to school on a frigid January morning. In those days, it was stylish to wear blue jeans that ended about an inch or two above the ankle. When in the riding position, that meant that there was about a one-inch gap between the bottom of my jeans and the top of my socks. One morning when the temperature was in the mid-twenties, I realized just how cold that one inch of exposed flesh could be. Instead of pulling over and stopping to make an adjustment, I decided to reach down with my left hand and attempt to pull up my sock to close the gap, while riding at about 35 miles per hour. When my body slid to a stop, I looked back to see that, based on the remnants of blue jean material, flesh, and blood, my bike and I had traveled a good twenty feet from the place where we hit the pavement to the point where we finally skidded to a halt. Despite wearing a heavy jacket and denim jeans, my skin was peeled from my left shoulder down to my elbow and from my left thigh down to my knee. It's called road rash and it hurts like crazy! I was lucky that there were no broken bones or internal injuries, and even more fortunate that there was no traffic coming from either direction since my body and the bike had traveled across both lanes of the street. On one other occasion about two years later, I was riding a Honda 305 Superhawk at about 40 miles per hour when an oncoming car decided to left turn in front of me. I evaded hitting the car broadside by crossing over the lane for oncoming traffic (again fortunate that there was none) and then traveling down an embankment into a ditch where I swerved back and forth for about fifty feet until the bike hit a large rock and catapulted me over the handlebars. I was pretty sure that I had broken my wrist and collarbone, although it turned out that neither was seriously injured. I was grateful that I had avoided hitting any cars and was treated to a "soft" landing compared to what might have happened had I stayed on the street. Other than those times I have had some terrifyingly close calls, but have been very lucky.

Almost every rider interviewed had experienced several near-mishaps, and most had been in a relatively minor accident; some had been in some fairly major ones. At the Republic of Texas (ROT) Rally in Austin, I spoke with a motorcyclist on crutches who said he had taken a nasty spill two weekends before on an interstate highway when an 18-wheeler pulled over into his lane forcing him off the road. He suffered a compound fracture in his tibia. At that same rally, a rider in a motorized wheelchair explained to me that he lost both of his legs in a motorcycle accident two years earlier. In Hot Springs, Arkansas, I met a rider with one leg who had rigged his motorcycle so that he could apply both his front and rear brakes with his right hand since he had lost his right leg in a motorcycle accident when he was 16. When asked why he did not give up riding after the accident, he replied, "My mom insisted that I quit riding, but my dad, who also rides, said, 'Hell, boy, you gotta be tougher than that." A former motorcycle racer recounted an accident that almost took his life, put him in a coma for weeks, and left him with pins in both legs, one of which is fused together in such a way as to be almost useless. His main goal: "find a motorcycle that [he] can ride for fun that does not require the use of [his] left leg." Countless other riders have recounted stories of both major and minor accidents, some no doubt exaggerating, but others modestly downplaying their physical toughness.

Motorcyclists may require even more mental toughness than their hardcore counterparts. Because of their lifestyle and their regular associates, probably very few one-percenters or hardcore bikers are asked why they ride or are ever chided or derided for doing so. Conversely, motorcyclists, especially middle- and upper-middle-class professionals, are routinely questioned as to why we have a "death wish," or we are derided for giving in to our "midlife crises." It takes a certain amount of mental toughness to climb aboard a high-powered two-wheeled machine, knowing the risks, and having to convince friends and loved ones that you do so not because you have a "death wish," but because you have a "life wish."

### Smartness

Miller (1958) contended that lower-class boys rejected the middle-class definition of smartness in favor of a lower-class version that valued "street smarts" over book learning and formal education. Watson (1980) concluded that hardcore bikers rejected smartness altogether and often proudly referred to themselves as "dumb bikers," whereas Quinn (2001) noted that outlaw motorcyclists valued knowledge of mechanics and the ability to work on engines.

Today's motorcyclists value all types of smartness. Most are well educated, many with university and postgraduate degrees and/or professional certifications. Many of the blue-collar motorcyclists have some college education or technical training beyond high school and also value knowledge and often work on their own bikes. Motorcyclists tend to subscribe to motorcycle magazines, study their owner's manuals, and constantly seek out new information about their motorcycles and other equipment. Two of the most common admonitions heard when motorcyclists part company are "ride safe" and "ride smart." Motorcyclists know these phrases may not be grammatically correct, but still give this advice regularly.

When interviewing middle-aged or older riders, I was struck by how many of them attributed their riding longevity to their riding experience and knowledge. One 51-year-old commented,

> I look back on my early riding days and realize I wasn't very smart. I never wore a helmet, rode in shorts and t-shirts, and took way too many chances. I got lucky on several occasions. Now, I rely on smarts a whole lot more than luck. I guess I figure you can always do the smart thing, but you can't always be lucky.

Another rider, in his early 60s, told me, "The main difference between how I ride now and how I rode when I was in my teens and twenties is that I'm a helluva lot smarter than I used to be back then — on a bike smartness is the key to survival."

Motorcycle magazines and Internet forums often contain articles or threads discussing how to avoid accidents and road hazards, or how to improve riding skills, with most participants exhorting the importance of "being smart." A number of posted comments begin with the phrase, "A smart rider would...." Nevertheless, as with hardcore bikers, much of the time, when motorcyclists get in trouble or have an accident, it is because they did something incredibly dumb. Almost every male has some humorous or semi-tragic story that starts with the words "Hey guys, watch this." Or, as one fellow motorcyclist posted on a forum, "Most motorcycle accidents are caused by the nut that connects the handlebars to the seat."

## Excitement

One of the standard questions asked of each interviewee in this study was "Why do you ride?" (the focus of chapter 10). Although there were numerous different specific responses to the query, answers could easily be grouped into one of four categories: fun, freedom, relaxation, or excitement, with most bikers including elements of at least three of the four as part of their motivation. A typical response can be seen in that of a fifty-something dentist who replied:

> I ride because I love it. My job is so tedious and usually boring — no fun, no thrills, and very little freedom to be creative or express myself. Plus, I'm cooped up inside all day. Riding lets me get outside and do all that. Going from zero to 60 in a matter of just a few seconds with the wind in your face and nothing between you and nature is exhilarating. It's the most fun and exciting thing I do, hands down.

Similarly, a physical therapist in his mid-forties responded:

> Why do I ride? The thrill, period. I know it's dangerous and I work with people every day who have been in accidents or otherwise do not have full use of their bodies, so I realize the risks. But still, it is so exciting to be sitting on 50 or 60 horses of sheer power. It's indescribable, and just incredible.

Ironically, although excitement is a prime motivation for riding, similar to riding in an airplane, the most enjoyable rides (flights) are those on which nothing exciting happens. Excitement on a motorcycle often translates into danger, and while the rider may experience a certain adrenaline rush, and perhaps gain an interesting story to tell, most motorcyclists try to avoid danger as much as possible. A classic example can be found in the conversation I had with my wife after just completing a 3,000-plus-mile roundtrip with friends to Sturgis for Bike Week. She asked, "How was the ride?" I replied, "It was fun — nothing really exciting happened, but we had a good time." Her response: "Good, you don't need any more excitement on a motorcycle." Later, when I told her about an encounter with a herd of bison in Custer State Park, and my brief but potentially dangerous nose-to-headlight standoff with a particularly protective bull who thought my bike and I posed a threat to a calf and its mother, she reminded me, "I thought you said nothing exciting happened."

Nevertheless, in the final chapter of this book when we look at why motorcyclists ride, it is clear that excitement is a prime motivator. There is something almost primal about traveling down a highway or back road with only two three-inch patches of rubber between you and the asphalt feeling each and every bump and the exhilaration of the wind and elements surrounding you. There is no question — it is exciting.

## Fate

Numerous studies indicate that members of the lower class tend to have fatalistic attitudes, often believing that they have little control over their lives, and attributing their life situations to happenstance, good or bad luck (mostly bad), and fate (Hurst, 2010). Working middle class and professional people, however, generally are "take charge" types who believe the outcome of situations are largely determined by their efforts and not by fate, chance, luck, or other mysterious forces. Yet, motorcyclists, even the most highly educated ones, are notoriously superstitious, and just by virtue of riding a motorcycle, are to some extent putting their destinies in the hands of fate.

Whereas one-percenters and hardcore bikers, and perhaps even neo-bikers, are more likely to throw caution to the wind and believe that "when your time is up, your time is up," today's motorcyclists are far more likely to take motorcycle safety courses, wear helmets and other protective apparel, purchase insurance (both motorcycle and life), and do everything within their power to reduce the dangers of biking. Still, many motorcyclists attach a "biker bell" to their motorcycle, which legend has it provides good luck to the rider. The bell is supposed to be attached to the lowest point of the bike in order to keep "road gremlins" from hopping up on the bike and causing problems for the motorcycle or rider. Supposedly, the bell provides double the good luck if a rider has received it as a gift as opposed to purchasing it. Although most said they thought it was just a silly superstition, of the 224 riders interviewed in this study, over half (126 or 56.3 percent) admitted they had a bell attached to their motorcycles, and 6 riders indicated they had more than one bell on their bikes. (I have two on my cruiser — one I purchased and one that was given to me.) When asked why they had the bell(s), most sheepishly replied, "I figure it can't hurt." A major insurance company that specializes in motorcycle policies appealed to this well-known biker superstition with a 2007 mail advertisement that said: "They're out there. Gremlins looking to take a crack at what you love best: your motorcycle. Before the Gremlins get you, get ... [name of insurance company] insurance." I am neither Catholic nor particularly superstitious, but every time I ride I wear a sterling silver chain with a St. Columbanus (the patron saint of motorcyclists) around my neck. When one of my friends asked me once why I wore it, I responded, "Why not? Can't hurt." Similarly, once after I witnessed a Native American "blessing of the bikes" before an organized ride, I asked one of the riders, "Do you believe in this sort of thing?" His response, "Not really, but hey, I'll take all the blessings I can get"—followed by a pause and then by, you guessed it, "Can't hurt."

## Autonomy

No single word epitomizes the motorcyclist subculture more than the word *freedom* — a synonym for autonomy. Hardcore bikers, one-percenters, neo-bikers, blue-collar riders, as well as middle- and upper-middle-class professional riders alike, refer to automobiles as "cages."[2] A motorcycle represents freedom from that cage. In *Zen and the Art of Motorcycle Maintenance*, Pirsig

(1974) described driving or riding in a car as a *mediated* experience, whereas riding a motorcycle puts a person *in* the environment as opposed to merely viewing it through a pane of glass. Every rider knows what Pirsig means. When asked why he rides, one biker responded, "for the same reason a dog sticks his head out the window of a car." Still another, replied, "Are you kidding me? Why not? It's such a sense of freedom." Another who emphasized the autonomy said, "When I'm riding, it's just me, the bike, and the road." Motorcycling represents and provides a sense of autonomy, even if only temporarily, that middle-class Baby Boomers can find in very few, if any, other areas of their lives—freedom from the stress and responsibilities of their careers, families, mortgages, taxes, and civic duties—freedom from their everyday lives. This particular aspect of motorcycling is explored in much greater detail in chapter 10 on why motorcyclists ride.

A popular song of the 1970s included a verse that proclaimed that freedom was another word for not having anything to lose, and while that may describe the feelings of the one-percenters and some of the hardcore bikers, it is hardly an accurate description of today's motorcyclist subculture.[3] While they may embrace the freedom experienced by riding, motorcyclists have plenty to lose. Their worlds and lifestyles include motorcycles and riding, but they do not revolve around them. Instead, families, jobs, careers, homes, mortgages, civic organizations, and a host of other personal and social responsibilities limit a true feeling of freedom when they take to the road. One motorcyclist acknowledged this sense of responsibility when he confessed:

> Since our baby was born, I haven't put a hundred miles on my bike. I just don't feel free to ride anymore. I mean, if something happened to me ... what would the wife and kid ... well, what would they do about the house, the mortgage? Don't get me wrong, I love riding, and will probably start up again at some time, but right now, I just don't feel like I can do it. It would be selfish.

Another rider, a 56-year-old surgeon, told me, "Every time I pull on my gloves to ride, I think: man, I need to take care of these hands—they're my livelihood." One other rider, a public school teacher and coach, confided, "I sometimes wonder if the risks are worth it, I mean, I've got a wife, a family, a mortgage ... but just about the time that speedometer hits 50, all my doubts go away."

## Meaningful Symbols for Motorcyclists

Every subculture has its own unique set of meaningful symbols that sets it apart from larger society and other subcultures (Thompson and Hickey, 2011). Watson (1980) noted that outlaw bikers adopt certain symbols, including extensive tattooing, beards, dirty jeans, earrings, skullcaps, boots, and cut-off jackets or vests with patches and pins attached — often with a club emblem or their "colors." He contended the single most important symbol for an outlaw biker was the Harley-Davidson V-twin motorcycle. Today, in the motorcycle subculture, if you replace "dirty jeans" with clean designer jeans, leather chaps, or expensive leather pants, and allow for the wide array of "Harley clones" made by Victory, Honda, Kawasaki, Yamaha, and Suzuki, the symbols are pretty much the same. In many ways, at least from a distance, it is difficult to distinguish today's motorcyclists and especially the neo-bikers from the hardcore bikers and one-percenters. There are important differences between these groups, however, though many of the symbols are similar.

## *The Motorcycle*

It may seem obvious that the most important symbol for motorcyclists is the motorcycle. It's hard to imagine a cowboy without a horse, a boater without a boat, or a skier without skis, but the motorcycle is far more than just a necessary component of motorcycling. Thomas Hauffe (1998) contended that as a design object the motorcycle has three functions: practical, to move a person about; aesthetic, to please the senses; and symbolic. to transmit social information about the rider. Or, as Alford and Ferriss (2007:8) explain, "the motorcycle is infused with cultural significance, tied up with complex issues of history, technology, engineering, consumerism, psychology, aesthetics, gender, and sexuality." To put it in simple terms, a 29-year-old Iraqi war veteran who rode a highly modified Heritage Softail painted in military camouflage told me, "You are what you ride." Perhaps more poetically, a 72-year-old rider of a fully decked out touring bike said, "My wife gets a bit jealous of Eileen,[4] but I always tell her — look, honey, you're my wife and the only real woman I love, but Eileen's my girlfriend, my mistress, my friend, and my companion." Then, looking around almost as if to see if his wife were in hearing range he added, "plus she don't ever say no when I want to ride her." When I asked this man how he came up with the name Eileen, he laughed and responded, "because whenever I want her to turn and go where I want her to go, 'I lean.'"

As mentioned in chapter 2, World War II veterans returned home from war with Germany and Japan, and many of them took up motorcycle riding, in part, because it provided excitement for young men who had risked everything in war. Out of work and fresh from the camaraderie of the military, many of the young men hung around motorcycle garages and bars and formed motorcycle clubs, some of which evolved into biker gangs. In his autobiography, Ralph "Sonny" Barger, founder of the Hell's Angels, admits that many of the Japanese motorcycles and the German-made BMW were faster and more dependable, but the Hell's Angels committed to riding Harley-

The motorcycle is the most powerful symbol in both the biker and motorcyclist circles followed closely by jackets, helmets, and other gear. The white DOT-approved helmet and the Kevlar-padded textile jacket reveal that these two bikes belong to motorcyclists and not one-percenters or hardcore bikers. One of these motorcycles is a Harley-Davidson Road King and the other is a Honda VTX 1300. Can you tell which is which? Could you differentiate between them if they passed you at 70 miles per hour?

Davidsons because they were American made (Barger, et al., 2001:53). In today's motorcycle subculture, however, Harley-Davidsons, Victorys, BMWs, Yamahas, Hondas, Kawasakis, Suzukis, and other brands of motorcycles are almost indistinguishable, especially from a distance. Sonny Barger, in fact, has been pictured on the Internet on a Victory Vision, Harley-Davidson's main American-made competitor. As noted in chapter 4, allegiance to the "brotherhood" of motorcycle riders seems to overcome some of the brand loyalties and previous hostilities of the past, although some hardcore bikers and one-percenters and even more neo-bikers still admonish, "If it ain't a Harley, it ain't shit." I doubt seriously that they have dissected that phrase to see how it could just as easily be interpreted as the exact opposite of what they mean by it.

Although research indicates that brand loyalty tends to be much stronger among motorcycle riders than automobile drivers (Schouten and McAlexander, 1995), motorcyclists seem more attached to motorcycles in general than any one particular brand of bike. As noted in chapter 1, however, there are some noticeable divisions between the riders of certain types of motorcycles, especially between the riders of cruisers or touring bikes and those who ride the sport bikes or "crotch rockets." The V-twin cruiser epitomizes the motorcycling subculture and symbolically represents an image that links the past with the present in the motorcycling world.

## The "Uniform"

Glynn Kerr (2011:38) contends that "while function may dictate the attire to a certain extent, much of it comes down to image and the desire for acceptance within the chosen group." He points out that much like the obligatory school uniforms he was required to wear as a schoolboy growing up in Great Britain, today's motorcycle riders, despite their air of rebelliousness, conform to a "uniform" linked to the particular type of bike they ride and identity they seek as a rider: "jerseys over armor on dirtbikers, Cordura two-piece touring suits on adventure tourers, black leather with skull patches on Harleys, one-piece leathers on sportbikers" (Kerr, 2011:38). Although most motorcycle riders would probably bristle at the word "uniform," motorcycle attire is clearly designed and marketed to appeal to certain categories of riders. Nevertheless, despite its variations, there is some uniformity in dress across all subcategories of motorcyclists that has symbolic ties to the motorcycle riders of yesteryear as well as the one-percenters, hardcore bikers, and neo-bikers of today.

## Leather Pants, Chaps, Jeans and Gloves

Doctors, lawyers, college professors and other white-collar professionals rarely don dirty jeans to mow the lawn or perform any other chore, much less to ride their $10,000–$30,000 motorcycles. Jeans are often part of the motorcyclist's wardrobe, but they are almost always clean and as often as not covered with leather chaps, or replaced with leather or some other form of protective pants, especially in cold weather. Leather serves both symbolic and pragmatic functions for motorcyclists. Symbolically, it is a visible link to hardcore biker subcultures and "personifies" the biker look. As the old saying goes, "There are two kinds of riders." Every motorcycle rider knows that they risk going down on a bike, which even in a best-case scenario, means coming into contact with gravel, blacktop, concrete, or worse. "Road rash" is a reality, and bikers know that if they go down, any fabric is better than bare skin, denim is better than most other fabrics, and leather is much more protective than denim. Many riders wear as much leather as possible both for looks and safety. Leather gloves provide a better grip on the handlebars, but more importantly, provide protection for the hands from flying insects and debris, and if a rider goes down, hands and fingers are among the first things to hit the pavement.

Leather chaps, pants, boots, vests, jackets, gloves, and skullcaps are an essential part of most bikers' and motorcyclists' wardrobes. Some pants and jackets are even fitted with rubber, plastic, or Kevlar "body armor" inserts at vital areas such as knees, crotch, spine, hips, elbows, and shoulders for additional protection should the rider be involved in an accident. Both women and men tend to wear similar attire and except for color schemes and some of the graphics, it often is difficult to distinguish male from female riders, especially at a distance.

## Helmets, Skullcaps and Bandanas

One-percenters and hardcore bikers tend to shun helmets in favor of skullcaps or bandanas, and if they do wear one, are more likely to wear what is referred to as a "novelty" helmet, which does not meet DOT requirements and is designed more for looks than safety. These helmets often resemble World War I Prussian helmets, or are modified half-helmets, usually plain black in color, or adorned with skulls and crossbones, or other intimidating symbols.

Motorcyclists are more likely than bikers to wear protective helmets, but skullcaps and bandanas are still part of the motorcycle subculture. Over half (116 out of 224) of the riders I interviewed said they always wear a helmet, and when combined with those who said they wear a helmet at least sometimes, approximately two-thirds (149) were included. Rarely does one encounter a bareheaded rider on a motorcycle. Motorcyclists' helmets are almost always Department of Transportation approved with the letters DOT clearly stenciled on the back verifying that they meet the minimum safety requirements established by the Department of Transportation for protective motorcycle headgear. Many helmets also boast of meeting Snell safety standards which are more stringent than those of DOT. Motorcyclists may spend anywhere from $50 to in excess of $1,000 for state-of-the-art protective headgear equipped with adjustable tinted visors, air vents, interchangeable cheek pads, and adjustable chinstraps. Some helmets can be fitted with or come equipped with headphones for music or communication with other riders. Helmets come in solid black, but may also be multi-colored in a wide array of fluorescent paints and designs. Often, motorcyclists' helmets are color coordinated to match motorcycles and many riders attach reflective motorcycle emblems or even school colors or mascots of their favorite university or teams to their helmets.

If not wearing a helmet, neo-bikers and some motorcyclists usually sport a leather skullcap or one made of brightly colored bandana material. Some wear baseball caps with the bill facing backwards. Even those who wear helmets can be seen wearing bandanas beneath them, or donning them when they remove the helmet at bike shows or rallies. One woman rider told me, "We [women] wear bandanas because helmets mess up our hair." Another said, "I wear a bandana under my helmet because I want to be safe, but I also want to be presentable." Skullcaps and bandanas tend to be either solid black or brightly colored and adorned with iron crosses, flames, skulls, dragons, and other symbols suggesting a throwback to the biker subculture.

## Boots

High-top leather boots are a mainstay of motorcyclists and serve both symbolic and practical purposes. Boots look "tougher" than shoes, because they are. Just as leather pants and jackets provide added protection, so do boots that come above the ankle, especially those equipped with steel toes. Bikers shift with their left foot, which usually involves stepping down on, hooking a toe under, and pulling up on a gear shift lever. Bikers also often put their feet down, not only at stops, but sometimes at slow speeds. No shoe and even few boots will stand up to that kind of wear, tear, and abuse. Motorcycle riders can almost always identify non-riders or "posers" at rallies by looking at their boots. A rider's boots, even if recently cleaned and polished are usually scuffed and worn, especially on the left toe area.

At one time, motorcycle boots were exclusively black, and designed almost solely for protection of the feet, but in today's motorcycling subculture, in addition to providing safety and practicality, boots are also another part of the fashion world. They come in a wide variety of styles and colors, and like helmets, can range in price from $50 to in excess of $1,000. Most riders are into comfort as well as safety and protection, so boot makers offer "custom fits," waterproof and rain protection, oil-resistant soles, gel inserts, and a wide variety of other extras so that the boots can be worn both on and off the motorcycle for extended periods. Moreover, motorcyclists are very likely to own more than one pair of motorcycle boots. For example, I own a summer pair that are made of leather and mesh for air circulation, a winter pair that are solid leather with insulated lining, and a waterproof pair for rides when I expect to encounter rain or standing water. Don't even ask how many pairs of motorcycle boots my wife and daughter own. Suffice it to say they have almost every riding and fashion contingency covered.

## Jackets and Vests

Other than a motorcycle, could any single item symbolize the motorcycle subculture more than a leather jacket? In fact, leather jackets with wide lapels,

zippered pockets, and belts at the waist are often called "motorcycle jackets."
Actually, hardcore bikers and one-percenters, especially those in warm cli-
mates, are more likely to wear sleeveless denim than leather. But in the motorcyclist subculture, leather jackets and vests are the norm. As with leather
chaps, pants, and gloves, jackets provide some protection if riders go down.
Just as important, however, jackets and vests provide walking "billboards"
for motorcyclists. They announce: "I ride a motorcycle." Moreover, it is rare
to see a motorcyclist wearing a leather jacket or vest that is not adorned with
at least one, and usually several, pins, patches, and insignias. Hardcore bikers
and one-percenters usually wear vests with only their "colors"—club insignias
or club logos—but motorcyclists often adorn their leathers with stick pins
and patches denoting motorcycle shows or rallies attended, as well as patches
bearing manufacturers' logos or "bumper sticker" slogans such as: "loud pipes
save lives," "$15 thousand and 15 miles does not make you a biker," and
perennial favorite, "Ride to Live—Live to Ride." Other frequently seen
patches denote local and regional riding clubs, MSF safety course completion,
and various religious riding groups, such as "Bikers for Christ."

As with boots, leather jackets and vests among motorcyclists are as much
a fashion statement as they are for protection. In fact, a leather vest offers
very little protection, except perhaps for the rider's back, and given the fact
that they are rarely snapped tight in front, they are not likely to even do that.
Jackets and vests, once almost exclusively leather and black, now come in a
wide array of synthetic materials and fabrics and almost any solid or combination of colors. Many riders have a lightweight mesh or fabric jacket for
warmer temperatures and heavier leather or synthetic jackets for colder rides.
Jackets come in water resistant and waterproof versions and such a wide array
of styles that some would hardly be identified as "motorcycle" jackets, except
for the fact that the person wearing them happens to be riding a motorcycle.
Lightweight pads, Kevlar, and other forms of body armor can be inserted in
strategic areas of many jackets for added protection of spine, shoulders, and
elbows. Many manufacturers offer full body suits for motorcycle riding that
no self-respecting one-percenter or hardcore biker would be caught dead in,
but are popular with some of the motorcyclists, who wear them precisely
*because* they do not want to be caught dead in them.

## Tattoos

"Getting tattooed in a motorcycle gang is considered good and conforms
to the rules—of a motorcycle gang" (Goode and Vail, 2008:xiii). But tattoos
are no longer symbols of gang or motorcycle club membership. A study shows
that between 12 and 20 million Americans, almost one-fourth of all those
between ages 18 and 50 have tattoos (Bridges, 2006), and my observations

imply that the proportion is noticeably higher among neo-bikers and motor-cyclists. It is not uncommon to find tattoo parlors located in the same build-ings, on the same property, or adjacent to motorcycle shops, garages, or motorcycle-friendly bars. Motorcycle shows and rallies not only attract ven-dors of all varieties, but also a number of tattoo artists who set up temporary shops on-site to accommodate bikers and motorcyclists seeking a memento of the event. One of the more popular bars in Sturgis, the Full Throttle Saloon, even offers free tattoos of their logo to customers. Why not? It is free adver-tising. When browsing through a Harley-Davidson apparel store that did not even sell motorcycles on the river walk in San Antonio, I spotted a young sales woman sporting a tattoo of the Harley-Davidson logo on her upper arm. "You ride a Harley?" I asked her. "No, I don't ride," she replied, and then added, "I just like the looks of the design, and it doesn't hurt me with cus-tomers any." Now that's brand loyalty, or marketing genius, or maybe just ... let's leave it at one of those two things.

Of the 224 riders interviewed in this study, approximately 36 percent (81) sported readily visible tattoos and another twenty-eight indicated they had tattoos hidden by their clothing (a total of 48.7 percent with tattoos). Some of the tattoos were motorcycle related (Harley-Davidson logos or other motorcycle insignias), but most were the run of the mill, from the person's initials or somebody's name to pop-ular designs such as roses, dragons, tribal designs, and Chinese characters that presumably stood for "freedom," "peace," or the rider's name. Four of the riders interviewed sported "family" tattoos with names of wife and/or children, and two men sported the breast cancer awareness ribbon, but not in its traditional color of pink. All but 7 of the 31 women (77.4 percent) in the study had tattoos— the most popular loca-tions being on the lower

This tattoo sported by a motorcyclist reflects some traditional biker values and shows a commitment to motorcycles, but at the same time is strategically placed on the upper arm so that even when wearing a short-sleeved shirt the tattoo is usually covered and cannot be seen by boss, co-workers, friends, or the public.

back just above the buttocks, on the shoulder, or near the ankle, although a few of the women had visible tattoos on their forearms, biceps, necks, or breasts. At motorcycle shows and rallies, both men and women sport a wide range of colorful tattoos, and in addition to the tattoo artists who set up temporary shop, there usually can be found numerous henna tattoos, temporary tattoos for both adults and children, and even face and body painters wherever motorcycle riders gather in large numbers.

## Facial Hair and Earrings

Moustaches and beards are also common in the motorcycle subculture with a large portion of the men sporting facial hair. While styles vary, and facial hair moves in and out of popularity among non-motorcyclists, it seems to be a staple among bikers and motorcyclists, both old and new. Long beards can be troublesome when riding at high speeds, so many who sport them either braid their beards or use some type of pony tail holder, rubber band, or other restraining device to keep their beards from flying up into their faces.

Many male riders wear an earring (usually in the left earlobe), and some, especially younger riders, wear earrings in both ears, and the crotch rocketeers often have pierced ears, eyelids, lips, noses, and probably many other body parts that are out of view. Additionally, when talking to middle-aged and older riders up close, I often notice that several of the men who do not wear earrings have tiny impressions in the left earlobe indicating that the ear had been pierced at some time. In talking with male riders sporting earrings, I found that in many cases, the riders' ears had been pierced in the 1970s or '80s and that today the only time the rider wears an earring is on weekends or special occasions when riding his bike, attending rallies, or otherwise fraternizing in the biker subculture. Conversely, some motorcyclists have a pierced ear, but do not wear an earring when they ride because it interferes with putting on and removing their helmets. Similar to tattoo artists, vendors selling earrings, necklaces, rings, and other motorcycle- and non-motorcycle-related jewelry are plentiful at motorcycle shows and bike rallies. In addition to t-shirts and other apparel, Harley-Davidson probably sells as much, if not more, jewelry as they do motorcycles.

## Argot/Language

Finally, as with any subculture, motorcyclists have their own language, or argot, that creates and provides what sociologists refer to as *boundary maintenance*. Riders can talk for hours about bikes, modifications, shows, rallies, bars, and other motorcycle-related topics that would provide little interest and even less information to *cagers* who would not know *ape hangers* from *jug huggers*, a *crotch rocket* from a *full-dress bagger*, or a *rice-burner* from an *Indian Chief* (see glossary at end of book for specific examples and definitions). Moreover, individual organizations, message boards, and other factions within the subculture often have their own language, slang, and nomenclature.

Language should not be underestimated as an important element of the motorcyclist subculture. Just as doctors, nurses, and other medical personnel communicate in such a way that excludes "outsiders" and establishes credibility within their occupational subculture, motorcyclists almost immediately know if they are speaking to another rider, or merely a poser, within a few minutes to even just a few seconds of entering into conversation. On several occasions at shows or rallies, I initiated conversations with what, based on dress and demeanor, appeared to be a fellow rider, only to discover that he or she was somebody who just happened to attend the show or rally for entertainment purposes. I am not talking about snobbery based on whether somebody rides a certain type of motorcycle or another, or whether they trailer their bike to/from a rally instead of riding it (yes, that is a big deal even in the motorcyclist subculture — see chapter 6), nor am I referring to the distinction that hardcore bikers and one-percenters make between themselves and other motorcyclists — a very important distinction that both groups recognize and acknowledge. I simply mean that, similar to any other hobby, activity, or occupation, those who are truly engaged in it readily recognize others who are also "insiders" and can easily distinguish them from those who are not. Drummers can easily recognize other drummers, attorneys other lawyers, and police officers other cops. Likewise, if you encounter motorcyclists, young or old, and engage them in conversation about their bikes, know instantly that they will recognize whether you are a fellow rider, simply interested in motorcycles (and that's okay), or just killing time (also okay, but be careful what you wish for as once motorcyclists start talking about their bikes they can kill a *lot* of time). If you encounter an outlaw motorcyclist or one-percenter, it might be best to not engage them in conversation at all. Odds are they will ignore you. If you are wise, you will play the odds and return the favor. That's what motorcyclists usually do. Nevertheless, the overlap in values, attitudes, beliefs, and meaningful symbols of the old motorcycle subculture and motorcyclists creates a "brotherhood" that somewhat bonds all two-wheeled riders and distinguishes them from those who traverse the road on four or more wheels. We explore this brotherhood in the next chapter.

CHAPTER 4

# Motorcyclists and the "Brotherhood of Bikers"

"Sorry about your mom, my brother — I love you" (Queen, 2007:189). When Billy St. John, full-patch member of the notorious one-percenter motorcycle club the Mongols, heard those words repeated over and over as each of the members hugged him and offered their love and support, he was truly moved, and tears welled in his eyes. It was obvious that these men, his brothers, were sincerely concerned for him in his time of loss and grief. Conversely, since his mother's death, Special Agent William Queen was surprised and disappointed that none of his fellow ATF agents bothered to voice any consolation; his immediate supervisor not only offered no condolences but seemed a bit perturbed that Queen had taken a few days off work to attend his mother's funeral. Nevertheless, Special Agent Queen, deep undercover as biker Billy St. John in an effort to expose the organized criminal activities of the Mongols, a well-known outlaw motorcycle gang, realized that if his true identity was discovered by his "brothers," he was a dead man [Queen, 2007].

From their beginnings, motorcycle clubs, especially those that evolved into one-percenter motorcycle gangs, formed closely knit brotherhoods — all for one and one for all (Barger, 2001). Hanging around, becoming a prospect for 1 or 2 years, and experiencing all the hazing, fighting, and proving oneself to the club, whether good or bad, creates a bond that cannot be duplicated by riding on weekends and special occasions with friends and colleagues. Nevertheless, albeit a sexist term, "brotherhood" is also an appropriate description for the motorcycle subculture as well, although not nearly to the extent of the one-percenter motorcycle clubs. Despite the fact that more women are riding than ever before and play several important roles in the motorcyclist subculture (see chapter 5), motorcycling is still predominantly a male enterprise, and the motorcyclist subculture is a male-dominated world, with men comprising approximately 88 to 90 percent of all riders, and women approximately 10 to12 percent (Box, 2007; Knol, 2010; Womenriders, 2010). My observations for this research confirm those rough approximations, and my more extensive interviews with riders had approximately the same proportions (193 men and 31 women).

The term *brotherhood* implies a bond that goes beyond mere acquaintance or simply participating in the same activity. Moreover, it is less about sex and gender than it is about camaraderie and *esprit de corps*. As one woman rider confided to me at a rally, "I love these guys," as she gestured toward hundreds of motorcycle riders. "I feel like they are my brothers, and they treat me like I'm one of them. One thing I know for sure, when I'm on the road, these guys have my back." Time and again, I heard similar comments about the brotherhood among both male and female motorcyclists. A 63-year-old male retired firefighter told me,

> I've been riding since I was about twelve or thirteen. Started out with a little old Cushman Eagle and have ridden almost every make or model of motorcycle at one time or another. I'm attracted to the bikes, but there's more than that. I'm also attracted to the people. There's something about a guy, or gal for that matter, that rides a motorcycle. They just seem more genuine to me. I feel an immediate bond with almost everybody I meet on a bike. It's kind of like in the department. I mean, it's different, but then again it's sort of the same.

Although he never used the words "brother" or "brotherhood," the sentiment is clear.

It would be naïve and incorrect to assume that all motorcyclists are part of one big happy family. As noted in chapter 1, because of wartime experiences of World War II veterans, longstanding "feuds" developed between riders of American-made motorcycles (mostly Harley riders) and those who rode Japanese or German bikes dating back to the late 1940s and early 1950s. Throughout my years of riding I have witnessed a noticeable evolution in attitudes of Harley riders toward riders of other brands of motorcycles. Early on, it was a bit intimidating to be riding a Japanese motorcycle and suddenly find yourself surrounded by Harley riders, and I had one up-close and personal experience with the Harley/Japanese bike dispute when I was about 16 years old. One afternoon, I pulled up to a red light on a Honda 305 Superhawk, a fairly fast and sporty bike for its time, and a legitimate full-sized motorcycle in those days. I heard the roar of pipes as about a half dozen Harley-Davidsons pulled up beside and behind me. These were not one-percenters or even hardcore bikers, mind you, just a few 25 to 30-year-old guys on Harley-Davidsons out for a weekend ride. Without acknowledging me in any way, one of the HD riders turned and spit on the gas tank of my bike. The light turned green, and he and his buddies rode off laughing as I sat there on my bike, stunned, trying to decide what to do. My decision: better wash my bike when I get home. If I was part of a biker brotherhood, I had at least one very mean sibling.

Some 40 years later, my daughter and I were on our way to Austin for the Republic of Texas (ROT) Bike Rally. We were riding two-up on a Honda VTX 1300, one of the V-twin cruiser motorcycles that many people refer to as a Harley "clone." About halfway there we stopped for a restroom break and a soft drink and my daughter mentioned that the left rear passenger floorboard was a bit loose and probably should be tightened before we continued on our ride. A Harley rider parked a few feet away overheard me tell her that since we were spending the night I had taken all my tools out of the saddlebag to make room for our clothes and toiletries. He walked over, and said, "Mind if I take a look? I've probably got a wrench that'll fit." I told him that I'd greatly appreciate that, and he squatted down, took a quick look at the bolt head, and sauntered back to his bike, rummaged through his saddlebag, and returned with a socket wrench and a couple of sockets. "It's probably a 12 millimeter or 14 millimeter," he mumbled as he knelt down and fitted the first socket onto the bolt. Within just a few seconds he tightened the bolt, stood and put his foot on the floorboard and tried to swivel it a few times. "Good as new," he reported, and started back toward his bike. "Hey, thanks," I said, and then added, "I'm surprised you carry metric tools." He turned, smiled, and responded, "You don't think I carry all these tools just to fix my bike, do ya? You never know when a brother will need some help." "Good point," I replied, and my mind flashed back to the grizzled Harley rider about this guy's age who had spit on my gas tank when I was a teenager. I thanked him again, and pondered just how much things had changed over the years. I have encountered a lot of helpful biker/motorcyclist "brothers" on the road and very few have been concerned about what type or brand of motorcycle I rode. Although brand loyalty and design or style of motorcycle may divide motorcycle riders into various subgroups, as one BMW rider acknowledged to another researcher (Austin, 2009:83), "I think all riders regardless of the style of riding or the make of the bike, feel a connection to each other. It is an unspoken understanding that we all share a passion. People who don't ride have no concept of that connection."

Today's cruisers and touring bikes dominate the motorcycle subculture. Whether made by Harley-Davidson, Victory, BMW, Yamaha, Honda, Kawasaki, Suzuki, or some other manufacturer, they are almost indistinguishable, especially from a distance. Despite some feelings of brand loyalty (especially among Harley-Davidson, Goldwing and BMW owners) as mentioned in the previous chapter, riders of all makes and models share the road and, at least to some extent, perpetuate a spirit of brotherhood among bikers. For example, one weekend when I stopped to refuel at a station along an interstate highway and encountered two couples on Harley-Davidsons, I asked, "You guys aren't the types who hate Honda riders are you?" One of the men responded, "Hey, as long as you ride, that's all that matters," as the other man nodded in agreement. Then, one of the women jokingly added,

"You're welcome to join us, but we do make the rice burners ride in the back of the pack."

On another occasion while at a Honda dealership getting my motorcycle serviced, I noticed a man who appeared to be in his early 50s looking longingly at the new models on the showroom floor. I approached him and commented on one of the new bikes. The man said, "I've ridden Hondas since the 1960s and absolutely love 'em — best bike ever made — but I finally broke down this summer and bought a Harley." When asked why, he ducked his head and confessed, "Peer pressure — all my buddies ride Harleys, and we formed a little club and they made it part of the bylaws that we've gotta ride a Harley to be a member." Then, he quickly added, "But hey, we still like all the brothers who ride and anybody can ride any kind of bike with us; they just can't wear our colors." Bottom line: brotherhood over bikes.

One year at the Hot Springs rally in Arkansas, an organized ride through the scenic Ozark mountains included several stops at area sponsors, most of which were restaurants or bars. One stop, however, was at the local Polaris/Victory motorcycle dealership. I noticed several riders congregated around a new Cross Roads, Victory's newest entry in the cruiser/touring line. The riders were obviously impressed with the bike's powerful 106-cubic-inch V-twin engine, sleek styling, and large capacity saddlebags. A salesperson walked over to the group and indicated that they were offering free test rides all weekend and that they had a similar bike out in the parking lot fueled up and ready to ride if anybody was interested. One man, decked out in Harley-Davidson t-shirt, vest, and belt, snickered and said, "It's a beautiful bike, but it ain't a Harley," as he turned and walked away. A couple of others followed, but at least two of the men in the group, one of whom was also decked out in Harley apparel, took the salesman up on his offer. Interestingly, when he returned and the salesman asked him his impression, the rider responded, "It's faster, smoother, and handles a lot better than my Road King." The salesman smiled and posited, "So, you might consider purchasing one?" "Nah," the rider quickly replied, "I'm a Harley guy."

In 2010, to gain some additional information about this whole brotherhood thing, I posted the following question on one of the online motorcycle forums: "As a motorcycle rider, do you feel like you are part of a 'brotherhood'?" Over a period of a couple of weeks there were over 600 viewers of the post and approximately 200 responses to this unscientific poll. Admittedly, the question was a bit leading, but I was still surprised by the overwhelming nature of the responses. All but one reply was a resounding "yes!" The individual answers were as varied as the people giving them, but most indicated that they believed there was a special "bond" among motorcyclists that they had not experienced in other aspects of their lives, including their jobs or careers. These responses usually included examples of when, how, and why the respondent had experienced this special "brotherhood." One unique response, but still representative of the entire group's sentiment, was,

> I'm not Will Rogers, so I'm not going to say that I never met a biker I didn't like. But, I will say this, of all the people I've met on motorcycles, most of them have been really decent people. I truly do think there is a brotherhood. Some brothers you might like better than others, but they are still all like family. Well, most of them anyway.

Several others voiced similar sentiments, most providing a caveat that they had met a few people on motorcycles that they did not particularly enjoy being around, but for the most part, their comments confirmed a sense of brotherhood among fellow riders. The one respondent who disagreed stated:

> Interesting topic, but it is no different with boaters, golfers, skiers, snowboarders, baseball players, hikers, skydivers, rock climbers, chess players, art lovers, Mozart lovers, or Gibson guitar lovers, ad nauseum [sic] you get the idea. Motorcycle riders are no different than anybody else. We like what we like. People with passion in common will gravitate to each other, and have a lot of stuff to talk about, and prefer each other's company over others who are non-participants. Motorcyclists are no different.

Almost immediately, responses began to pour in disagreeing with this post. "You gotta be kidding!" one said. "You think boaters, golfers, and chess players have the same type of brotherhood as us bikers?" the post continued. "When have you ever seen a chess geek come to the aid of another chess player, or for that matter, a boater stop and go over and help another guy in a boat?" Several others chimed in with exhortations that riding a motorcycle was very different than the other interests mentioned by the sole dissenter. One respondent summed up many of the others' feelings with:

> I respectfully disagree with _____. Riding a motorcycle is very different and sets you apart. I can't speak for other countries where more people ride bicycles, scooters, and motorcycles, so it's more common, but here in the states, if you ride a motorcycle, you are set apart. I don't know if it's the danger, or being in a minority, or what, but it's more than just a common interest. We have a bond. Yeah, I think — no, I know there is definitely a brotherhood.

In an effort to put the "feud" between Harley and other brands of motorcycle riders to rest, at least 25–30 respondents indicated, "It doesn't matter *what* you ride, only *that* you ride. Although not all riders feel that way, I have heard that phrase over and again at motorcycle shows, rallies, and other places where motorcyclists gather that it almost seems to be the mantra for those who truly love riding motorcycles. And, yes, there is even a patch with that phrase stitched on it.

Over the years, and particularly during the five years of participant observation research for this book, I have ridden in groups, attended bike shows and rallies, and visited biker shops and bars that included all makes and models of motorcycles. Although from time to time there are numerous jokes, and some good-natured chiding about type or size of motorcycle ridden, other than with a few neo-bikers and on websites and in chat rooms, I have not witnessed many meaningful divisions between Harley riders and other motorcyclists. Moreover, I have noticed almost as much brand loyalty among BMW and Goldwing riders as I have among Harley riders. Some riders are so enamored with one particular make or model of motorcycle that they refuse to ride any other type of bike. Lifelong rider and writer Fred Rau (2011:47) calls this blind brand loyalty "motorcycle snobbery," and says that in his experience, it is strongest among riders of Harley-Davidsons, Honda Goldwings, and BMWs. Still, the most important dividing line in the motorcycle subculture is whether you ride or not. Perhaps a 50-something motorcycle enthusiast I interviewed put it most succinctly when he said, "I've learned over the years that it ain't *what* you ride or *where* you ride, but *who* you ride with that matters."

Clearly, nothing binds together motorcyclists in the fashion that hardcore one-percenters bond through being a prospect, hazing, earning a patch, and becoming part of a club/gang committed to colors, turf, and a way of life. Nevertheless, motorcyclists feel a strong affinity toward one another that they do not share with others on the road. As one study noted, "The motorcycle serves as the site for the production and maintenance of communal identity" (Packer and Coffey, 2004:643). This feeling of community and connectedness manifests itself in several ways.

## The "Biker Wave"

Motorcyclists almost always acknowledge one another on the road. As one author noted, "...there is only one thing that makes you a 'real' biker ... it's whether you give 'the wave' to every rider you pass" (Pierson, 1998b:66). The so-called "biker wave," widely used by motorcycle riders of all types, consists of extending the left arm out from the body at or below waist level, usually showing two fingers (the index and middle finger like a horizontal peace sign). I have heard some bikers say the "V" made with the two fingers represents the V-twin engine so popular among motorcyclists who ride cruisers. Since I have seen riders of motorcycles with one cylinder, two cylinders, four cylinders, and even in-line or opposed six cylinders all give the same wave, I am a little dubious of that explanation. Others say it hearkens back to the "peace" symbol of the 1960s and '70s, but given some bikers' penchant for violence, as well as the large number of military veterans who ride, I'm not convinced by that explanation either. Whatever the meaning, this gesture, like many other elements of the motorcycle subculture has both symbolic

**Two motorcyclists exchange the well-known two-fingered "biker wave" as they pass and acknowledge each other on the highway.**

and pragmatic elements. Symbolically, it is a very casual and nonchalant gesture befitting the "coolness" associated with riding a motorcycle. One can hardly imagine a biker raising and waving his or her hand like an excited schoolchild or a celebrity in a parade. It also is a symbolic form of acknowledgement and acceptance. *I see you, and although I may not know you personally, I relate to you, and feel somewhat of a connection to you.* Moreover, the wave serves as a form of boundary maintenance and symbolizes the sense of being an "insider," or a meaningful part of a particular group. As David Preston (2011:2) notes, waving at each other signifies our "separateness from those with the convenience and comfort of the automobile ... [as well as] the recognition of a kindred spirit and a dollop of respect for the commitment and grit of a fellow rider." The specificity of the wave is only known by fellow riders, thus, if somebody in a car or truck waves to a cyclist in that manner, the rider immediately knows that person is also a member of the "brotherhood." Pragmatically, riding a motorcycle with two hands firmly on the handlebars is dangerous enough. Removing the right hand is impractical because it releases the throttle, and although removing the left hand is much safer because it does not affect the speed of the bike, any waving motion is likely to affect the rider's and the motorcycle's balance. Consequently, if you are going to acknowledge somebody from a motorcycle, the "biker wave" is the simplest and safest method.

Not all motorcyclists wave to each other. Sometimes it is impractical or dangerous to wave. When riding to rallies or shows, there generally are so many motorcycles traveling in both directions that it would be nearly impossible to acknowledge each and every one. Sometimes when passing large groups of riders, the lead riders will wave and most of the following riders forego the ritual. When riding around sharp curves or encountering other circumstances that require keeping both hands on the handlebars, waves are usually omitted. I once encountered a fellow rider coming toward me on a hairpin curve in the mountains of Arkansas and was shocked to see his left hand extended in the familiar gesture and felt a little guilty that I was gripping the handlebars too tightly to return the gesture.

As with any subculture, not everybody follows the normative practices. Some riders are undoubtedly less friendly than others, some may not see the oncoming rider, especially on divided highways or where other barriers exist, and some may prefer to just ignore the ritual altogether. Ironically, despite the reference to bikers, the riders least likely to initiate or return the so-called biker wave are the hardcore bikers. Nevertheless, if you ride a motorcycle very far or very often you will undoubtedly experience what might be better termed the "motorcyclist wave."

## Warning Other Motorcycle Riders

In addition to the "biker wave," motorcycle riders use a wide array of other hand signals to communicate with each other. I am not referring to the standard hand signals for right turns, left turns, slowing, and stopping. Although all of those are important ways in which motorcyclists communicate, they are not unique to motorcyclists as almost every schoolage child who rides a bicycle learns them and they are usually included in driver's training manuals and on state exams to obtain drivers' licenses. Similarly, the "thumbs up" sign is commonly used to indicate that things are okay and is widely understood by both riders and non-riders. Motorcycle riders have developed a variety of additional hand signals, however, some of which are shared by others, but many of which are unique to their subculture or have different specialized meanings for riders. For example, pointing to one's gas tank usually signifies "low on fuel," indicating to other riders that the pointer needs to stop at the next opportunity to refuel his or her bike. While it does not take a genius to figure that one out, I have ridden with novice riders who did not understand the gesture and seemed puzzled when another rider or I made it. Perhaps a bit more obtuse is the signal used to notify another rider that his or her turn signal is on. Many motorcycles are not equipped with self-canceling turn signals so the rider must remember to turn off the signal after making a turn. Although most bikes have a flashing light somewhere in sight of the rider to indicate a turn signal is on, since riders cannot hear the signal blinking, it is common for riders to forget to turn it off. When a fellow rider notices the flashing blinker, he or she extends either the right or left hand (whichever one is consistent with the blinker) and cups his thumb to the four fingers opening and closing the hand (mimicking the flashing of the blinker) until the rider notices and turns off the signal.

When automobile drivers want to warn an oncoming vehicle that a speed trap is ahead or that a police car is approaching or is parked on the roadside, they often flash their headlights. Motorcycles manufactured in the United States after 1986 are required to have a headlight that remains on anytime the motorcycle engine is running. Motorcyclists could probably switch from dim to bright to warn an oncoming rider, but the change might be too subtle to notice, particularly in the daytime. Moreover, several states have laws prohibiting the flashing of bright lights at oncoming motorists, so the motorcycle giving the warning could be pulled over and cited for using their bright light inappropriately. Instead, when a motorcycle rider sees a fellow rider reach up with the left hand and pat the top of his head or helmet, it is understood that a law enforcement officer is nearby. Although almost every motorcycle rider recognizes this gesture, very few automobile drivers and even many police officers do not understand its meaning.

Finally, one of the biggest hazards faced by motorcycle riders (other than automobile and truck drivers) is debris on the road. Sand, gravel, rocks, sticks, boards, small road kill, tire treads, and other fragments that cars and trucks routinely speed over with little or no consequences can spell big trouble for motorcyclists and bikers. Just imagine what large obstacles that often litter the roads can do. I have seen lawn chairs, step ladders, mattresses, sofas, wooden dressers, car bumpers, and almost anything and everything imaginable in the road, sometimes blocking entire lanes. When motorcyclists ride in pairs or larger groups it is the responsibility of the lead rider to warn those behind of such obstacles in the road. Experienced riders stagger their positions so that no two riders are beside each other or directly behind each other and space their bikes at intervals large enough so that they can see and heed the warnings of riders ahead of them. If time allows and the rider can do so without endangering himself/herself, the lead rider takes the hand on the side of the bike where the obstacle is and points down at the road in an exaggerated manner. If he/she cannot safely remove his/her hand, the foot on the appropriate side is used in the same manner. Almost every motorcycle rider can cite numerous examples of times that they have avoided major accidents by being warned by a fellow rider about some impending danger awaiting them. There is no way to know how many accidents have been averted and how many lives have been saved by these simple acts of "brotherhood."

# The "Biker Code"

More evidence of the brotherhood among motorcycle riders can be found in the so-called "biker code," which also applies to motorcycle riders of all types—in fact, maybe more to motorcyclists than to hardcore bikers. I suppose the aforementioned warning signals could be considered part of this code. There is an unwritten, informal understanding among motorcyclists that you never leave another biker stranded. If motorcyclists see a fellow rider on the side of the road, they generally stop to check on the rider's well-being, help with repairs, provide a ride to the nearest service station, or at least offer to make a phone call or provide other assistance. Often they will hang around until help arrives. As one rider told me, "One thing I can always count on is if my scoot goes down, there's always a brother who will stop and help." A female rider, approximately 30 to 35 years old, elaborated,

> It's funny, but if I'm in my car and it breaks down, I immediately get on my cell phone and call my husband or Triple A. I actually hope that nobody stops and offers to help, because it scares me that they might be up to no good. But when I ride my bike, if it breaks down, I just wait for another biker to ride by. I know they will always stop, and I never fear for my safety. I just know that another biker would never hurt me.

Male riders expressed similar sentiments. A fifty-something male rider confided,

> When I was younger, I used to pick up hitchhikers and stop for other motorists on the road whether I was on my motorcycle or in my truck. But these days, if I see a hitchhiker or a person in a car or truck stranded, I just pass right on by. Sometimes I feel a little guilty, but I figure with cell phones and everything else that they will probably get help. To be honest, I'm about half afraid to stop for a stranger. On the other hand, if it's a guy on a bike, I'll pull over no matter what. I figure if he's riding a motorcycle, he's one of us. I know that may be stupid, but just the same, I'm not going to leave a fellow rider stranded on the road. I figure he'd do the same for me.

On numerous occasions I have passed riders stopped alongside the road. When approaching them, I always raise a hand and shrug my shoulders as if to gesture "Do you need help?" If they are indeed broken down or in need of help, they usually point to the bike or wave wildly, indicating they want me to stop. If they are simply resting, or are not in need of help, they either shake their heads, give the "thumbs up" signal, or gesture for me to keep going. Similarly, I have been stopped alongside the road and had other riders approach and I have signaled them that I did not need help. While there are no uniform standardized gestures for all this nonverbal communication, it usually works quite well. On those occasions of miscommunication, or if the signals are vague, more often than not a motorcyclist will pull over and ask if the stopped rider needs help. This sometimes involves two or more riders meeting and greeting and then going their separate ways—having symbolically acknowledged and reinforced the "brotherhood" of motorcycling.

When motorcyclists ride in groups, it is common to put one of the most experienced riders at the front of the group and another experienced rider at the rear of the group. Newer or less experienced riders generally ride in the middle of the pack. For safety purposes, experienced riders never ride side-by-side sharing one lane. Instead, motorcycle riders tend to divide a single street or highway lane into three imaginary lanes. Lane one is where the left tire of an automobile usually tracks, lane two is in the middle, and lane three is where the right tire of an automobile runs. Riders stagger themselves so that the lead rider takes the lane one position, followed by the next rider who takes lane three. The third rider takes lane one, and the fourth lane three, and so on. Motorcyclists usually avoid the center of the lane (lane two) altogether unless moving to dodge an object or an oncoming vehicle. Lane two is the most likely area to catch oil drips and other debris from automobiles and on most highways and streets there is a slight crown so that lane two is a little higher than the other two lanes allowing for water runoff. All riders in a group try to keep track of other riders. As already mentioned, if a person is low on fuel, he or she usually points in an exaggerated gesture toward the fuel tank of the bike letting others know that a stop at the next filling station is order. If the lead rider encounters an object in the road, he or she generally points at it letting all those trailing that they need to avoid something in the road. If one rider makes a sudden move, dodging an object without letting the others know, or if the trailing rider suddenly pulls over or takes an exit without notifying the others, problems usually ensue. Part of the unwritten code is that: if one rider has to stop, all the riders stop. If a lone rider peels off from the group, nobody proceeds until he or she is accounted for even if that requires riding several miles to the next exit and turning around to go back and find them. Almost every rider can tell you about some frustrating time when he or she had to circle back to find someone or sat waiting alongside the road waiting for somebody to catch up, not knowing if the person was lost, injured, broken down, or simply off sightseeing. If the wait is precipitated by one of the first three reasons, it is understandable. If it is because of the last, it might be tolerated once, but if repeated, that person will soon find himself/herself riding alone.

Another example of the "brotherhood" among motorcyclists can be found in their sense of trust in other riders. Austin (2009:81) noted that when in the company of other motorcyclists riders often leave expensive helmets, jackets, gloves "and motorcycles with keys in the ignition unguarded for hours or even overnight." My research confirms this observation. The norm among riders is clearly to leave other's motorcycles and possessions alone observing an unspoken "look, but don't touch" rule and trusting other riders to do the same. As one interviewee in this study said, "Every rider knows you never throw your leg over another man's wife or another man's bike." I have no data to support this, but I suspect there is more heed paid to the latter portion of that admonition than the first part.

I have attended numerous motorcycle events where hundreds and even thousands of riders were in attendance, some of whom were readily identified with one-percenter motorcycle clubs, others who came from all walks of life and rode all types of bikes. I have left my keys in the ignition, my jacket, gloves, and helmet on the seat, and have never had an item stolen. On the other hand, one afternoon while my bike was parked in the university police-patrolled parking lot reserved for faculty members only, someone rifled through my saddlebags and helped themselves to a sixty-dollar pair of riding gloves. Who would guess that bikers are more trustworthy than college students or faculty?

As with any subculture, however, such blind trust may be misplaced. There is much variation in the norm of mutual assistance among riders of different types of motorcycles. And, just because a person rides a motorcycle does not mean he or she is immune to thievery. Some riders do not stop to help others. These variations are often based less on the *make* of motorcycle and more on the *model* or *type*. As previously mentioned, the Harley versus non–Harley feud of the past has largely been resolved. If nothing else, it's hard to tell one brand of V-twin cruiser from another off the showroom floor, much less after numerous modifications have been made with various brands of aftermarket pipes, windshields, saddlebags, and other paraphernalia. Pass a V-twin cruiser going down the highway at 70 miles per hour and they all pretty much look alike. Conversely, it is very easy to distinguish a cruiser or touring bike from an off-road "dirt bike" or the high-powered, streamlined "crotch rockets." Many who ride cruisers or touring motorcycles shun riders of sport bikes, and vice versa. Most automobile drivers have experienced situations where one or more riders of these high-powered performance bikes come screaming down the highway and pass us at speeds in excess of 100 miles per hour while the rider is either popping wheelies (pulling the bike up on the rear wheel), texting, or talking on a cell phone. I've experienced such events both in my car and while riding my cruiser, and despite the fact that I also ride sport bikes, I can assure you that it elicits the same feelings in both situations. I have never wished a fellow rider ill will, but those folks give all motorcyclists a bad name, and they inflate the motorcycle accidents and deaths statistics.[1]

It must be acknowledged that, brotherhood or not, just as there are differences among teachers, police officers, doctors, musicians, or any other subculture, so too all motorcycle riders are not alike. There are numerous reasons why a biker or motorcyclist may or may not stop to help a fellow rider. For example, it would be rare for a one-percenter or hardcore biker to stop and assist a member of a rival club/gang. They also might be reluctant to stop and help an ordinary "citizen" (what they call a non-club affiliate rider), and the typical motorcyclist, if stranded helpless along the road, might feel more threatened than relieved if a one-percenter club member, a hardcore biker, or a group of them stopped to help. Sonny Barger (2001) contends, however, that if another rider ever stops and helps a Hell's Angel, he or she will always be considered a "friend of the club" and the assistance will be returned if possible.

What about the other 99 percent of bikers, though — the fellow motorcyclists who might ride on by without rendering assistance? Sometimes riders are just too busy, might be on the way to work, or traffic patterns and other circumstances may make it impractical or impossible to stop and offer assistance. In at least one situation a rider told me that he was stranded on the interstate with a flat tire. He said that he had been marooned for over an hour, and at least a dozen motorcyclists rode past him, and although a couple of them waved, none stopped or offered assistance. Evidently, he had pulled off the interstate onto a one-way service road. Riders, passing on one side of the interstate could have seen him, and that is probably why some waved, but it would have taken considerable effort for one of them to stop and help. Riders going in the opposite direction could not even see him from the highway. Nevertheless he was surprised that nobody stopped to see if he needed help. I related this experience to a motorcyclist at a rally who was touting the virtues of the "biker brotherhood." He simply acknowledged, "Hey, there are assholes in every group, and just 'cause they're ridin' a bike don't change that — still, I ain't never seen a rider pass a brother up, and I know I never would." His dichotomy of motorcyclists into "assholes" and "brothers" is overly simplistic, as there is a wide range of riders that could be categorized between those two ends of the spectrum. Nevertheless, the sentiment acknowledges that the brotherhood exists but certainly is not absolute or perfect.

Today, more and more motorcyclists are members of AAA, motorcycle riding clubs, and riders' associations, or have motorcycle insurance that provide 24-hour roadside assistance and/or towing services. Most riders carry cell phones, and thus, brotherhood or not, help is never far away. Still, it is reassuring to most motorcyclists to know that their fellow riders "have their backs." As one rider said to me, "Isn't it funny that cagers have to pay a fee and carry AAA cards to receive the kind of assistance we provide each other for free?" It is indeed, but the brotherhood of bikers extends beyond merely waving to one another, warning other riders, helping each other in distress, and informal rides and gatherings. There also is a fairly extensive array of formal clubs and organizations to which many riders belong that in addition to providing certain types of information or services, also contribute to a feeling of belongingness, mutual respect, and camaraderie among motorcyclists.

# Motorcycle Organizations

As with many subcultures, in addition to countless informal associations, networks, and support groups, the motorcycle subculture offers a host of formal organizations. Although many motorcyclists are not members of any formal organization or association, they often benefit from some of these organizations in various ways. Almost half (103) of the 224 riders interviewed for this study indicated they either were or had been members of one or more motorcycle associations or organizations and almost all were aware of various organizations created for motorcyclists. It would be impossible to name or describe all of them, but some of the better known examples are worthy of mention and description.

## American Motorcycle Association

Nationally, the largest motorcycling organization is the American Motorcycle Association (AMA), founded in 1924. I interviewed one medical doctor who joked, "I'm an official member of two AMAs—one that is fun, and one that isn't—the bad part is that the one that is no fun costs the most." According to their website, the AMA has "an unparalleled history of pursuing, protecting and promoting the interests of the world's largest and most dedicated group of motorcycle enthusiasts" (AMA, 2010). The AMA focuses on motorcyclists' rights through lobbying efforts and government relations work, and also sanctions both on-road and off-road riding activities, as well as oversees professional and amateur racing events. Remember from chapter 1 that it was allegedly a representative of the AMA who in 1947, after the infamous Hollister event, inadvertently gave one-percenters their nickname when he declared that 99 percent of all motorcyclists were decent law-abiding citizens and only one percent might be outlaws.

Despite its size and international stature, few (only 13 or 5.8 percent) of the riders in this study claimed membership in the AMA. Virtually all the interviewees were aware of the organization, however, and almost all of them supported its agenda.

## Motorcycle Riders Foundation

The Motorcycle Riders Foundation (MRF) serves as "an aggressive, independent national advocate for the advancement of motorcycling and its associated lifestyle" (MRF, 2010). This organization acts as an advocate before national, state, and local legislative, executive, and judicial bodies as well as with private or public entities regarding issues affecting motorcycles, motorcyclists, or motorcycling. They also help train national, state, and local motorcyclists' rights activists. State and local chapters of MRF often lobby for motorcyclists and attempt to ensure motorcyclists' rights are recognized when traffic laws and other pieces of legislation affecting riders are involved.

Slightly under one-fourth (52 or 23.2 percent) of the riders interviewed were or had been members of either the national MRF or one of its state or

Many local, state, and national organizations promote motorcycle safety among riders. This booth at a motorcycle rally in Arkansas challenges riders to test their skills on a simulator.

local affiliates. Several of the rallies and shows I have attended have had MRF booths or tables where representatives of the organization passed out literature and offered membership forms to attendees. In addition to dues, MRF gains some financial support from rides, shows, or other motorcycle-related events designed as fundraisers. Many local chapters of MRF hold fundraisers for injured motorcyclists, riders with cancer, or other worthy causes in their community or surrounding areas.

## Motorcycle Safety Foundation

Almost all motorcyclists are aware of the Motorcycle Safety Foundation and many are familiar with the safety courses it conducts in major cities, suburbs, and small towns around the globe. The Motorcycle Safety Foundation (MSF) is an internationally recognized non-profit organization that provides leadership to the motorcycle safety community through its expertise, safety courses, and partnerships. The major message of the MSF (2010) is:

- Get trained and licensed
- Wear protective gear — all the gear, all the time — including
    a helmet manufactured to the standards set by the DOT
- Ride unimpaired by alcohol or other drugs
- Ride within your own skill limits
- Be a lifelong learner by taking refresher courses.

Hardcore bikers and the one-percenters routinely ignore these admonitions (Smith, 2006), but motorcyclists are much more likely to adhere to them. One of my riding buddies called to tell me that his son had wrecked one of his bikes. He was riding on a curvy road and the pavement was a bit wet and he entered a turn a little too fast and lost control of the bike. He laid the bike down and slid about thirty feet on the asphalt. When I asked if his son was hurt, my friend responded, "Nope, A-T-G-A-T-T," the common acronym for "all the gear, all the time." My friend indicated that his son had borrowed a pair of his riding pants and a jacket, both equipped with Kevlar inserts. And, like his father, the son never rode without a DOT approved helmet. He suffered some minor road rash but no serious injuries. His son had taken an MSF course much earlier, and though not an active member of the organization, he was well aware of and routinely practiced MSF standards for riding.

In this study, almost two-thirds (137 or 61.2 percent) of the motorcyclists indicated they had taken a certified MSF safety course, and over one-half (116 or 51.8 percent) of them reported that they routinely wear a DOT (Department of Transportation)-approved helmet when they ride. Another 27.2 percent (61) said they occasionally wear a helmet, and 47 (21.0 percent) said they rarely or never wear a helmet. Forty-nine (21.9 percent) of the 224 admitted, however, that they drank alcohol and rode on a fairly regular basis, and 167 (74.6 percent) said they had drunk at least one beer and ridden. Although somewhat lower in each category, these numbers are comparable to those found in online polls where one poll showed that out of 381 riders, 269 (70.6 percent) reported they had taken a certified MSF course, 255 (66.9 percent) said they wore a helmet at least some of the time, and 301 (79 percent) said they had ridden after consuming alcohol. Chapter 6 explores the world of motorcycle shows and biker rallies where alcohol is a staple, drugs are readily available, and riding after consuming alcohol is widespread. Like members of many organizations, some MSF-trained riders may not necessarily practice what they preach, or at least had preached to them. Nevertheless, when it comes to riding skills, many MSF-trained riders do practice what they (MSF) teach.

## Iron Butt Association

The Iron Butt Association (IBA) claims to have over 24,000 members dedicated to safe long-distance riding. Membership in the IBA must be "earned" by completing a 1,000 (or more)-mile motorcycle ride within a 24-hour period. Although based in the United States, the IBA claims to have thousands of members around the globe, and one of its more popular slogans is "The World Is Our Playground." The IBA website boasts that it is "home for hundreds of excellent stories about long-distance riding ... [and] a vast amount of technical information regarding the art and science of endurance riding." The site includes an "Archive of Wisdom," that contains the "collective wisdom and knowledge of some of the most experienced, seasoned Endurance Riders in the world!" (IBA, 2010).

In 2009, I rode from Texas to Sturgis, meeting up with several friends in Oklahoma. We took three full days to make the ride, stopping frequently for coffee, soft drinks, restroom breaks, and fuel as well as just to stretch our legs and even sightsee along the way. We were all experienced riders and we averaged a little over 400 miles per day. At the end of each day, we were exhausted. Two other riders had intended to go with us, but because of a family obligation of one of them, they decided to join up with us a couple of days later. Those two ended up leaving at 5:00 A.M. and riding straight through from northeastern Oklahoma to Sturgis, South Dakota (approximately 1,100 miles), arriving in our camp approximately twenty hours later, stopping only for mandatory fuel and restroom breaks. They even encountered a major thunderstorm two-thirds of the way through the trip and rode at least a couple of hours through driving rain. As soon as they arrived, one of them dismounted his bike and proudly proclaimed, "I've finally earned an Iron Butt patch!" One of the riders in our group responded, "I'm assuming it also comes with a Dumbass patch."

I've logged well over a hundred thousand miles on motorcycles, but I've never earned or attempted to earn an Iron Butt patch. Moreover, I do not anticipate ever doing so. In chapter 3 we discussed toughness as a motorcyclist value, but riding a thousand miles in 24 hours or less stretches most riders' definition of toughness beyond reach — or, as the "dumbass" quote suggests, might change the definition altogether. Exhaustion and fatigue on a motorcycle often lead to disastrous results.

## ABATE and State Motorcyclists' Rights Organizations

State Motorcyclists' Rights Organizations (SMROs) exist in almost every state, and often go by the acronym ABATE, which stands for American Bikers (or Brotherhood) Active Toward Education. SMROs are affiliated with the AMA and MSF, but take a somewhat different stance on issues such as mandatory helmet laws, required motorcycle safety inspections, mandatory rider training and licensing, and other similar regulations. Most SRMOs favor optional or voluntary motorcycle rider safety courses and other training. State chapters of ABATE and other SMROs actively lobby legislatures, conduct letter writing campaigns, put up billboards along highways, and sponsor public service announcements to increase public awareness of motorcycle safety issues. They also lobby for stronger penalties for automobile and truck drivers who cause accidents that injure or kill motorcyclists.

Almost half (98 or 43.8 percent) of the riders in this study were current or former members of an SMRO, with most of them having been affiliated with a state chapter of ABATE I have rarely attended a motorcycle rally or organized ride where some type of SMRO was not represented. Members often wear t-shirts or patches on vests or jackets that identify them and, in my experience, most members are fairly active proselytizers for their organization and its causes.

## Military Veterans' Motorcycle Organizations

Since World War II, there has been an affinity between military veterans and motorcycles, motorcyclists, and motorcycle clubs or organizations. A national organization called the Combat Veterans Motorcycle Association offers full membership to veterans who served in combat from all branches of the United States military as well as "supporter" status to members or veterans of the armed forces who served in non-combat roles. A more high-profile motorcycle organization comprised mainly of military veterans is the Patriot Guard Riders who attend funerals of veterans of Iraq and Afghanistan wars at the invitation of their families. This group extends free membership to anybody who rides and even those who do not as long as they respect the service and sacrifice of fallen veterans. Their motto is simple and succinct: "an unwavering respect for those who risk their very lives for America's freedom and security" (Patriot Guard.org, 2011), and they list two goals in their mission statement:

1. Show our sincere respect for our fallen heroes, their families, and their communities.
2. Shield the mourning family and their friends from interruptions created by any protestor or group of protestors.

There are several other national motorcyclists' organizations including clubs for Vietnam veterans, Korean veterans, and World War II veterans. Additionally, almost every state has chapters of motorcycle clubs or associations for military veterans.

## Other Organizations and Associations

There are far too many other national, state, and local motorcycle organizations to mention them all, and almost every motorcycle manufacturer offers an organization or "club" for its riders. These organizations not only promote brand loyalty, but also develop a spirit of solidarity and legitimacy for the motorcyclist subculture that may or may not have previously existed. A prominent example is HOG (Harley Owners Group) that in addition to promoting Harley motorcycles, apparel, and paraphernalia, also sponsors rides, safety courses, motorcycle shows, and a host of other events and activities that promote both brand loyalty and a sense of camaraderie. Manufacturers and other groups also sponsor websites, message boards, forums, and chat rooms where riders can be updated on safety recalls, new models, rallies, and events, as well as communicate with one another, buy and sell motorcycles and accessories, or discuss a wide variety of topics both related and unrelated to the world of motorcycles (see chapter 9).

There is a "Brotherhood of Gray Beard Bikers" that maintains a website devoted to meetings, events, activities, and information of interest to older motorcyclists. Similarly there is a "Brotherhood of Old Bikers" who use the acronym "BOOBS," which probably provides a hint of some of the interests of their group. More than one group operates websites under the heading "Brotherhood of Bikers," which is a motorcycle "club" whose motto is "Striving Toward a Better Biker Image." This organization works to diminish the stereotype that all motorcycle riders are outlaws or hardcore bikers by emphasizing charity rides, as well as rallies and shows that are geared more toward motorcyclists than bikers. Packer and Coffey (2004:662) indicate that "as a

Despite numerous admonitions against drinking and riding, it is not uncommon to see motorcycles parked outside bars all hours of the day and night. I have ridden past taverns at 10:00 P.M. and seen the same motorcycles parked in front that were there when I rode past at 10:00 A.M.

stereotyped marginal population one can understand why there would be an investment in altering the assumptions which have led to unfair legislation, insurance exclusion, police brutality, public scorn, and vigilantism," and why both motorcyclists and motorcycle manufacturers work so hard to change and enhance the image of motorcycle riders.

## Women in the "Brotherhood"

Not included in the previous list of motorcycle organizations are those created by and for female motorcyclists. They will be discussed in chapter 5, "Women and the Motorcycling 'Sisterhood.'" As previously noted, "brotherhood" is a sexist term, but despite the fact that motorcycling is primarily a male activity, there are thousands of women who ride their own motorcycles, and well over a million others who participate in the world of motorcyclists in some form or fashion (Box 2007). Women's motivations for riding seem very similar to those of men and despite their numerical minority, females

sense that they are part of the "brotherhood" of motorcyclists. Veno and Winterhalder (2009:62) surmised that "biker chicks certainly are women who
choose to live an unconventional lifestyle ... there are attractions to the motorcycle, the adrenaline high obtained by riding and, for many, the sisterhood
of riding motorcycles collectively." But women in today's motorcycle subculture play far more important roles than that of "biker chicks," and I certainly would not recommend referring to women motorcyclists in that fashion
(Thompson, 2012). The "brotherhood" among motorcyclists clearly includes
women, many of whom ride their own bikes. Men interviewed in this study
overwhelmingly indicated that they like for their wives or girlfriends to ride
with them either two-up or on their own motorcycles. Moreover, the women
I interviewed indicated that they felt like they are a meaningful part of motorcycling scene. "There's a camaraderie among cyclists that you just don't find
with automobile drivers," one woman told me. Another echoed, "There's
definitely a biker brotherhood and I feel like I'm part of it." then, after a
slight pause, she added, "But there's a sisterhood in biking like no other."
Chapter 5 takes a closer look at this sisterhood and women's roles in the
motorcycle subculture.

# Women and the
# Motorcycling "Sisterhood"[1]

"Excuse me sir, but you can't park that motorcycle there." Because the bike was still running and the leather-clad rider was wearing a full-face helmet, the admonition went unheard and unheeded. "I'm sorry," the teenager stammered, "but my boss told me to come out and tell you that you can't park your motorcycle in front of our store." The rider turned and for the first time saw the boy standing about three feet away wearing a dark green apron and a matching baseball cap. "This parking is for our customers only," he continued, and pointed at the sign in the coffee shop window that indicated parking spaces in front of the business were indeed for customers only. "Sorry, it's not me, but my boss doesn't like it when you guys park your motorcycles in front of the shop — he thinks it's bad for business." The coffee shop employee was stunned as the rider stood and slowly removed a pair of black leather gloves revealing two slender hands accentuated by bright red manicured nails. The hands then loosened the chin strap on a black helmet adorned with a reflective silver skull on the back and a smoke-colored face shield on the front that obscured the rider's face. The rider removed the helmet revealing a woman in her mid-to late thirties wearing lipstick that matched the nails and sporting a long blonde-streaked mane. "Tell your boss that I am a customer, and so are my girlfriends." The rider nodded toward two approaching motorcycles as they pulled into the lot and parked in the adjoining spaces.

Ask any American to name two or three famous motorcyclists, and there is a good chance they will mention Tom Cruise, Jay Leno, Evel Knievel, Gary Busey, or perhaps the late Malcolm Forbes. If they are movie buffs, they may be more likely to name Marlon Brando, Steve McQueen, Peter Fonda, and maybe John Travolta or Nicholas Cage (see chapter 6), and if they happen to be motocross fans, they might name Ryan Dungey, Ricky Carmichael, or James Stewart. All of these high-profile men are associated with riding motorcycles either in films or in real life. Ask any American to name even one famous female motorcycle rider, however, and there is a good chance you will get a blank stare (Boslaugh, 2006). Despite their long-term connection to the world of motorcycling, women generally are not associated with the two-wheeled subculture except in the most stereotypical roles. As one author noted, "Although times have changed with more and more people taking up riding — including women — one thing that has remained implicit in motorcycling is the association it has with masculinity" (Ilyasova, 2006:6).

The "brotherhood" of bikers has always included women. In traditional biker culture, especially in one-percenter motorcycle clubs, the role of women was clearly defined: although equally tough as the men, the equality stopped there. They were considered property to be used (for sexual and servant purposes), traded, and given or thrown away at the biker's discretion (Thompson 1967; Watson 1980; Hopper and Moore 1990). Watson's (1980:42) research found women to be viewed with contempt by most outlaw bikers and regarded as "necessary nuisances." He concluded that the women were just as tough as the male bikers, but saw themselves as subservient to the men and usually referred to themselves as "old ladies." James Quinn (1987; 2001; 2003) rode with a one-percenter motorcycle club and conducted research on several others. He identified three distinct roles for women in the hardcore biker subculture: *mamas, sweetbutts,* and *old ladies.* Mamas were at the bottom of the food chain in biker gangs. They were considered to be the property of the club and in exchange for shelter, protection, and transportation, were expected to serve any and all members' needs — sexual and otherwise. Sweetbutts were generally younger than mamas, and were more likely to provide regular sexual services to one, or in some cases a few members, while providing a source of income to both him/them and the club — usually through topless dancing, prostitution, and/or drugs. An old lady was the exclusive property of one club member — her old man. She might still be expected to provide a source of income to the club through dancing or prostitution, but all members understood that she was "off limits" to everybody except her old man, unless he decided to trade her off or sell her services.

Other studies on women in one-percenter motorcycle clubs confirmed the same three roles as described by Quinn, with a few minor differences and modifications. Some clubs also had *sheep* — young women brought in by new initiates as a "gift to the club" (Hopper and Moore, 1990). These young women, often strippers and/or prostitutes, were offered to all the members of the club during initiation, and many of them became sweetbutts after initiation. Betsy Guisto (1997) offered a unique look at women in the one-percenter subculture as she conducted an ethnographic study and wrote a doctoral dissertation on the subject while serving as an old lady to a one-percenter biker for approximately 20 years. Clearly, the one consistency in all the studies of women in the hardcore biker subculture is that females play a subordinate and usually subservient role, or as one author put it, they are generally viewed as "leather-clad sexualized accessories" (Boslaugh, 2006:1).

This chapter is not about these women. Instead, it focuses on women who participate in the American motorcycling subculture.

# Women in the Motorcycle Subculture

Despite decades of feminist progress in larger society, some females still play subordinate roles in today's motorcycle subculture, although not nearly as degrading as those described in the studies on hardcore bikers. Other women are essentially full-fledged members of today's motorcycle subculture, although a few (some might say many) lingering patriarchal attitudes and activities persist. Based on my participant observation and interviews, women who participate in today's motorcycle subculture roughly fall into four distinct but not mutually exclusive categories that I call leather lovers, biker babes, two-uppers, and female riders. As with any typology, these categories are not necessarily exhaustive, discreet, or mutually exclusive. For descriptive purposes, however, they provide some valuable insight into women's participation in today's motorcycling world.

## *Leather Lovers*

At the fringe of the motorcycle subculture are women who do not ride, and are not married to a rider, but are attracted to motorcycles and the motorcycle scene. Basically motorcycle groupies, probably a more accurate descriptor for these women would be "hang-arounds" as they simply hang around biker bars, motorcycle shops, rallies, shows, or anywhere else there are motorcycles and motorcyclists. I do not refer to them as "hang-arounds" because that term has meaning in the one-percenter biker subculture denoting one of the first stages of joining a motorcycle club: novices usually hang around a club for a while, then develop into prospects, and eventually become full patch members (Montgomery, 1976, 1977; Quinn, 2001). Leather lovers are never going to be full participants in the biker or motorcycle subculture, but can be found almost anywhere motorcycle riders gather. Their presence is most noticeable at large bike rallies such as Laconia, Daytona, Sturgis, and Fayetteville, but can also be seen at smaller rallies and shows. They typically wear biker-related attire, especially flimsy tops and bare midriff motorcycle t-shirts, usually accompanied by leather vests or bustiers, leather pants or chaps, or perhaps shorts, and biker boots—clothing that attracts a lot of attention, but most definitely is not designed for riding.

Leather lovers may accept rides from bikers or motorcyclists, but they are not in attendance to ride. They are mostly there to see and be seen. Many are local single women, college students, or sometimes even married women out for a little fun. I spoke to one twenty-year-old leather lover in Sturgis who said, "I live here, and this town really sucks 11 months out of the year, but for one month, it's a lot of fun." I asked her if she rode, and she replied, "Hell no, I'd be afraid to," and then she added, "but there is something about motorcycles and the guys that ride them that just fascinates me"— a common theme echoed in Veno and Wenterhalder's (2009) book, *Biker Chicks: The Magnetic Attraction of Women to Bad Boys and Motorcycles*. She indicated that she had worked in a few of the local bars since turning 18, but preferred to just come downtown and "enjoy the scene" as opposed to working and actually being part of it. Those leather lovers who eventually become part of the biker or motorcycle subculture are most likely to participate as biker babes.

## Biker Babes

No motorcycle rally, large or small, would be complete without *biker babes*, young women who participate in bikini bike washes and wet t-shirt contests, or serve as beer girls or "models." Although these women, usually ranging in age from late teens to mid-thirties, may be attracted to motorcycles and the men who ride them, make no mistake about it, their primary interest in the motorcycle subculture is monetary. These young women are often college students working part time for tuition, books, and spending money, or young single mothers capitalizing on their youthful good looks (and good shapes) to make far more money than most jobs they could take based on their educations and work skills. In some cases, they may be topless dancers, models, or waitresses and bartenders who "moonlight" at biker events to pick up additional revenue, usually in the form of tips and other forms of untaxed and untraceable cash. A huge custom motorcycle shop and biker bar in Dallas holds a number of special events and rallies throughout the year to celebrate holidays and other special occasions. At one such event, I asked a young "beer girl" decked out in a bikini top, a pair of camouflage short shorts with numerous strategically located holes, black fishnet stockings (also with holes), and a pair of biker boots how she got the job. She replied, "Oh, I dance at [one of the topless bars in Dallas] and one of my girlfriends (another dancer) told me about this gig — several of us from the club come over for these events and work for tips." She pointed to a large fish bowl marked "TIPS" that must have contained somewhere between $200 and $300 in crumpled bills. Next to it was what appeared to be a large pickle jar with a sign that read "PHOTOS $5" taped to it. There must have been 15–20 five dollar bills as well as several tens and a couple of twenties inside. "You sell photos, too?" I asked. "No, the guys pay me to pose with them, or they just pay me to take my picture — easy cash." "So, what are the qualifications for this job?" I asked. She did a little 360 degree pirouette, smiled, and said "You're lookin' at 'em."

**This "biker babe" bartender entertains the customers at a rally by doing one-handed pull-ups on a metal rafter above the bar.**

At Laconia, Fayetteville, Daytona, Sturgis, Austin, and other large motor-cycle rallies, major beer distributors (and sometimes other companies such as energy drinks or soft drink manufacturers) hire girls in bikinis or skimpy biker attire to hand out flyers, serve samples, or sell their products. The "Coors Light Girls," "Budweiser Bikini Team" and others are often in attendance posing for photos, signing calendars and/or posters, and otherwise flirting with the riders and encouraging them to spend money. At those venues, it also is common for "Miss July" or some other centerfold from a men's magazine to be on hand signing photos and posing for photos with bikers and motorcycle riders.

Bikini bike washes are popular attractions at most motorcycle shows and rallies. Riders line up for hours and sometimes even make appointments to have their motorcycles washed by young local women clad in bikinis. Others simply stand around and watch. Sometimes the girls are raising money for a sorority or some charity, but more often than not, they are enterprising young ladies who, much like the beer girls, are simply taking advantage of a testosterone-laden event where men will pay to see young lithe female bodies on display. In fact, sometimes the beer girls and the bikini bike washers are interchangeable. At a biker bar in Hot Springs, Arkansas, I asked a bikini bike washer who was on break approximately how much money she made washing motorcycles. "On average, "she said, "I'll make 2–3 hundred bucks ... on a good day, maybe 4." "Not bad," I replied. "Oh, I'd much rather sell beer," she countered. "I can make twice as much, and it's a lot less work!" She continued, "Plus, there's no risk — scratch a guy's bike, and there's hell to pay."

Biker babe apparel includes leather bras, leather bustiers, and sexy outfits accentuated by low-cut bodices, bare midriffs, and lots of leather, lace, and fringe. Biker babes and beer girls in halter tops and Daisy Duke shorts, bikinis, or other scanty outfits not only serve beer to bikers and wash motorcycles, but often pose for photos on motorcycles for tips. Clearly, their wardrobes are designed for posing and flirting, not for riding. Motorcycle advertisements often exploit women as sex objects and use biker babes and other forms of blatant sexuality to recruit men into the motorcycle subculture. At live venues, these "fantasy women" come to life.

Wet t-shirt contests are very popular events at motorcycle rallies. Usually sponsored by a local bar or one of the vendors, these contests typically offer cash prizes of anywhere from $25 to $1000. Winners are most often determined by "vote" as a crowd of leering men yell and scream for the contestant they believe has the most "talent." Many of the contestants are local girls and "amateurs" who get caught up in the moment or are encouraged by the crowd to participate, but many are "ringers" who are topless dancers and strippers who routinely "work" these events as beer girls, waitresses, or bike washers, and are regular participants in the wet t-shirt contests. The topless dancers and strippers often win these contests as they have little reluctance to remove their t-shirts, or raise them to flash the crowd, and what started as a wet t-shirt contest often ends as a topless dancing contest. Some of the dancers are daring enough to remove their shorts or bikini bottoms and some will have g-strings or other stripper attire underneath, while others are totally nude. Bar and club owners have to be cognizant of local city ordinances and state statutes covering nudity and must be ever-vigilant in protecting their liquor licenses. More than once, I have seen club owners or security people rush a stage to cover a woman, make her put clothes back on, or even escort her out of view, much to the chagrin of the crowd of onlookers.

Unlike the one-percenter and hardcore biker subculture, biker babes are just as likely, if not more likely, to be doing the exploiting as to being exploited. As opposed to being the bikers' property and sex slaves, through flirtation and sexual titillation, biker babes manipulate men into spending money on things they don't want, and into wanting things they don't need. In most cases, despite capitalizing on sexuality, no actual sex act or even physical contact will take place. Like strippers and topless dancers, these women are in total control of the situation, and they tease male bikers and motorcyclists alike into spending money on them with a wide variety of fantasies and promises that for the most part remain unfulfilled. It is not surprising that many topless dancers and strippers fill the role of biker babes since the roles are not all that different (Thompson and Harred, 1992; Thompson, et al., 2003).

## Two-uppers

In stark contrast to biker babes, today's motorcycle subculture also includes a number of wives and girlfriends who ride two-up with their husbands or boyfriends (or, in some cases, girlfriends), and like today's riders, are often well-educated middle- or upper-middle-class professionals who participate in the motorcycle subculture primarily on weekends and holidays. It would not be wise to refer to these women as riding in the "bitch seat" as the one-percenters often call it, but there is a subordinate dimension to their role despite their level of education and independence in their everyday lives. In addition to the 31 female riders interviewed for this research, 24 two-uppers were interviewed who are not included in the total N of riders since they only ride on the backs of motorcycles as passengers.

Women who ride on the backs of motorcycles are special types of people. As a motorcycle rider, I am very uncomfortable riding as a passenger on the back of a motorcycle. A number of other riders, both male and female, have told me they feel the same way. Maybe it is about being in control, perhaps it is a matter of trust, or maybe those who have ridden motorcycles are more acutely aware of the inherent risks involved in being a passenger on a motorcycle. Another factor may be that men find riding on the back of a motorcycling somewhat emasculating. Whatever the reasons, riding on the back of a motorcycle requires a tremendous amount of trust, devotion, courage, and submission. Riding a motorcycle is dangerous. As a rider, you must be constantly alert and vigilant, watching for debris on the roadway; animals, people, and vehicles that might dart into your path; articles being thrown from vehicles or blowing out of the backs of trucks; and the biggest threat: cars and trucks whose drivers either don't see you or don't respect that you have as much right to be on the road as do they. Riding on the back of a motorcycle can be even more dangerous.[2] The two-upper faces all the same risks as the rider, but additionally, must rely solely on the riding skills and the judgment of the person sitting in front of her to keep her from harm. My wife's view is: "I feel totally safe riding with you. I know you're a good rider and I know that you are going to be extra careful with me on the back. I totally trust you, so I can just sit back, relax, and enjoy the ride." My daughter expresses a similar sentiment, saying that despite the fact that she would rather be riding her motorcycle, she has no reluctance to ride behind me. On several occasions she has said, "You are my father and I have total trust in you." She knows I would never take any unnecessary chances with her aboard. Interviews with other two-uppers indicate similar feelings. One woman in her early 70s who has ridden with her 78-year-old husband for over 50 years, may have said it best: "He ain't killed me yet." Later, in a more serious tone, she said,

> We started riding when we were just kids in our 20s. I didn't know any women that rode motorcycles then, and I had no interest in riding on the front of one or riding by myself. It just seemed natural to climb on behind [her husband] and just hang on. If I trusted him enough to marry him, I trusted him enough to ride a motorcycle with him.

Perhaps one of the more interesting and grim comments about riding two-up as a couple came from a young wife and mother who said,

> I used to ride on the back all the time, but since the children came along I'm not too big on it anymore. We bought me my own bike and we prefer riding separately. We figure it is less likely for both of us to be critically injured on separate bikes. Of course, if one of us gets hurt badly, the other one will have to store their [sic] bike until the kids grow up.

## Female Riders

In the past, women primarily rode on the backs of motorcycles driven by men, but the motorcycle subculture includes a large number of women who own and ride their own bikes. Women have been riding motorcycles for a very long time, but the number of female motorcyclists has always been relatively small compared to that of male riders (Pierson 1998a). In 1998, a little less than half a million women, or approximately 9 percent of all riders, were included among the 5.7 million motorcyclists (Williams, 1998), but five years later, that percentage increased to approximately 10 percent — 635,000 women out of 6.6 million riders—and in 2007, estimates put female riders at approximately 10–12 percent (Motorcycle Industry Council, 2007; Box 2007). Estimates from 2010 mirrored that same 10–12 percent estimate (Knol, 2010; Womenriders, 2010). An unscientific online poll conducted in 2009 as part of this study discovered that out of 225 respondents, only 16 (7.1 percent) were female, but it is difficult to conclude whether that figure is an accurate reflection of the percentage of women who ride, or merely more reflective of those who participate in the particular online forum in which the poll was conducted. As noted in chapter 2, 31 (13.8 percent) of the 224 riders interviewed for this book were women. As with male riders, the median age for female riders has increased over the past decades (approximately 42 years of age); nearly 60 percent of women riders are married, 28 percent have college or post-graduate degrees, and 35 percent are in professional or technical jobs/careers (Box 2007; Womenriders, 2010). The women in this study approximated those national trends.

## Sexism and the Macho-Motorcycle Subculture

Despite the increasing number of women riders, today's motorcycle subculture is a male-dominated and somewhat macho domain. When I was looking at motorcycles for purchase after my riding hiatus, salesmen[3] chided me when I looked at 750cc motorcycles (one of the largest motorcycles made when I had last ridden). They remarked that the 750s were good "girls' bikes" or "good bikes for the little lady," but if I wanted a "man's starter bike," I needed to look at the 1100cc, 1300cc, or even larger models. At a Harley dealership when I asked about a new Sportster, which is usually considered an "entry-level" bike, the salesman asked, "You interested in the woman's version (883) or the men's model (1200)?"

I usually ask women at rallies what they think of the male-dominated and sexist environment that permeates such events, and a typical response can be summarized by one woman's answer, "It's no big deal, I've seen and dealt with a lot worse." Another indicated,

> I'm a teacher and my husband is an architectural engineer. Sometimes we're both appalled at what we see and hear at biker events, but overall, it's a whole new world for us, and we have met the most interesting and nicest people on motorcycles. Maybe it's like everything else, you have to take the bad with the good. For us, it's well worth it.

Nevertheless, some women are offended, but either decide that the benefits of motorcycling outweigh the drawbacks, or perhaps those most offended no longer participate. One woman, a realtor who rides, summarized her feelings,

Men are men. Sometimes they say and do stupid things. When a bunch of them get together, they seem to become adolescents again. Men on bikes don't strike me as much different or any worse than men at work, or anywhere else. They're just a little more open about everything. At least most of them respect the fact that I ride and treat me more like an equal than even some of the men I work with.

## Feminizing a Male-Dominated Activity

Although motorcycle attire tends to be masculine in appearance, most women riders in this study "feminized" their appearance in noticeable ways. Some wore pink leather jackets instead of the traditional black, and one even wore pink leather chaps. Others wore leather jackets in white, blue, or black adorned with floral patterns, butterflies, and other decorations such as rhinestones or fringe that identified them as women's attire. All but one of the women riders wore helmets, but only two of those were black. Most wore white, silver, or black helmets with colorful graphics, some obviously chosen to match or complement the color of their motorcycle. Often, ponytails, long hair, or various types of visible jewelry also served to identify the riders as women, although these potential identifiers can often be found on male riders as well. Consistent with other research, many of the women riders in this study seemed to "go out of their way to accessorize and feminize their appearances in order to communicate unambiguous femininity and heterosexuality" (Martin, et al., 2006:190). Even the motorcycles the women ride hint at femininity.

Whereas the majority of men in this study rode Harley-Davidson motorcycles which have been boldly linked to a macho image, only three women in this study rode Harley-Davidsons, and two were the smallest Sportster model offered (883); one was blue and one was red in color; one woman rode a white softail.[4] The other women rode Japanese model (metric) bikes— Hondas, Yamahas, Kawasakis, and Suzukis— in that order. Only one of the women rode a black motorcycle, and it had red pinstriping on the gas tank and fenders. The other women's bikes were usually white, silver, or red, or had two-tone paint jobs. Most of the women's motorcycles in this study were between 650cc and 900cc in size; one woman rode an 1100cc motorcycle that was identical to her husband's bike, except that his was black in color and her bike was silver with maroon trim. And, there was the aforementioned rider of the HD softail. Although I have observed women riding large and powerful motorcycles of all makes and models, the majority of women seem to ride smaller motorcycles and be less concerned about the macho-image of the motorcycle than their male counterparts. Pragmatic reasons for the smaller motorcycle may be that because it weighs less, women believe it "fits" them better and is easier to control — although most riders discover that heavier bikes provide a much

These two female motorcyclists, a professional artist and an elementary school teacher, ride large high-powered cruisers but still manage to feminize their appearance while participating in a male-dominated activity.

smoother ride and are much easier to control once moving. Symbolically, the smaller motorcycles may seem more "appropriate" for women riders, and manufacturers now openly aim specific models at the emerging female market.

The sexism and association with masculinity that permeates the motorcycle subculture has not dissuaded women from being full participants. A fairly typical female rider told me,

> I used to only ride on the back of my husband's motorcycle, I guess because I grew up always hearing that riding motorcycles was for men only. But I never could understand the male-only thing — guess it was just the way I look at things. I enjoy riding my own bike and love to see other women riding.

In order to get a larger response and perhaps wider view of the sexism that permeates predominantly male activities like motorcycling, I conducted an online poll on one of the motorcycle forums to which I belong. The poll question was placed under the heading: "For Women Riders Only," and stated: "Just curious about how women motorcycle riders feel about being part of a male-dominated activity. Do you feel fully accepted as a female rider?" A total of 47 people responded to the poll. That would not be a disappointing number except for the fact that 41 of those were *men* and a total of only six women responded. Although that percentage may be fairly representative of the ratio of men to women riders, since the poll question was clearly addressed to "women riders only," it may speak volumes that almost 90 percent of the respondents (87.2 percent) were men! Responses from men included, "I see more and more women riding these days, and that's fine with me." Another said, "Why wouldn't women feel accepted?— it's a free world, they have as much right to ride as men do." More typical responses from men, however, reflected tolerance more than acceptance, and hinted at sexism. For example, "I don't have any problem with women riding, as long as they know what they're doing," which implies that he believes women often may not. Another said, "I like the fact that more women ride, especially if they're good looking." Perhaps the most telling response: "Who cares if they feel accepted or not? If they choose to ride, that's their business, but it's not called a 'brotherhood' for nothing."

The six women who responded all indicated that they enjoyed riding and had never experienced any serious forms of harassment, hazing, or overt discrimination. Yet, each indicated that they were very much aware that motorcycling was considered a "man's world," and that a certain amount of sexism was to be expected. One woman responded,

> Hey, I knew when I started riding that some of the men wouldn't like it, but who cares? It's my bike and I have as much right to the highways as anybody else. Overall, I've not had any problems. Of course, I usually ride with my husband, and not too many guys are going to give me any trouble as long as he's around.

Another female rider indicated, "I notice there aren't too many women on this forum and that's too bad, because I know there are a lot of women out there who ride." Perhaps the most straightforward response and one that may represent the sentiments of today's modern female motorcycle rider more than some of the others since the final three female respondents all indicated agreement: "Brotherhood, schmotherhood [sic], I ride a motorcycle and love it. Most guys seem okay with that. For the ones who aren't —fuck 'em!"[5]

It seems that many of the same attributes that lure men into riding are also appealing to women riders. One female rider told Veno and Wenderhalder (2009:143–144):

> From my observations, it seems that women riders are of the mindset that there's more to life out there and they want to experience it. It's a sensation of freedom, independence and, for many, rebellion from the stereotypical molds women are supposed to embrace.

Women in today's motorcycle subculture are very confident and independent, and as one woman rider commented to me, "I can tolerate a lot of the macho nonsense that goes on at these events, because I love the whole motorcycle experience, but don't call me a 'biker chick.'" Another female rider probably in her late 50s or early 60s responded to my wife's question as to whether she considered herself a "biker," "I don't know what I am — biker, motorcyclist, or whatever. As far as I'm concerned I'm just a wife and grand-mother who rides motorcycles. I'll say this though, I'm not a 'chick,' or any-body's 'old lady.'" Another female rider told me, "I don't consider myself a 'biker'— I'm a 30-year-old school teacher who happens to ride a motorcycle." Perhaps these two responses, and several similar ones from other women rid-ers, provide valuable insight into the "new breed" of both male and female motorcyclists. They are not posers or wannabes as so often suggested in biker literature, because riding a motorcycle is not a *master status* (Hughes and MacGill, 1952) for them. Riding motorcycles is *what they do, not who they are*. Rather, like most Americans, their strongest sense of identity is related to their age, race, sex, family roles, and occupation. Consequently, riding a motorcycle is only one of many social statuses and roles women riders fulfill. Conversely, "biker" implies commitment to a lifestyle, and is much more likely to be viewed as a *master status* accompanied by *role engulfment* (Lemert, 1951) by those who fit into that category. This particular aspect of riding is further explored in chapter 10.

# Women's Motorcycle Organizations

Many women are members of the American Motorcycle Association and several of the other motorcycle organizations described in chapter 4. Today there are also numerous motorcycle clubs and associations exclusively for women and several of these groups have their own rallies, sponsor rides for charitable causes, and provide information to women riders in the form of magazines, brochures, and online websites (Womenriders, 2010). A few of the better known and larger groups include Motor Maids, Women on Wheels, Chrome Divas, and Women in the Wind. Lesbian bikers can join the Women's Motorcycle Contingent which is more commonly known as Dykes on Bikes.

## *Motor Maids*

Motor Maids was chartered by the American Motorcycling Association in 1940 and offers membership to women in the United States and Canada who own and ride their own motorcycles. The main purpose of the organi-zation is to promote safe motorcycle riding by women and to foster a positive image of women who ride (Motor Maids, 2010). Motor Maids cite as their prime objectives:

- To unite women motorcyclists and promote interest in riding
- Maintain pride as a motorcycle club/organization
- Maintain their heritage and traditions
- Promote a positive image of women riders [Babchak, 2010].

None of the women in this study was a member of Motor Maids, although all had heard of the organization and one rider indicated that her mother had been a member.

## Women on Wheels

Founded in 1982, Women on Wheels (WOW) boasts over 3,000 members in the United States, Canada, and several other countries (Women on Wheels, 2010). Its mission is to unite all women motorcycle enthusiasts for recreation, education, mutual support, and recognition, and to promote a positive image of motorcycling. The stated goals of Women on Wheels (2010) are:

- To unite women motorcyclists with friends of common interest
- To promote a positive image to the public of women on motorcycles
- To help educate its members on motorcycle safety and maintenance
- To have a good time riding.

There were no current members of Women on Wheels included in this study, but one of the women interviewed had been a member when she first started riding.

## Chrome Divas

Chrome Divas was formed in Tallahassee, Florida, in 2002 for women who ride their own bikes, ride as passengers, or simply love motorcycles. Chrome Divas are incorporated and have a logo shared by organization chapters throughout the United States, Canada, Australia, and parts of Europe, but they do not wear "colors" and are not considered to be a "motorcycle club" (Chrome Divas, 2010). Members are female motorcycle enthusiasts who support a wide range of charities and host motorcycle and motorcycle-related events. One of the founding members of Chrome Divas indicated that she and fellow founders envisioned a motorcycle club comprised of professional women and their associates. "Our message was clear: if we can do it, so can you!" (Veno and Winterhalder, 2009:102). No active members of Chrome Divas were interviewed in this particular study.

## Women in the Wind

Women in the Wind (WITW) strives to educate its members in motorcycle safety and maintenance, unite women motorcyclists with friends of common interest, and promote a positive image to the public of women on motorcycles (Women in the Wind, 2010). Founded in 1979 in Toledo, Ohio, Women in the Wind boasts over 80 chapters in the United States and Canada. They hold two national meetings/rallies per year, and local chapters sponsor a wide array of motorcycling and motorcycle-related events.

I interviewed a 63-year-old woman in Texas who had ridden motorcycles since she was 15. She said she had joined a local chapter of Women in the Wind a few years earlier, but did not maintain her membership, since she preferred to ride with her husband. When a freshman in high school, her mother taught her to ride an old Harley-Davidson motorcycle as well as how to change the oil, adjust the belt, and fix a flat tire. She commented,

> I thought it was perfectly normal for women to ride their own bikes since my mother had ridden a Harley all my life. I didn't ever question it, until when I was about 20, my boyfriend said that girls don't ride motorcycles—they belong on the back. I ditched him 'cause I figured he was too old-fashioned for me. Since then, I've learned that most men feel that way. I'm not sure why. Maybe it threatens them, seeing a woman riding, I don't know. I heard a comment at this very rally that really burns me up. I overheard a woman talking to her husband say, "Look at all the women riding motorcycles. Why don't you teach me to ride?" His response: "Honey, all them [sic] women are lesbians."

Most of the women I have met and interviewed who ride their own motorcycles started out riding two-up with their husbands or boyfriends and then made the transition to riding alone. These straight women seem to be simultaneously amused and irritated by the stereotype that all or even most women bikers are gay. Nevertheless, as with any activity, there are homosexual women who ride motorcycles, and consequently, there is a biker organization especially for them.

## Women's Motorcycle Contingent/"Dykes on Bikes"

In 1976, a group of about 20–25 women on motorcycles made their way to the front of the Gay Pride parade in San Francisco. These women were organized under the name of Women's Motorcycle Contingent (WMC), but a reporter from the San Francisco Chronicle overheard one of the female riders refer to the group as "Dykes on Bikes" (Dykes on Bikes, 2010). The nickname stuck, and the Women's Motorcycle Contingent, more commonly referred to as Dykes on Bikes, is an organization committed to creating a local, national and international community of women motorcyclists and friends of women motorcyclists. Their mission is to "support philanthropic endeavors in the lesbian, gay, bisexual, transgender and women's communities and beyond, and reach out to empower a community of diverse women through rides, charity events, Pride events and education" (Dykes on Bikes, 2010). For several years, the Women's Motorcycle Contingent has tried to register "Dykes on Bikes" as their trademark, but have run into legal and bureaucratic battles over the use of what is widely considered a derogatory term for a group of people. Meanwhile, women in the group continue to call themselves "Dykes on Bikes" and local chapters sport a common national logo on the backs of their vests and jackets with individualized chapter logos and colors on the front (Dykes on Bikes, 2010). I interviewed one active member of Dykes on Bikes as well as her partner, who was a two-upper.

## Why Do Women Ride?

Women's motivations for riding seem very similar to those of men. According to Veno and Winterhalder (2009:62), "Biker chicks certainly are women who choose to live an unconventional lifestyle. There are attractions to the motorcycle, the adrenaline high obtained by riding and, for many, the sisterhood of riding motorcycles collectively." The "brotherhood" among motorcyclists clearly includes women. Men in this study overwhelmingly indicated that they like for their wives or girlfriends to ride with them either two-up or on their own bikes. Although clearly in a minority, women in today's motorcycle subculture seem to sense this inclusiveness. "There's a camaraderie among cyclists that you just don't find with automobile drivers" one woman told me. Numerous other women echoed that sentiment.

If the motorcycle has always represented a symbol of rebellion for men, that must be even more true for women. A woman rider interviewed by Veno and Winterhalder (2009:106) indicated that, as a Baby Boomer, she grew up in an era of *Leave It to*

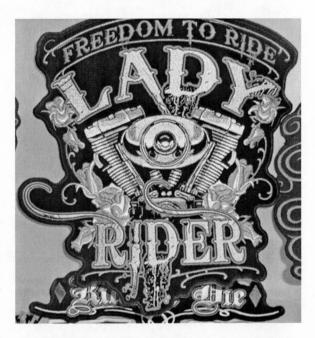

This Lady Rider patch on the back of a female rider's vest makes clear that she feels like she is a meaningful part of the motorcycling world.

*Beaver* and *The Donna Reed Show,* and for her, "the motorcycle is an icon of rebellion and freedom from those traditional stifling values." Women I interviewed expressed similar attitudes. "Nobody expects a woman to ride her own bike," one female attorney who rides told me, "and I like to do the unexpected." Another woman rider told my wife "I'm 62 years old, a mother and a grandmother, and I'll be damned if I'm going to let anybody tell me I can't ride a motorcycle if I want to."

Much like discussions with male riders, the word "freedom" came up time and time again in conversations about why women ride. "I've never felt so free," said one female rider. "Riding is freedom personified," said another. When asked, "Freedom from what?" she responded, "Freedom from everything ... freedom to be me." When I asked one woman rider her primary motivation for riding, she simply turned, lifted up her t-shirt, and revealed a one-word tattoo in red, white, and blue ink across her lower back that read "FREEDOM." As Martin and associates (2006:181) note, "The move from pillion seat to the front seat of a motorcycle results in a quantum leap in status for a woman in a biker subculture." Moreover, Roster's (2007) research indicates that this increase in status is accompanied not only by increased feelings of freedom and exhilaration, but also a sense of empowerment.

Findings from this study are consistent with both of those studies' assertions. As one woman revealed to the author,

> I used to think riding on the back of a motorcycle was one of the coolest feelings a person could have. Then I moved up to the front seat. Wow! What a difference! The wind in my face ... I can see everything, and I'm actually in control of the bike. Me. What a feeling!

The thrill and excitement of riding is also a prime motivator. As a female rider from Arkansas told Veno and Winterhalder (2009:108), "The magic of the motorcycle for me is that it allows me to face my fear head-on and just go for it." A female rider when describing why she rides told me, "It's the most exhilarating thing I do." "It's a rush," said another. "Most fun I've ever had with my clothes on," chimed in another female rider. When her husband looked over at her with raised eyebrows, she added, "Or off, for that matter" with a laugh. Several of the women spoke of the thrill of riding a powerful machine and feeling totally in control of it. One woman summarized this feeling by comparing it to driving a car.

> In my car, I feel like I'm not doing much of anything. It's so highly technical and controlled by computers. I don't have any idea how anything works. It's so space-age. I sit in climate-controlled comfort, push a few buttons, put on the cruise control, pop in a CD, and talk on my cell phone. It's like being at home. Now, my bike is something totally different. It's a machine. I start it, I control it, it responds to even my slightest movement. I shift the gears, I downshift, I

brake.... It's exciting. I feel the air, the dust, the dirt, and although I don't care much for them, even the bugs and the rain. Riding a motorcycle makes me feel alive.

This feeling of exhilaration and excitement will be pursued in chapter 10, "Why Motorcyclists Ride: Motorcycling and Life on the Edge." In that chapter, the common threads of fear, risk-taking, exhilaration, and living life on the edge are explored as possible explanations for why millions of Americans, both male and female, participate in the motorcycle subculture.

# CHAPTER 6

# Motorcycle Shows, Rallies and "The Pilgrimage"

One August, my family and I decided to leave the hubbub of work and school life for a week of peace and quiet offered by the Black Hills of South Dakota to be followed by a week in Yellowstone National Park. We packed the mini-van with a couple of week's worth of soft drinks and snacks and had already booked motels and hotels along the way, surprised at how many hotels had no vacancies. We planned to visit the beautiful town of Hot Springs and stop for photos at the partially completed Crazy Horse Memorial mountain sculpture. After a drive through Badlands National Park as well as Custer State Park, we would spend the night somewhere near spectacular Mount Rushmore. The kids wanted to visit the infamous town of Deadwood and see the legendary saloon where Wild Bill Hickok was gunned down, and the entire family looked forward to spectacular underground expeditions into some of the many famous caves in the area. Mostly, we were seeking peace, quiet, and except for a few other tourists, solitude. As we made our way through Nebraska, the kids were excited to see a small group of motorcyclists approach the mini-van from behind and they waved frantically as the leather-clad riders passed us, roaring pipes temporarily breaking the serenity of the seemingly endless cornfields on both sides of the highway. As the mini-van approached the South Dakota border, it seemed that we encountered an unusual number of motorcyclists, most headed north. When we passed the "Welcome to South Dakota" sign, we were surprised to see more than a dozen motorcycles parked around it with their riders striking various poses as one wielded a camera. "Why all the bikers on the road?" my wife wondered aloud. I was too stunned to answer. As I looked in the rearview mirror, a seemingly endless stream of motorcycles trailed behind the mini-van as far as I could see. Up ahead, a sea of motorcycles spread across both lanes. The roar of their pipes was almost deafening. Peace, quiet, and solitude? Dream on. It finally occurred to me; it was "Biker Week," and over the next 10 days approximately a million or more motorcyclists would descend on the Black Hills as they made the "pilgrimage" to the tiny town of Sturgis, South Dakota.

If hardcore bikers, or at least one-percenters, are somewhat "loners" except for their allegiance to their particular motorcycle club (Quinn, 2001;

Barker, 2007), motorcyclists are anything but. Motorcyclists love motorcycles and therefore most of them love motorcycle shows, rallies, and just about any other event or excuse to meet, greet, congregate, show off their "scoots," and ride. If, in the process, they inadvertently rub elbows with a few of the one-percenters, so be it. Those somewhat rare occasions make for great stories to be told around the water cooler at work or at the next bike show or rally, as long as the motorcyclists are smart enough to keep their distance, show proper respect, and keep their mouths shut. Motorcycle shows and bike rallies are similar in nature and composition, but are distinctive in many ways and attract somewhat different but certainly not mutually exclusive patrons and crowds. Both are important fixtures in the American motorcyclist subculture.

## Motorcycle Shows

Motorcycle shows are primarily about the bikes. There are a host of international motorcycle shows around the world in London, Paris, Amsterdam, and other European cities as well as in major cities in the United States including Chicago, Dallas, Daytona, Long Beach, Minneapolis, New York City, Seattle, and Washington, D.C., to name but a few. Vendors from around the globe attend these shows eager to display their products to hundreds, thousands, and sometimes millions of potential customers. Often these shows are scheduled to coincide with the introduction of manufacturers' new lineup of motorcycles for the upcoming year. At the same time, many of these shows include vintage motorcycles from bygone eras that document pivotal design and engineering changes as well as provide a nostalgic view of motorcycling's past.

Other vendors represent manufacturers of a wide array of products that may or may not be directly related to motorcycles and riding. In addition to the obvious vendors for helmets, boots, riding apparel, motorcycle insurance, and motorcycle parts and supplies, I have seen booths for everything from general household cleaning products to marital/sexual aids. At one rally, my daughter and I approached a booth surrounded by dozens of eager onlookers who were spellbound by a man selling gun holsters that could be hidden inside a rider's chaps or vest, and one that was disguised as a wallet. Although he could not display guns in the booth, he clearly implied that no rider should ever be caught without one.

In addition to the numerous vendors, depending on the venue and size or type of show, prominent names in motorcycle racing are often present, as are television personalities, movie stars, rock music performers, and other celebrities associated with motorcycles or motorcycling. Most motorcycle shows include a bevy of "biker babes" (see chapter 4) who hand out brochures, demonstrate products, pose for photographs, or otherwise call attention to the motorcycles

Motorcycle shows feature all types, makes and models of vintage and customized bikes. Riders can enter their motorcycles for prizes, get their bikes pinstriped or outfitted with custom lights, and mingle with other motorcyclists who share their love of two- (and three-) wheeled vehicles.

or motorcycle-related products, or to themselves. Also in attendance is a wide array of "leather lovers." Since motorcycle shows are often held indoors at civic centers or fairground exhibition halls, often during what is considered the "off season" for riding, they may attract almost as many non-riders as motorcyclists and even committed motorcycle enthusiasts often do not ride to shows, preferring to drive their 4-wheeled vehicles so they can take along family or friends. Rallies, on the other hand, are usually held at much larger outdoor venues, and motorcyclists usually ride their bikes to them, often disparaging those who trailer their bikes or dare to venture in on four wheels.[1]

## Motorcycle Rallies

Whereas motorcycle shows are all about the bikes, rallies are mostly about the riders. All of the same accoutrements associated with bike shows can also be found at rallies—vendors, celebrities, biker babes, leather lovers, and even motorcycle shows—but the real "stars" of rallies are the motorcyclists themselves. Rallies generally feature concerts by well-known rock 'n' roll, country, and blues artists, as well as the ever-popular "poker-runs," and various motorcycle games and skills competitions. Poker runs usually involve a scenic ride of 75 to 100 or more miles where participants make five designated stops to pick up playing cards that comprise a poker hand at the end of the run. Cash or prizes are usually awarded to the highest hand and sometimes a lesser prize is given to the rider with the lowest poker hand. Depending on state or local gambling ordinances, the "poker run" may consist of riders drawing numbers as opposed to playing cards, or they may be awarded tickets that are placed in a tumbler for a drawing with winning numbers for "door prizes" given in lieu of cash. At large rallies, winners may win as much as a thousand dollars or more, or valuable prizes such as motorcycle trailers, or even a new motorcycle donated by one of the local dealerships (or paid for by the entry fees for the run). Games and skill events may include riders completing some type of obstacle course, "reverse races" where the slowest time wins, or skill competitions where riders lean down and pick up tennis balls or pull flags from posts while making strategic maneuvers.[2]

Sociologically speaking, "attending motorcycle rallies is an important component of social life for many motorcyclists and serves to bond members of the group, reinforce their identity, and distinguish members of this subculture ... from the larger social world" (Austin, 2009:70). In plain English, if you are a motorcycle rider, motorcycle rallies are the place to be. As one female rider put it, "For people who long to be with other like-minded people, in however large or small dose, rallies fit the bill" (Pierson, 1997:114).

Since much of the observation and most of the interviews for this research took place at motorcycle shows and rallies, it comes as no surprise that almost all of the participants indicated that they at least occasionally attend such events, and a little over half (116, 51.8 percent) said they regularly do so. On average, the 224 riders interviewed indicated they attend between 2 to 3 motorcycle shows and/or rallies per year. While a few riders said they only attend 1 or 2 such events, one retiree in the group indicated that he attended at least one per month, saying,

> I live for these things. I've ridden most of my life and always wanted to attend shows and rallies, but because of my job [plumber] I just couldn't do it. Once I retired, my wife and I bought a touring bike and we make as many of them as we can. We've been to all the big ones—Sturgis, Daytona, Laconia, and the like—and many that you've probably never even heard of. If a bunch of bikers are getting together, we're there. If my wife's busy, the grandkids are sick, or the weather's bad, I go alone.

There are far too many motorcycle rallies, especially when those organized by and for specific makes and models of motorcycles are included, to try to provide any type of comprehensive list, but some are so large and well-known even among non-riders that they deserve mention. Although everybody's list might be different, based on interviews and participant observation, the "big five" rallies (at least in the United States) would probably be those held annually in Laconia, New Hampshire; Daytona Beach, Florida; (R.O.T., or Republic of Texas) in Austin, Texas; Fayetteville, Arkansas; and Sturgis, South Dakota. Australian, Canadian, and European riders would no doubt offer a very different list.

## Laconia Motorcycle Week

One of the oldest organized motorcycle rallies in the United States is held annually in Laconia, New Hampshire. Officially recognized by the American Motorcycle Association in 1923, Laconia Bike Week traces its roots to the Loudon Class Motorcycle Race of 1916 (St. Clair and Anderson, 2008). Laconia Motorcycle "Week" started out as a weekend event, but grew in popularity until it expanded to a full week and eventually ten days. Attendance increased over the years, but dwindled significantly after violence between rival biker gangs erupted at the event in the mid–1960s, causing officials to limit the length of the event to three days and seriously curtail some of the events and activities. Law enforcement urged shutting down the rally entirely, but at the urging of local merchants, an agreement was struck with the Federation of American Motorcyclists to sponsor the rally and a race to help self-regulate the event in order to attract more of a motorcycle enthusiast than a hardcore biker crowd. Today, motorcyclists of all types attend the nine-day event in early to mid–June that usually ends each year on Father's Day. Most estimates put attendees at around 400,000 to one-half million motorcyclists in recent years.[3]

Perhaps because of geography,[4] fewer interviewees in this study had attended Laconia than Daytona, Fayetteville, or Sturgis. Only four (1.8 percent) of the 224 riders in this study had actually been to Laconia, but almost every one of them was aware of the New Hampshire rally, and several indicated intentions to attend at some time. Of those four who had attended, all said they enjoyed the rally and would like to go again, but probably would not, simply because it was too long of a trip and too expensive. For them, Daytona, Fayetteville, and Sturgis (and a few smaller and geographically closer rallies) were more likely destinations. Moreover, despite being one of the oldest and largest rallies, there is probably less public awareness and/or mystique about Laconia than some of the more glamorous and highly publicized rallies such as those held in Daytona Beach, Florida.

## *Daytona Bike Week and Biketoberfest*

Like Laconia Motorcycle Week, Daytona Bike Week, which is held annually at Daytona Beach, Florida, traces its origin to a motorcycle race. Starting in 1937 as the Daytona 200 race, the warmth, beauty, and the beach of Daytona was a natural gathering site for motorcyclists emerging from winter hibernation in other parts of the country. The Daytona rally took a brief hiatus during the World War II era, but has grown in popularity, notoriety, and attendance almost every year since. Usually held the last week of February into the first week of March, over half a million riders descend on Daytona Beach for the races, bike show, concerts, parade, and other festivities. There is some debate as to whether Daytona or Sturgis is the largest motorcycle rally in the United States, as crowd estimates at both sites range from just over 500,000 to approximately one million over the course of the events— numbers as previously noted that are almost impossible to accurately determine.

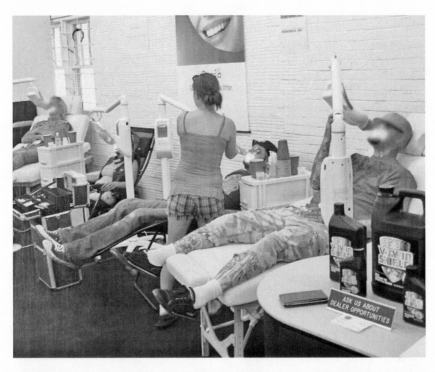

One of the more unusual vendor booths I have seen at a motorcycle rally was this one that featured teeth whitening. This booth was so popular that riders were required to make appointments in advance for its services. This hardly fits the public's stereotype of bikers.

Also held in Daytona Beach each year is the popular "Biketoberfest," started in 1992. Usually much smaller and less spectacular, Biketoberfest claims to attract approximately 100,000 riders from all across the United States. Several states hold "Biketoberfest" motorcycle rallies, but Daytona is one of the better known and better attended events probably because of its location, perceived association with Bike Week, and events that are held at the Daytona Speedway.

Almost one-third (69, 30.8 percent) of the riders in this study had attended at least one of the Daytona rallies—several had attended both, and some more than once. Most attendees thought Daytona was a great experience and indicated they planned to go again, although two who had gone together to Bike Week in February said they would never do it again. "Too cold and too crowded" was their take on the event. Others thought Bike Week in Daytona was a fabulous way to break up winter and begin the riding season. Another big attraction, as more than one male rider proclaimed, was "the most beautiful and scantily clad women you will ever see at a bike rally."

## R.O.T. (Republic of Texas) Rally

Despite claims that "everything is bigger in Texas," the Republic of Texas Rally (R.O.T.), which began in 1995, is not the largest motorcycle rally in the United States. It is, however, the largest rally in Texas and its sponsors claim annual attendance to be in excess of 200,000 (R.O.T. Rally, 2011). Held in Austin the first weekend after Memorial Day, R.O.T. Rally attracts bikers and motorcyclists from all over the United States. The four-day event includes bike shows, live concerts, stunt riders, skill-riding contests, tattoo artists, vendors, and a motorcycle parade from the Travis County Expo Center to downtown Austin that its website claims "in 2006, the *Guinness Book of World Records* certified as the 'Longest Parade of Motorcycles Known to Mankind'" (R.O.T. Rally, 2011). Living in Texas, I have attended the Republic of Texas Rally more consistently than any of the others, and have interviewed a number of riders at that venue. Of the 224 interviewees, over half (119, 53.1 percent) had attended the R.O.T. Rally at least once and some had attended several times. One rider from Louisiana indicated that he had attended all the major motorcycle rallies in the United States but found the Republic of Texas Rally most appealing because of its location in Austin, stating: "Austin has some of the best music, prettiest women, and friendliest riders in the country — in my view this beats Sturgis and Daytona, hands down." Another popular motorcycle rally in that area of the country that is growing in size and stature is held annually in Fayetteville, Arkansas.

### Bikes, Blues and BBQ—Fayetteville, Arkansas

First held in 2000, a relative newcomer to the motorcycle rally scene is the Bikes, Blues and BBQ (BBB) rally held every fall in the university town of Fayetteville, Arkansas. Nestled in the heart of the Ozark Mountains, the Fayetteville rally offers scenic rides, a parade, a motorcycle show, poker runs, motorcycle games, and all the major vendors, combined with a barbecue cook-off, legendary blues bands, and a Miss BBB pageant. The event began as a fundraiser for a number of local charities and continues in that vein, raising upwards of one-half to three-quarters of a million dollars per year in addition to stimulating the local and surrounding economies. In its newsletter, BBB boasts over 400,000 participants and claims to be the third largest motorcycle rally in the United States behind only Daytona and Sturgis in attendance. Almost sixty percent (133 or 59.4 percent) of the participants in this study had attended the Fayetteville rally, and although some in the study had never heard of it, once it was mentioned, most expressed interest in attending. One rider who had attended commented, "I've been to Sturgis, and I've been to Daytona, but I'll take Fayetteville any day. Friendliest people I've ever been around, beautiful scenery, and beautiful town." While in attendance, another rider told me,

> Man, there's nothing like a university town for bike event. People here seem to want us here, and it doesn't just seem to be all about the money, or all about the show. This is a more genuine place to be. The food's great, the music is great, and they ought to add another B to the title for beer.

Perhaps one of the most interesting comments I heard at Fayetteville was from a rider who lived in Missouri and attended the Fayetteville rally every year since its inception. He indicated:

> This is one of my favorites, but even it is just getting too damned big. Too many people. I prefer the smaller rallies, personally. I've been to Daytona and always go to Sturgis, but they are just wall-to-wall people. People seem to go there just to be seen and to get a t-shirt. This place is a little different. People seem to kick back, enjoy the food and the music, and just enjoy being here, but I'm afraid it's changing.

In response, I asked, "So are you no longer going to attend the bigger rallies like Sturgis and Daytona?" After a brief pause, he grinned, and said, "No way, man — Daytona maybe, but Sturgis — well, you know, it's Sturgis; I've just gotta go."

## The Pilgrimage to Sturgis

First held in 1938, the Sturgis motorcycle rally is not the oldest, and it may no longer be the largest (although annual attendance allegedly approaches the 1-million mark), but without doubt, Sturgis is probably the most famous and/or infamous motorcyclist/biker get-together in the world. As the afore-mentioned rider in Fayetteville put it, motorcyclists and bikers alike "just gotta go." The trip to Sturgis, South Dakota, is indeed a pilgrimage — "a jour-ney to a sacred place or shrine; any long journey or search, especially one of exalted purpose or moral significance" (*American Heritage Dictionary*, 2009: 993). Slightly fewer than half the interviewees (109, 48.7 percent) in this study had attended Sturgis with most of the other half pledging their intent to do so at some time in the future.

The pilgrimage to Sturgis is a mixture of myth, merriment, marathon, and with apologies to the Islamic faith, Mecca. As a motorcycle rally, Sturgis has it all — bike shows, leather lovers, biker babes, organized rides, unorgan-ized rides, races, burnouts, parades, celebrities, midget wrestlers, bikini bike washes, wet t-shirt contests, concerts, motorcyclists, bikers, booze, outlaws, law enforcement, family entertainment, biker bars, vendors, beautiful scenery, and more. If it is in any way associated with or remotely related to motorcy-cling, it can be found at Sturgis.

The real excitement and mystique of Sturgis may have less to do with the rally itself, and more to do with traveling to and from the event — the "journey to the sacred place or shrine." Although a number of participants trailer their bikes, or even have them shipped to Sturgis, attending the rally is only one component of the pilgrimage. As noted in footnote 1, a clear-cut hierarchy exists between those who "make the ride" and those who just attend the event. A substantial part of the Sturgis experience is the trip itself, and the further the ride, the higher the sense of accomplishment and the more prestige accorded the attendee. As with many rallies those who travel the longest distance are often exalted and rewarded in some way for their demon-strated commitment to the event. Two common questions at every motorcycle rally are "Where you from?" and, "did you ride all the way?" I was amazed the first time that I attended the Sturgis rally at people's reactions when they discovered I had ridden my bike from just outside Dallas. Responses ranged from amazement and curiosity to admiration and almost deference. That is, of course, unless I was talking to someone who had ridden a further distance. I encountered numerous Texans who had ridden from the Austin, San Anto-nio, and Houston areas, and they were quick to point out the added mileage of their treks. In one bar several of us from Oklahoma and Texas were talking about our experiences on the ride up when a patron from a nearby table ambled over and joined our conversation with the entrée: "I heard you guys talking about ridin' up from Texas and just thought I'd let you know that I came all the way from Orlando, Florida." This was said without bravado or a sense of competitiveness; more just a statement of fact that he assumed we would all be interested in knowing. We invited him to join us and discovered

**During Bike Week, the sleepy little South Dakota town of Sturgis is transformed into a booming 24-hour-a-day party as anywhere from half a million to a million motorcyclists, vendors, and tourists descend on this rural community with a population of less than 7,000 residents.**

that he had made the "pilgrimage" from Orlando to Sturgis four times. "I prefer Sturgis over Daytona," he said. "There's something more genuine about it." Then, upon reflection, he surmised,

> Maybe it's just the fact that I live so close to Daytona that I really don't appreciate the significance of the trip. I dunno. I always grew up hearing about Sturgis, and me and my buddies always talked about riding up here if we could get the time and the money. I have a job where it's hard to take off two weeks in August [he owned and operated a landscaping and lawn service], but a few years back, I decided, hell, I'm not getting any younger and Sturgis ain't getting any closer. If I'm going to go, I better do it now. So, me and one other guy I rode with just bit the bullet and did it. We spent 5 nights on the road coming up and 4 on the way back, so we really only had a couple of days in Sturgis. Still, it was one of the best experiences of my life. I've ridden for over 25 years [he was in his 40s], but it seemed like coming to Sturgis somehow validated me. It was the trip up and back more than being here. Once I'd done it, I figured I'd never do it again. But then, I'd tell other people about it, share some of the stories, and by the time the next year rolled around, I was ready and willing to do it again. Still, it costs too much time and money for me to do it every year. This will probably be the last time I do it.

Austin (2009) uses sociologist Emile Durkheim's *The Elementary Forms of Religious Life* as a theoretical framework for analyzing BMW riders' participation in motorcycle rallies organized for those who ride that particular brand of motorcycle. Durkhiem ([1915] 1965) contends that society uses the basic components of religion (e.g., rituals, belief, commitment, and conversion) to transform secular activities into sacred ones. The same theoretical perspective can be expanded far beyond BMW riders, as the same (or perhaps even a stronger) case can be made for the reverence to which many riders refer to the Sturgis motorcycle rally — itself a very irreverent event.

RITUALS. Rituals at Sturgis are almost too numerous to count. One in which almost all riders either knowingly or unwittingly participate is what some refer to as the *ride-through*. At Sturgis, and many other motorcycle rallies held in small towns, a major street (sometimes the only major street in the town) is blocked off to all traffic except for motorcycles and pedestrians. Motorcycles will be parked, sometimes two or even three deep along each side of the street and usually down the center of the street leaving two lanes essentially just wide enough to allow riders safe passage single file in each direction on either side of the middle row(s) of bikes. As riders enter this street, they rarely pull into the first available parking space although parking is at a premium and there is a good chance that if they pass up a spot there may not be another one available unless they happen to catch someone pulling out at the precise moment they approach.[5] Instead, riders typically enter at one end of the "main drag" and ride slowly in one direction the entire length of cordoned off area, make a U-turn, and then proceed in the opposite direction until they find a suitable space. Sometimes riders pass up available spaces in each direction until they have ridden the entire length and are on their second "ride-through" and find a suitable space. A few riders seemingly never park their bikes, preferring to simply ride up and down "the strip," but most eventually end up parked somewhere in order to partake in the activities of the event. I had noticed this phenomenon at a number of rallies but never thought much of it until my first trip to Sturgis when a 40-year-old male rider who had attended Sturgis 7 or 8 times met up with our group at our campsite the night before and told us newbies,

> Just follow me into town and do what I do. We will all go up and down the main drag at least once. Parking will be at an absolute premium and don't be discouraged if you have to ride up and down the street several times to find a spot. More than likely some of us will have to go over onto one of the side streets and park there — maybe even two or three blocks away. Don't worry, you'll find a place. Still, don't take the first empty space you come across. You need to ride the entire length of the strip just to fully appreciate this thing.

Other rituals include walking up and down the streets, both seeing and being seen, a visit to the many vendors, purchasing the obligatory Sturgis t-shirt, patch, or commemorative pen, and spending anywhere from a few minutes to several hours in one of the many famous/infamous Sturgis bars.[6] Some attendees feel like they have not fully experienced the Sturgis rally unless they have participated in ritualistic "burnouts," wet t-shirt contests, or concerts that comprise part of the annual entertainment. Each year several big-name bands and celebrities perform at Sturgis and some of them participate in one or more of the organized rides.

Many participants contend that the real "action" and appeal of the Sturgis rally is not found in Sturgis at all. Rather, it takes place in the numerous camping venues that surround the town, some up to 30 or 40 miles away that capture much of the attention and provide much of the entertainment. While some campsites are designated as "family-oriented," many others are notorious for rocking concerts, wild parties, rampant nudity, free-flowing alcohol and other drugs, races, burnouts, fights, and almost anything else that bikers and motorcyclists might find fun and exciting. As one attendee told me, "Hell, Sturgis ain't nothing, but the _____ campground, now that's something else — that's why I come every year."

BELIEF/COMMITMENT. While some view going to Sturgis as a once in a lifetime event —"Now, that I've done it, I can check that off my bucket list," one attendee told me — it is amazing how many motorcyclists attend the Sturgis rally as often as possible with some committed to attending every year. I was standing in line to pay for my meal at a small café in Deadwood when I started counting the Sturgis patches on the back of a man's vest standing in front of me. There were 17 of them all in rows of consecutive years from 1992 to 2009 with the exception of one blank space between patches for the years 1994 and 1996. Since there was a blank space the size of a patch, I assumed there had been a patch there but it had fallen or been torn off. As the vest wearer turned to leave, I asked, "so what happened to your '95 patch?" A sullen expression descended on the man's face, and he replied,

> Oh man, 1995 was a bad year for me. I lost my job, my ol' lady left me, and I had to sell my bike. I didn't get to make it up here that year, and I've regretted it ever since. I swore I'd never miss another Sturgis, and I haven't. I leave the hole there in my patches as a reminder.

In another incident, we were camped several miles outside of Sturgis when a motorcyclist, probably in his early 40s, with a woman about the same age riding two-up pulled into our campsite. As it turned out, he was the son of one of the riders we had joined up with in Oklahoma for the ride to Sturgis. That night around the campfire, he began talking about his previous Sturgis experiences, as he had attended each of the past eight years. "I tell you, I'm a firm believer that Sturgis is the ultimate biker rally. I can't imagine anybody who ever comes here not wanting to come back every year. You come once, and you're hooked."

CONVERSION. Nobody is as devout as a recent convert. The long-time smoker who finally quits, the reformed alcoholic, the recently baptized, and the middle-aged Baby Boomer who takes his/her first road trip on a newly purchased motorcycle are something to behold. A first-time Sturgis attendee who had been riding for less than a year told me,

> I always wanted to own and ride a motorcycle, but I never understood the whole "biker image" thing. I mean I'm a loan officer in a bank. I wear suits to work every day. So when I bought my bike, I thought, "This is not going to change me, or who I am." I started out riding in blue jeans and t-shirts. Then, for protection, I bought my first pair of chaps and a jacket with some protective padding. Then, I attended a little motorcycle rally a few miles from where I live. For the first time, I felt like I was part of something, but I didn't quite fit in. Now, I've been to Sturgis. This is the ultimate "initiation ritual." I'm never going to be a "badass biker," and don't want to be, but I feel like I've "come of age." I'm a *legitimate* rider now. I've got buddies who've said I was crazy to make the trek all the way up here, but when I tell them about this experience, they're going to want to come next year. I bet I bring four or five guys with me next year.

Another rider who was attending Sturgis for the second time commented,

> I've ridden motorcycles for 30 years and never even considered coming to Sturgis. I live in southern Kansas, and even though I've taken much longer rides, the idea of riding all the way through Kansas and Nebraska in August just to go to a bunch of biker bars and get a t-shirt did not appeal to me. Then, my buddy at work made the trip. You should have heard him after he got back. He talked about the atmosphere, the bands, the vendors, but mostly the feeling of being here — it was like some kind of religious experience — it was like he met God or something. So, I came with him last year. I don't think it was as big a deal to me as he made it out to be, but I have to admit, it was cool. I guess you can say I'm a convert. I'll probably come back again, and may even try to bring a few of my buddies with me.

Perhaps the most telling comment from a rider on his first visit to Sturgis: "Okay, I'm done now; I've been to Sturgis; I can die a happy man."

While most attendees at Sturgis are not ready to die anytime soon, the rally does represent a "bucket list" entry for many. Time and again, I heard comments to that effect. "I finally made it to Sturgis." "This is the ultimate biker experience." So on, and so forth. It would be misleading, however, to give the impression that all motorcyclists are infatuated with the Sturgis experience. While the vast majority of the riders I interviewed were very positive about the rally and most indicated they would attend again, at least a few felt differently. One rider from Oklahoma is representative of the dissenters with his comment, "This is it? I can't believe I rode this far to see essentially the same thing that takes place every Saturday night at a biker bar in my home-town."

## Other Rallies and Destinations

There are other motorcycle rallies and destinations too numerous to mention that are somewhat famous or infamous among riders. One of the more famous national motorcycling events is the Cannonball Run, named after Erwin "Cannonball" Baker, who first crossed the United States on a motorcycle in 1912, and then repeated the accomplishment 142 more times. Participants in this event ride classic motorcycles, many 100 years old or older, some 3,200-plus miles in 17 days across the United States, collecting points as they reach predetermined checkpoints along the route. One participant who was asked why he would make such a trek on a 1947 Knucklehead hardtail chopper after having had hip replacement and artificial knee surgeries, replied, "How often do you get to experience something like this? ... Life can get so structured. This really does it for me" (Hathaway, 2011:45).

Most organized rides are shorter and far less arduous than the Cannon-ball Run, and unorganized and informal rides are far more common among motorcyclists. Almost every state boasts a twisty or hilly highway that chal-lenges motorcyclists' skills and many popular motorcycle magazines rate var-ious roads or destinations for their scenic beauty, challenging hills or curves, and other components of interest to motorcyclists. Many riders believe the ultimate ride experience can be had at "the Dragon," a 14-mile stretch of highway U.S. 129 that begins at the "Fugitive Bridge" in North Carolina (the bridge off which Harrison Ford jumped in the movie *The Fugitive*) and ends across the Tennessee state line at the Tabcat Creek Bridge. Others believe the ultimate motorcycle challenge is to ride to the summit of Pikes Peak in Col-orado, especially the last few miles of gravel road that offers no guardrails or protection of any kind. Still others rave about stretches of coastal highway in Washington, Oregon, and California. The bottom line is that motorcycle riders, regardless of where they live and where they ride, all have a favorite place or memorable riding experience that, for them, defines what motorcy-cling is all about. What all of these sites share in common is that motorcyclists find them opportune places to show and share their skills and to meet other like-minded two-wheeled enthusiasts. As we will see in chapter 10, these types of challenging rides also provide some of the motivation for riding motorcy-cles.

Motorcycle rallies feature bike shows, poker runs, a host of vendors and various events and contests for attendees. Here, pillion riders traveling on a motorcycle at 10–15 miles per hour compete to take the biggest bite out of a hotdog suspended six feet in the air. The contest is usually limited to male riders and female passengers, but this male contestant donned a wig for the event and despite a few good-natured protests, took home the trophy.

## The Mingling of Motorcyclists and Bikers

Motorcycle rallies, especially large ones such as those held in Laconia, Daytona, Fayetteville, Austin, and Sturgis provide occasions for today's motorcyclists to mix and mingle with hardcore bikers and one-percenters, at least on a limited basis. For the most part, however, very little mixing or mingling actually takes place. Invariably, the two groups may come into limited contact on the streets, in bars, or at concerts and campsites, but generally, the one-percenters and other hardcore bikers tend to stick to themselves and ignore other riders. Although curious, motorcyclists generally return the favor. At one rally I attended in Texas, a well-known one-percenter club operated a vendor booth selling bandanas, leather pouches, and other motorcycle-related paraphernalia. They wore their colors, and while not as commercially aggressive as some of the other vendors, they were polite and friendly to those few who visited their booth. For the most part, motorcyclists showed little interest in them and vice versa. At Sturgis, the Hell's Angels operate a store on the main drag, and my observations indicated that while most attendees seemed curious, few were seen entering or leaving the store. Many took photos of the shop, but only a few ventured inside. The few club members in and around the store either ignored passersby altogether, or briefly acknowledged those who entered the store. A "live and let live" philosophy seemed to guide both group's behaviors and I neither saw nor heard of any confrontations during the rally.

The potential for confrontation and violence, however, is ever present, although it usually takes place between rival clubs as opposed to between club members and "civilians." For example, in 2007, newspapers reported, "Two Hell's Angels, one a prospect of a Canadian chapter, were arraigned for shooting five members of the Outlaws at Custer State Park in South Dakota" (Walker, 2006). "It was the first violence between one-percent biker gangs at the rally [Sturgis] since 1990 when a bar brawl between the Outlaws and the Sons of Silence left an Outlaw shot and two Sons of Silence members stabbed (Barker, 2007:166). In 2009, when I was in attendance at Sturgis, a newspaper reported, "A member of the Hell's Angels motorcycle club was shot early Saturday morning at the Loud American Roadhouse on Main Street in Sturgis, Sturgis police said, and the Seattle Police Department said one of its officers [a member of the Iron Pigs] was involved" (Woodard, 2009). In both 2009 and 2010, widespread rumors circulated that several Sturgis attendees who purchased and wore t-shirts bearing the colors and insignia from the popular television series *Sons of Anarchy* were brutally beaten by some one-percenters, but I never found confirmation of those stories.

Part of the appeal and mystique of motorcycle rallies may be related to media portrayals of them. Several popular biker movies have shown scenes at various rally venues, and cable and satellite networks have produced several documentaries on the Sturgis and Daytona rallies, to name but a few. Whether fact or fiction, the media and how they have portrayed bikers and motorcyclists over the years have had tremendous impact on how the non-riding public views them, and even how the riders view themselves. In the following chapter we turn our attention to motorcycles, motorcyclists, and motion pictures.

# CHAPTER 7

# Motorcycles, Motorcyclists and Motion Pictures

"Do you think stuff like that really happens?" the young wife asked as she and her husband emerged from the dark theater out into the bright sunlight. "I don't mean running into the real estate sign or the surfboard, but I'm talking about jumping up over curbs, running into bales of hay, or getting hit in the face by a bird, and things like that." "Naw, that's strictly Hollywood," he answered. "Most of that was ridiculous—no bird would ever fly into a motorcycle rider like that, and besides, if somebody got hit in the face by a bird while going 70 miles an hour down the highway it would probably kill him and the bird." The couple had just seen the popular 2007 comedy movie *Wild Hogs*, and since neither rode motorcycles, both were attracted to the film by its well-known cast, John Travolta, Tim Allen, William H. Macy, and Martin Lawrence, and not by its theme, which focused on four middle-aged Baby Boomers seeking to recapture some of their lost youth via a cross-country adventure on motorcycles. Also, since neither rode motorcycles, both were guessing as to the accuracy of the riding experiences portrayed in the movie.

As a longtime rider, let me answer the young wife's questions about the authenticity of *Wild Hogs* by saying, first, it was very difficult to watch expensive motorcycles being damaged just for the sake of a few laughs. Second, William H. Macy getting knocked off his bike by a real estate sign and Travolta, Allen, and Lawrence running head-on into a surfboard were pretty far-fetched, and smacked much more of Hollywood creativity than reality, but they are not beyond the realm of possibility. Third, I can state unequivocally: yes, riders sometimes lose control and jump the curb (I've done it a few times and have seen others do it many times); yes, if there were hay bales stacked on or near the road there is a good chance that a motorcycle rider would hit them and go flying over the handlebars (I have had some near misses with hay bales that have fallen off trucks on some of the back roads I've ridden); and yes, a rider can get hit in the face or chest by a bird (as well as by a bat, a grasshopper, a June bug, a rock, a stick, an empty beer can, a

121

wasp, and/or a trash bag as well as a lot of other miscellaneous objects) at 70 miles an hour and live to tell (or write) about it. Sometimes motorcyclists must decide in an instant whether it is safer to try to dodge an animal (such as a deer or large dog) or to go ahead and hit it (for example, a squirrel or chipmunk). An old motorcycle adage admonishes, "If you can eat it in one sitting, hit it" (Kresnak, 2008:403). I have learned, however, that hitting any object while riding a motorcycle, large or small, living or dead, is seldom funny, and can be disastrous for both the motorcycle and the rider.

## Motorcycles in the Movies

The media, especially motion pictures, have long been fascinated with motorcycles and the people who ride them. Since the 1950s, the public's image of motorcycle riders has been shaped largely by atypical riders portrayed by the media (Barker, 2007). Usually, these stereotypical media bikers wore leather jackets, boots and bandanas; displayed skulls and cross bones, iron crosses and swastikas; sported tattoos; drank heavily; cursed; and brawled with rival gangs, law enforcement, or anybody else who got in their way. Rarely were women ever featured as motorcycle riders in movies. "One reason women and motorcycles are infrequently associated in American popular culture is because most stories involving motorcycles fit into one of two genres, both of which reserve the major roles for men: the macho world of biker gangs and the road trip journey of discovery" (Boslaugh, 2006:2). Still, as one scholar notes, and as we discovered in chapter 4, "This virtual absence of independent women bikers from popular culture is puzzling because in fact many women in America ride motorcycles" (Boslaugh, 2006:1). Whether accurate or not, the macho image and demeanor portrayed by media helped redefine masculinity and shaped public perception of bikers and motorcyclists for decades (Willett, 2009).

During the 1950s and 1960s movies capitalized on these stereotypical images of bikers with several major motion pictures that featured rebellious teenagers and young adults battling society's values, social norms, and the established social order. Motorcycles and motorcycle gangs played an important role in these movies, as did the underlying themes of rebellion, defiance of authority, pursuit of freedom, and the desire for autonomy. There is general consensus among scholars that biker movies of this period "created a 'folk devil' image and moral panic about bikers" (Barker, 2007:11). Some of the most prominent so-called "biker" films of that era included *The Wild One* (1953), *The Great Escape* (1963),[1] *The Wild Angels* (1966), *Hell's Angels on Wheels* (1967), *Hell's Angels '69* (1969), and, at the end of that period, a different kind of rebellious biker image was portrayed in *Easy Rider* (1969).

During the late 1960s, 1970s and 1980s, the popularity of motorcycles waned (Perlman, 2007), resulting mostly in "B-movies" with entries such as *Stone* (1974) and *The Loveless* (1982), but one notable "biker" movie of this era was *Electra Glide in Blue* (1973) in which Robert Blake played a motorcycle patrolman on the highways of the northern Arizona desert. A central "character" in the movie was the Harley-Davidson Electra Glide that Blake's character rode day in and day out policing the highways. In some ways, this movie helped reinforce Harley-Davidson motorcycles' role of cultural icon (Perlman 2007; Coffey and Packer, 2009), and transformed the Harley from being almost solely identified with outlaws and rebels to also being associated with law enforcement.

During the 1990s and the dawn of the 21st century, the world of motorcycles and motorcyclists, like almost everything else in America, became dominated by Baby Boomers, that huge segment (approximately 70 million) of the population born roughly between 1945 and 1964 (National Safety Council, 2007; Box, 2007). The motorcycle became acknowledged as both art and cultural artifact (Packer and Coffey, 2004) and motorcycle manufacturers, dealers, and even motorcyclists strove to eradicate negative stereotypes and images associated with outlaw motorcyclists and the hardcore biker subculture (Coffey and Packer, 2007). At first, media were slow to acknowledge the new motorcycle subculture, but eventually evidence of the changing trends appeared in movies, on television, and in the print media (Schouten and McAlexander, 1995; Thompson, 2009). Although there were still a wide array of "B" movies featuring outlaws and gangs, popular movies of that period included *Born to Ride* (1991), *Harley Davidson and the Marlboro Man* (1991), *Beyond the Law* (1992), *The World's Fastest Indian* (2006), and *Wild Hogs* (2006). Of those films, *The World's Fastest Indian*, starring Anthony Hopkins as real-life New Zealand motorcyclist Burt Munro who set several motorcycle land speed records, garnered the most critical acclaim.

## A Brief Synopsis of Three Popular "Biker Movies"

In order to provide a more in-depth look at media portrayals of motorcycles and the people who ride them, a content analysis was performed on three of the most popular and box-office-successful "biker" movies spanning a 50-year period: *The Wild One* (1953), *Easy Rider* (1969) and *Wild Hogs* (2006). Two methods were used to determine which movies to be analyzed. First, during the interviews for this research, conversations often turned to movies and television shows and how motorcyclists are depicted in those media. With no prompting, these three movies were mentioned over and

First introduced by Marlon Brando's character in *The Wild One,* leather jackets with multiple zippers and belted waists soon became known as "motorcycle jackets" and today are meaningful symbols among modern American motorcyclists.

again as representing three distinct eras and three vastly different portrayals of motorcycling. Second, I posted an open-ended poll question on three popular message board websites for motorcycle riders and enthusiasts. One message board was established and maintained almost exclusively for Harley-Davidson riders, the most popular and largest selling motorcycle in the United States (Motorcycle Industry Council, 2009). A second message board was established and maintained for riders of Honda motorcycles, the second best-selling motorcycle in the U.S. (Motorcycle Industry Council, 2009). The third was a generic message board established for motorcyclists in general. The poll question asked: "What do you think are the three best motorcycle/biker movies of all time?" Respondents simply hit a "reply" tab and listed their three favorites. In a few cases, respondents listed only one; others listed four, five, or more; and in one case, a respondent typed a link to a website entitled "Best Biker Movies." Admittedly, an unscientific method, nevertheless, the results of these polls were amazingly consistent. Over 3,000 responses generated a list of over 60 different motorcycle movie titles, but three movies appeared on over three-fourths (78 percent) of the lists: *The Wild One, Easy Rider,* and *Wild Hogs.* The next closest movie in popularity (ranking 4th) was *The World's Fastest Indian,* which appeared on just under one-half (47 percent) of the lists. The distance between the top three and the fourth movie seemed like a "natural" breaking point for determining the three most popular movies. The *Wild One* and *Easy Rider* are widely acknowledged as cult classics (Barker, 2007; Perlman, 2007), and *Wild Hogs,* despite being panned by critics, was a huge box-office success and spawned an immediate following among "new bikers" and motorcyclists (Thompson, 2009).

## *The Wild One* (1953)
*Length: 79 minutes; Format: black and white; Rating: not rated*

One of the earliest motorcycle movies, now considered a classic, *The Wild One* was based on a short story, "The Cyclists' Raid" by Frank Rooney, that appeared in the January 1951 issue of *Harper's* magazine. The story was later published in book form as part of *The Best American Short Stories 1952.* The story was loosely based on an actual biker street party on the Fourth of July weekend in 1947 in Hollister, California, that was elaborately embellished in an article that appeared in *Life Magazine* as the "Hollister riot," complete with staged photographs of wild motorcycle outlaws and their even wilder women. The movie featured a young Marlon Brando as the gang leader and juvenile delinquent, Johnny Stabler. Brando sported a black leather jacket, which immediately became dubbed a "motorcycle jacket," leather boots (soon popularly referred to as "motorcycle boots"), and a paramilitary style cap, and he rode a 1950 Triumph Thunderbird 6T. He mumbles his words, swaggers when he walked, swigs beer, and soon became the archetype American teenager/young adult that parents everywhere warned their sons and daughters to avoid. After disrupting an organized motorcycle race and stealing a trophy, Johnny's "gang" rides into a small town and almost immediately begins terrorizing its citizens and openly defying the town's one police officer. One of the most famous scenes and lines in the movie take place in a local diner when Brando's character, Johnny, leaning on a jukebox and sipping a beer, is asked, "What are you rebelling against?" His answer, "Whadda ya got?" epitomized the outlaw biker persona for generations to come. A young Lee Marvin played a rival gang leader in the movie. This low-budget production included real-life motorcycle riders/gang members and had Brando playing a "rebel without a cause" two years before the movie by that title starring James Dean hit the screens in 1955.

## Easy Rider (1969)
*Length: 95 minutes; Format: color; Rating: R*

In 1969, a different breed of motorcyclist emerged in the media and, to a lesser extent, in real life, personified by Peter Fonda and Dennis Hopper in *Easy Rider*. Fonda wrote and produced the movie and it was directed by co-star Hopper. These motorcyclists were also rebels, and wore many of the same symbols as their earlier biker counterparts, but sported long hair, beards, and peace symbols, and were as likely to smoke marijuana and take LSD as to drink alcohol and smoke cigarettes. "Make love not war" served as their mantra, and fighting among these "hippie" bikers was rare. The movie begins with a scene in which the two main characters culminate a major drug transaction and then purchase a couple of choppers upon which they begin a cross-country jaunt from Los Angeles to New Orleans with the goal of attending Mardi Gras. Along the way, the two bikers encounter a hippie commune, a small-town down-on-his-luck attorney (played by a young Jack Nicholson), a couple of hookers, and a bevy of southern rednecks—two of which ultimately end the journey and the movie when they kill the two young motorcyclists with shotgun blasts through the window of a pick-up truck.

## Wild Hogs (2006)
*Length: 100 minutes; Format: color; Rating: PG*

*Wild Hogs* starred Tim Allen, John Travolta, Martin Lawrence, and William H. Macy as middle-aged, middle-class motorcyclists on a midlife-crisis cross-country trip designed to help them recapture their youth. On their journey, the four motorcyclists stop at a bar where they encounter a band of "hardcore bikers" who show their resentment and contempt for these four posers by humiliating them, taking one of their motorcycles, and sending them back home. Travolta's character refuses to be denied this rite of passage on which the men have embarked, and in trying to retrieve the stolen motorcycle, inadvertently causes an explosion and burns down the biker bar. A comedic cross-country chase ensues with the bikers seeking revenge as the motorcyclists attempt to elude them. The story ends in a small New Mexico town where the four motorcyclists along with Macy's love interest, a diner-owning innocent played by Marisa Tomei, a local sheriff, and the rest of the intimidated townspeople finally take a stand against the motorcycle gang who had bullied them for years. An interesting twist in the movie's finale includes a scene where *Easy Rider* star Peter Fonda makes a cameo appearance as the father of the leader of the hardcore biker gang. He admonishes his son (and the gang) for forgetting the true spirit of riding which is all about freedom, which means everybody has a right to the road. He then takes off his wristwatch and throws it in the dirt, reminiscent of a scene from *Easy Rider*. Earlier in the movie, the *Wild Hogs* threw away their cell phones in a similar fashion before starting their adventure.

## Content Analysis of *The Wild One,*
## *Easy Rider* and *Wild Hogs*

Through the use of qualitative content analysis (Neurendorf, 2002; Berg, 2009) couched within a symbolic interactionist framework, common themes, settings, and meaningful symbols as well as unique features of each of these movies can be identified. Four independent raters (three other people and I) viewed each of the three movies. Two of the raters were males aged 24 and 57, one of whom rode motorcycles and one who did not. The other two raters were females aged 28 and 54. One of the women rode her own motorcycle, and both had ridden on the backs of motorcycles numerous times. All four of the raters were familiar with two of the movies (*Easy Rider* and *Wild Hogs*) and had seen them before. The two younger raters were not familiar with *The Wild One*, although one had heard of the movie, but neither had seen it. All four of the raters were white and college educated, and all but one of the raters (the 54-year-old female) had taken a course on sociological research methods that covered content analysis. The rater who had not taken such a course was familiar with content analysis from an introductory sociology course and an art history course.

All raters were provided DVD copies of the movies and were given the same instructions. The first task was to watch each movie twice and identify and write down what they believed to be "dominant themes" in each movie. Also, as they watched the movies, they were instructed to make note of what they considered to be "meaningful symbols" of the biker/motorcyclist sub-culture (Blumer, 1969). Four separate lists of dominant themes were compiled for each movie. In order for a theme to be included for the next step of the study, it had to appear on all four raters' lists. After compiling the lists of six common dominant themes identified by the four raters (discussed later), each rater was instructed to watch each movie again; this time armed with a stop-watch and a tally sheet with each dominant theme listed and a place for them to record the number of scenes and time devoted to each theme. They were instructed to time the sequences or scenes that depicted each of the six dom-inant themes and to note the time in minutes and seconds as accurately as possible. If two or more dominant themes overlapped, they were to note the time for each. In some cases this required the raters to stop/start and replay scenes several times in order to record the amount of time devoted to each of the dominant themes. Times from each rater were compiled for each movie. Where there were discrepancies of more than one minute, the author and the three other raters watched that section of the movie and discussed when they thought each theme under question started and ended. Consensus was reached rather easily, and it was discovered that most discrepancies were more related to the logistics of operating the stop watches, especially when two or more themes overlapped, than in actual disagreement over what theme was being depicted and how long it lasted.

A list of meaningful symbols was also identified by each rater for each of the movies. The lists from the four raters were remarkably consistent for each movie, with only minor discrepancies. Interestingly, the two females tended to note more meaningful symbols in clothing and apparel-related accessories, whereas the two males tended to note more symbols related to the motorcycles and their accessories— a finding worthy of note for perhaps another study.

## Dominant Themes

The six dominant themes identified in each of the three movies were 1) motorcycle riding; 2) confrontations; 3) fighting or other violence; 4) drugs and/or alcohol; 5) love/romance/sex; and 6) biker(s)/motorcyclist(s) as sym-pathetic character(s). The second dominant theme, confrontations, was divided into three sub-categories: confrontations with law enforcement, con-frontations with non-riders, and confrontations with other bikers or motor-cyclists. These subdivisions evolved out of discussions with the raters as all four noted confrontations as a major theme, but some initially differentiated the types of confrontations when others did not. The tally sheet included these three different types of confrontations to make it easier to time various scenes. Similarly, the raters agreed that "fighting and other violence" needed to be separated from other types of confrontations which primarily involved verbal confrontations, heated disagreements, and verbal threats. If the action escalated to actual physical contact such as shoving, punching, kicking, or other forms of fighting or violence, the scene then became classified as fighting/violence and the stopwatch was reset to time that portion of the scene. Table 7.1 summarizes the number of scenes, time in minutes and seconds, as well as the percentage of total movie time that each film devoted to each dominant theme.

Since the three films were all considered "biker" movies, it is not surprising that one of the six dominant themes identified in each of the movies was motorcycle riding. This theme was expanded to include any scenes in

| Table 7.1— Time and Percentage of Total Movie Time Devoted to Dominant Themes | | | |
|---|---|---|---|
| | *The Wild One* | *Easy Rider* | *Wild Hogs* |
| | (length: 79 min) | (length: 95 min) | (length: 100 min) |
| Motorcycle Riding | 20 scenes<br>18 min; 22 sec<br>(23.3%) | 12 scenes<br>12 min; 56 sec<br>(13.6%) | 16 scenes<br>22 min; 33 sec<br>(22.5%) |
| Confrontations | 28 scenes<br>19 min 33sec<br>(24.7 %) | 8 scenes<br>6 min; 31 sec<br>(6. 8%) | 16 scenes<br>15 min; 20 sec<br>(15.33%) |
| With law | 10 scenes<br>8 min; 00 sec<br>(10.1%) | 3 scenes<br>3 min; 01 sec<br>(3.2%) | 6 scenes<br>3 min; 04 sec<br>(3.0%) |
| With bikers | 3 scenes<br>4 min; 41 sec<br>(5.9%) | 0 scenes<br>0 min; 0 sec<br>(0.0%) | 9 scenes<br>12 min; 11 sec<br>(12.2 %) |
| With non-bikers | 15 scenes<br>6 min; 52 sec<br>(8.7%) | 5 scenes<br>3 min; 30 sec<br>(3.7%) | 1 scene<br>0 min; 5 sec<br>(0.5%) |
| Fighting/Violence | 8 scenes<br>3 min; 34 sec<br>(4.5%) | 3 scenes<br>1 min; 32 sec<br>(1.6%) | 12 scenes<br>2 min; 36 sec<br>(2.6 %) |
| Drugs/Alcohol | 14 scenes<br>14 min; 04 sec<br>(17.8%) | 17 scenes<br>26 min; 02 sec<br>(27.4%) | 4 scenes<br>9 min; 42 sec<br>(9.6 %) |
| Love/Romance/Sex | 12 scenes<br>14 min; 42 sec<br>(18.6%) | 6 scenes<br>10 min; 23 sec<br>(10.9%) | 8 scenes<br>4 min; 24 sec<br>(4.4 %) |
| Bikers as Sympathetic Character(s) | 5 scenes<br>5 min; 33 sec<br>(7.0%) | 2 scenes<br>1 min; 40 sec<br>(1.7%) | 5 scenes<br>12 min; 18 sec<br>(12.3 %) |

which the focus of the action was on motorcycles, such as riding, sitting on motorcycles, working on motorcycles, and other activities related to riding motorcycles. Nevertheless, as table 7.1 indicates, a relatively small amount and percentage of time in each of the movies is relegated to motorcycle riding. *The Wild One* has the largest portion of time at 23.3 percent of the movie, but that is still only 18 minutes and 22 seconds. *Easy Rider*, which many think is the quintessential "motorcycle movie" with the entire plot revolving around two men riding motorcycles cross-country, devotes the least number of scenes (12), least amount of actual time (12 minutes and 56 seconds), and lowest percentage of time (13.6 percent) to the riding of motorcycles, prompting one reviewer to ask: "What happened to my motorcycle movie?" (Semack, 2005). *Wild Hogs* has 16 scenes and 22 minutes and 33 seconds of motorcycling (22.5 percent of the movie).

Bikers have almost always been characterized as confrontational, and two of these movies reinforce that notion. The *Wild One* devotes 28 scenes (plus another 8, if fighting and violence are included) and a total of 19.5 minutes (23 including fighting/violence) or a little over 29 percent of the movie to biker confrontations of one type or another. *Wild Hogs* weighs in with 28 scenes and approximately 18 minutes of violence when verbal and violent confrontations are combined. *Easy Rider*, however, deviates from the confrontational portrayal of bikers with only 3 fighting and/or violent scenes and 8 verbal confrontations, totaling a mere 8 minutes out of a 95-minute movie (less than 9 percent). Paradoxically, the violent confrontations portrayed in *Easy Rider* are more graphic than either of the two other films, including a brief but horrifically brutal beating scene in which Jack Nicholson's character is clubbed to death in his sleep, and another scene in which the two stars of the movie are brutally murdered by shotgun blasts, one of which ends in a violent explosion. These scenes, along with language, drug usage, and nudity, no doubt earned the movie its R rating. *Wild Hogs*, probably best described as a comedy, included 28 scenes totaling almost 18 minutes of verbal confrontations and fighting and violence, but most of the confrontations and violence, including a violent explosion, were couched within a comedic context, evoking laughter as opposed to horror.

Strictly based on time allotted, *Easy Rider* could be more accurately classified as a "drug movie" than a "biker movie." While 12 scenes and just under 13 minutes or 13.6 percent of the movie was devoted to motorcycle riding, twice that much time (just over 26 minutes) and 17 scenes were devoted to drinking and drug usage — mostly drug usage — including a nightmarish almost-8-minute-long acid trip filmed in a Louisiana cemetery. Several scenes and minutes of pot smoking along with cocaine snorting and acid-tripping made *Easy Rider* a cult film among hippie types and anti-establishment youth. The drinking/drug scenes in *The Wild One* and *Wild Hogs* are prominent, but less frequent and shorter in duration, and are limited strictly to the consumption of beer. *Wild Hogs*, in fact, only has 4 scenes in which alcohol is consumed for a total of 9 minutes and 42 seconds, despite the fact that several scenes take place in and around bars. Even that figure is a bit misleading, in that one scene includes an extended conversation where beer bottles are visible on the table but no drinking is shown.

While bikers are often portrayed as loners, no movie would be complete without a love interest. A large part of *The Wild One*'s plot focuses on the forbidden romance between the wild and deviant biker Johnny and the innocent and beautiful waitress in the local diner, who just happens to be the town's only police officer's daughter. Twelve scenes and almost 15 minutes (18.6 percent of the movie) are devoted to this subject. A little over 50 years later, *Wild Hogs* portrays a spontaneous romantic relationship between the only unmarried biker (Bill Macy's character) and an innocent and beautiful waitress in a diner (that she happens to own) — perhaps an intentional or unintentional homage to *The Wild One*. While much less time is devoted to this relationship (only 4 minutes and 24 seconds) it dominates 8 scenes in the movie, and plays a central role in the movie's plot. A sequel to the movie, *Wild Hogs 2*, was scheduled to be released by Disney's Touchstone Pictures in 2010, with a plot that focused on one last cross-country ride taken by the four men before Macy's character married that of Tomei's. Disney scrapped the movie after a new CEO decided it did not represent the "appropriate" family values upon which Disney had built its reputation. Probably nothing in *Easy Rider* could be categorized as love or romance, but there are 6 sex scenes, including nudity and simulated coitus, that cover approximately 10 and one-third minutes (10.9 percent of the movie). While it does not feature a love interest, it is notable that there is a small-town diner scene in which some local innocent and beautiful girls flirt with the bikers, something that is frowned upon by some of the local men, and ends in the beating death of Jack Nicholson's character.

While not a persistent theme, each of the movies devote a portion of the movie (ranging from just under 2 percent in *Easy Rider* to 7 percent for *The Wild One* and 12.3 percent for *Wild Hogs*) to portraying the motorcyclist(s) or biker(s) as sympathetic characters, or in some ways as "anti-heroic" heroes. After the first two viewings of the movies, one of the male raters did not include this category as one of the dominant themes, and although he admitted that he picked up on that theme in *The Wild One* and *Wild Hogs*, he could not see any way in which the bikers in *Easy Rider* could be seen as deserving of viewer sympathy. While he conceded that nobody deserved to be killed in cold blood on the highway, he also thought that the characters had put themselves in that situation by selling and using drugs, challenging dominant values and norms, and by making an obscene gesture at the offending truck passenger. After discussing it with the other three raters, when timing the various segments under other themes, he admitted that he felt sorry for the motorcyclists in a couple of scenes (the consensus among the other raters were that there were two such scenes), especially when the Nicholson character was savagely beaten and in the final scene when the two main stars were shot and killed. A previous study of biker movies underscores this theme in *Easy Rider*:

> The violence in *Easy Rider* is not ambiguous, nor is it performed by the bikers in the film. Instead, citizens brutally murder first George and later Billy and Wyatt. The film defines the motivation for these acts as prejudice against the bikers based solely on their appearance. The killers are demons, sadistic "weirdo hicks." The violence is morally wrong, as the victims are helpless and guilty of no crime [Perlman, 2007].

Marlon Brando's character in *The Wild One*, despite his bravado and open resentment and hostility toward authority figures and the law, also comes across as somewhat sympathetic. Johnny is not only misunderstood, but seems decent and downright benevolent when he is falsely accused of harming an older citizen and hunted down by a hostile mob, but is willing to take the blame rather than jeopardize the reputation of his love interest. Several scenes in *Wild Hogs* (5) evoke simultaneous laughter and sympathy for the middle-aged motorcyclists experiencing midlife crises: one experiences a false heart attack; another is being divorced by his wife; the third is mercilessly henpecked; and the fourth is afraid of women. These attributes hardly conform to public or media stereotypes of bikers.

## Meaningful Symbols

As noted in chapter 3, early on, hardcore and one-percenter bikers adopted certain symbols: tattoos, beards, dirty jeans, earrings, skullcaps, boots, cutoff jackets or vests with patches indicating their "colors," and most importantly, the Harley-Davidson motorcycle (Thompson, 1967; Watson, 1980; Quinn, 2001; Smith, 2006). Subsequent research shows that most of these symbols have been adopted or co-opted by motorcyclists (Schouten and McAlexander, 1995; Thompson, 2009). The most obvious and important symbol for bikers in all three movies is the motorcycle. *The Wild One* placed its central star on a British-built Triumph as opposed to the ubiquitous Harley-Davidson featured in the other two films, but few viewers other than motorcycle enthusiasts note the difference. In all three movies the motorcycles are prominent, loud, and accessorized in a way that accentuates the characters who ride them. Brando's bike, like his character, is rather plain, rough-looking, and, in one scene, adorned with the stolen trophy Johnny seems to simultaneously desire and yet care little about (feelings he seems to share toward the motorcycle itself, and the girl in the diner as well). The garishly chopped and painted Harley-Davidson motorcycles featured in *Easy Rider* can almost be considered co-stars in the film. In fact, the bike ridden by Fonda's character, custom-painted in an American flag design, was called "Captain America" and is perhaps more recognizable today than either of the film's two main human stars. The bike ridden by Dennis Hopper was bright yellow with reddish-orange flames, and is also considered a film icon by movie buffs. All four stars of *Wild Hogs* rode Harleys and if they did not, Harley-Davidson should have paid product-placement fees for all the visual and even verbal advertising they received.

Leather is a common symbol for bikers and motorcyclists in both fact and fiction. Marlon Brando made the leather jacket he wore in *The Wild One* famous almost overnight. Peter Fonda wears a little "hipper" version of the leather jacket replete with the American flag in *Easy Rider*, and the jackets worn by the four *Wild Hogs* would have allowed their characters to have ridden alongside Brando's character in *The Wild One* without raising an eyebrow. While almost all the riders in all three movies wore black, there are two notable exceptions. One of the "gang" members in The *Wild One* wore what appears to be a brown leather or suede jacket with fringed sleeves (the movie is in black and white, so since the jacket is obviously not black, it is reasonable to assume that it is a light shade of brown). He topped his outfit with a coonskin cap (presumably also brown) in the style worn by Davy Crockett. In *Easy Rider*, Dennis Hopper's character wears an almost identical-looking brown leather/suede jacket with fringed sleeves. He also wears a brown leather cowboy-style hat with one side of the brim pinned back in stark contrast to the bandanas, leather skull caps, custom helmets, and other headgear worn by the bikers in the three movies (Brando's character wears a black captain's hat).

Regarding headgear, none of the three films promotes motorcycle safety. No helmets are to be found in *The Wild One*. Although *Easy Rider*'s Peter Fonda is shown with a helmet on the back of his motorcycle, it is rarely seen on his head. Jack Nicholson's character, who is not a biker but rides on the back of Dennis Hopper's motorcycle, wears what one can only assume is his old high school football helmet. *Wild Hogs*' riders are usually shown wearing bandanas on their heads, although Bill Macy's character wears an ancient leather motorcycle helmet at the beginning of the movie, and throughout the remainder of the movie, each of the four riders are shown with and without helmets (mostly without) at various times. None of the rival "old school" bikers in the movie wear protective helmets, preferring either bare heads, bandanas, or skullcaps. Black "motorcycle boots" can be seen in all three movies, the notable exception being Billy (Dennis Hopper) in *Easy Rider*, who wears brown square-toed cowboy/motorcycle boots that match his fringed coat. Because of its black and white format, it is difficult to tell if the fringe-coated rider in *The Wild One* wore black or brown boots. Riders in all three movies also don black leather gloves in most of the riding scenes (except for Billy, who wears brown).

Sunglasses abound in all three films, ranging from the aviator-style worn by Brando's character and some of his comrades in *The Wild One* to the stylish wrap-arounds worn by Peter Fonda in *Easy Rider* and the Oakley and Ray Ban brands worn in *Wild Hogs*. Most of the riders in all three movies wear blue jeans, the notable exception being Peter Fonda's memorable black leather pants in *Easy Rider*. Leather is functional in the real-life biker world, as it protects the skin in case of a spill, but Fonda's leather pants are clearly more for style than safety. In fact, all of the aforementioned symbols — leather jackets, helmets, bandanas, skullcaps, boots, gloves, and sunglasses — serve some functional purpose in the real world of motorcycling, but their symbolic purpose seems far more important (Watson, 1985; Schouten and McAlexander,

Exotic customized choppers designed more for show than for riding are thought by some to have been inspired by the motion picture *Easy Rider* which featured Peter Fonda and Dennis Hopper riding cross country on customized bikes that became almost as famous as the actors who rode them.

1995; Quinn, 2001; Thompson, 2009). These symbols all portray bikers as tough, independent, cool, and unapproachable, or as Hell's Angels founder Sonny Barger puts it, "someone not to be messed with" (Barger, et al., 2001).

Finally, the "girl in the diner" can also be viewed as a meaningful symbol in all three of these movies. Whereas the bikers portray the toughness, rudeness, and crudeness of the macho-dominated world of motorcycles, she portrays its antithesis—pure, innocent, and in need of protection.

Volumes of research document the fact that the media, especially television and films, both reflect a society's cultural attitudes, values, and beliefs, and at the same time help shape them (e.g., Campbell et al., 2009). This being the case, these three movies may provide some insight into the world of motorcyclists of their particular time frame. Rather than accurate portrayals of the biker and/or motorcyclist subculture, however, creative license, box-office aspirations, and potential commercial revenue assure that all of these portrayals sensationalized, idealized, and stereotyped the world they supposedly portrayed, and probably had some impact on public perceptions of motorcycle riders. Moreover, as one researcher noted, they incorporated at least two themes that would appear in most biker movies to follow: an emphasis on cohesion among bikers and motorcyclists' disdain for conventional lifestyle (Perlman, 2007). No doubt, they also encouraged some who did not own or ride motorcycles, especially those who believed themselves to be "free spirits" and nonconformists, to give it a try. Art imitates life; life imitates art.

*Easy Rider*, while far from an accurate portrayal of bikers of that era, furthered the portrayal of the aimless, rebellious, freedom and thrill-seeking biker, modifying it to conform to the establishment's biggest threat of the 1960s, the hippies. These bikers were fundamentally different from those depicted in *The Wild One*. First, there was no gang, only two bikers—not wearing gang colors, but one wearing a buckskin jacket and the other a leather jacket adorned with the American flag. The freedom from authority and the appeal of the open road were combined with free love and the appeal of dope, all of which were anathemas to America's political leaders and "decent, hardworking, law-abiding" citizens. Drugs were indeed a staple of the biker world during that period, and the cross-country ride by the two main characters probably was played out in real life by hundreds, if not thousands, of bikers, but the flamboyant choppers and garish outfits of the two "easy riders" were pure Hollywood. Their influence, however, can be seen today at almost any motorcycle rally from Fayetteville, Arkansas, and Austin, Texas, to Daytona, Florida, and Sturgis, South Dakota. Chopped motorcycles, many designed more to be looked at than ridden, adorn every motorcycle show and rally; likewise, drinking and the consumption of illegal drugs are staples. Still today, a poster depicting Peter Fonda and Dennis Hopper astride their choppers is a popular seller both in stores and on the Internet. It has been suggested that *Easy Rider* may have been the inspiration for the popular Discovery Channel's television show *American Chopper* (Packer and Coffey, 2004)

Every weekend, American motorists are surrounded by "wild hogs"—doctors, lawyers, dentists, college professors, and other middle- and upper-middle-class professionals who take to the roads on their $10,000–$20,000 motorcycles to recapture their youth, express their manhood, or merely to escape the drudgery of their weekday existence (Packer and Coffey, 2004; Thompson, 2009). *Wild Hogs* reflects a trend in the motorcycle subculture, and no doubt, after seeing the movie, many middle-aged non-riders used the film as leverage to try to convince their wives and children that they should take the plunge and purchase that motorcycle they had wanted for so long. Although the movie portrayed the conflict between hardcore bikers and the new suburban middle-class motorcycle riders, today these two groups tend to avoid each other as much as possible and, when they inadvertently cross each other's paths, tend to practice civil inattention. Nevertheless, brand loyalty tends to be much stronger to motorcycles than automobiles, and some tension still exists between Harley-Davidson riders and those who ride Japanese or German bikes (Schouten and McAlexander, 1995: Coffey and Packer, 2009).

## Bikers and Motorcyclists as Modern-Day Cowboys?

Perlman (2007) contends that biker movies can primarily be categorized as modern-day Westerns. Despite the camaraderie of fellow riders, the motorcyclist often emerges as a lone figure. Replace the horse with the raw horsepower of the motorcycle and the barren frontier with the urban jungle, and "the cowboy of yore has become the contemporary biker; no longer is he the agent of civilization, but the man whom civilized society has left behind" (Perlman, 2007). Just as most Westerns did not accurately portray cowboys, most biker movies do not accurately reflect motorcyclists or the motorcycle subculture.

The comparison of motorcyclists to cowboys may or may not be accurate. If today's motorcyclist is a modern-day cowboy, the middle-aged, middle-class novice motorcycle rider may be analogous to an urban cowboy with all the appropriate accouterments, but in accord with a popular expression, perhaps "more hat than cowboy."[2] Just as "real cowboys" today resent the cowboy hat–and boots-wearing urban and suburban pseudo-cowboys, many motorcycle riders who consider themselves to be real bikers and even some motorcycle enthusiasts resent the weekend warriors or RUBS who take to the

Could this lone motorcycle rider on the American prairie be reminiscent of the free-spirited motion picture cowboys who used to ride their horses across this same isolated terrain?

highways on expensive motorcycles on weekends and holidays, but often lack the riding skills to handle the motorcycles they ride.

Still, whether bikers, motorcyclists, modern-day cowboys, or whatever, real-world motorcycling is far different than motion pictures would lead us to believe. Similarly, the resurgence in popularity of motorcycles is reflected on the small screen. Chapter 8 looks at bikers and motorcyclists on television.

# CHAPTER 8

# Bikers and Motorcyclists on Television

A biker clad in black leather exits a small diner in a remote area surrounded by a stark landscape. A young innocent waitress (à la *The Wild One* and *Wild Hogs*) follows behind him waving a dishrag and desperately begging him to take her with him. The biker stops, slowly turns, shakes his head, and responds, "No, I'm a loner, an island — I always fly solo." The camera shot opens wider and as the biker straddles his motorcycle we discover that he is surrounded by hundreds of people, some wearing hard hats, other white laboratory coats, and still others in a wide array of apparel. We discover these are the support personnel associated with his wireless provider as he explains, "Well, except for my network — I like to check my e-mails and get GPS directions if I get lost"[Thompson, 2009].

This humorous and paradoxical portrayal of "new bikers" depicts only one of the hundreds, if not thousands, of television commercials that capitalize on the renewed interest in motorcycling in American society. Whether television merely reflects cultural values, attitudes, and behaviors, or dramatically influences and creates them is open to debate, but there is virtually no disagreement that television and culture are inherently linked.

Bikers, motorcyclists, and motorcycles have received less attention from television than motion pictures, but they have been featured from time to time, especially since the widespread involvement of Baby Boomers in motorcycling. During interviews for this study, conversations often turned to movies and television and how motorcyclists are depicted in those media. Unlike the case with movies, when asked about their favorite television shows or characters associated with motorcycles and motorcycling, there was no general consensus as to which ones were "the best." Hundreds of television shows and commercials were mentioned, far too many to warrant content analyses of each. Nevertheless, a few trends and patterns could be identified that are worthy of discussion.

# Motorcycles and Popular Television Series

The wide variety of motorcycling and motorcycle-related television programs cited by the riders interviewed in this study was a bit surprising. Obviously, television has been and is acutely aware of the popularity of motorcycling riding and, as with motion pictures, has depicted riders in both stereotypical and non-stereotypical fashion — liberally combining fact with fiction and reality with fantasy. While it would be impossible to describe or discuss all of them, some of the more popular television portrayals suggested by the riders in this study merit mentioning. These television programs are not listed in the order of popularity, since that determination was not part of the research. Instead, they are discussed in approximate chronological order of their appearance on television.

## *Then Came Bronson* (1969–1970)

The television series *Then Came Bronson* featured actor Michael Parks as a disenchanted nomad who traveled cross country on a Harley Sportster, taking temporary odd jobs on his quest to discover the meaning of life. Despondent over the suicide of his best friend, Bronson bought the motorcycle left by his friend and, much like earlier stars of American television Westerns, traveled the countryside helping people and rescuing women in danger. Bronson embodied both the loner qualities so often associated with motorcycling as well as a reflective "do-gooder" quality not usually associated with bikers. Despite the transitory nature of their relationships, Bronson typically had positive impact on almost everyone with whom he came in contact. Shot in and around Jackson, Wyoming, the limited amount of motorcycling included in *Then Came Bronson* featured beautiful scenery depicted in a way that can only be experienced on a motorcycle. Several of the interviewees in this study mentioned this series as being one of their favorites because the Bronson character seemed both stoic and reluctantly heroic — two characteristics that they believed shed a very positive light on motorcyclists.

## *Happy Days* and "the Fonz" (1974–1984)

The popular television series *Happy Days* was not about motorcyclists or motorcycling. Nevertheless, many of the interviewees mentioned "the Fonz" as being one of their favorite television characters who rode a motorcycle. Arthur "Fonzie" Fonzarelli, rode a motorcycle (initially a variety of Harleys and later a Triumph), and although he was never depicted as a "bad guy," his character, a high school dropout and former gang member, was portrayed as the "coolest" and yet most non-conforming to adults' and society's expectations. He also was a tremendous hit with the girls and was clearly idolized by the other male characters. Fonzie was a high school dropout who rode a motorcycle, wore a black motorcycle jacket, combed his pompadour into a ducktail, and was so cool that he merely had to hit the jukebox in a particular spot known only to him to set the local teenage hangout hopping. Rarely was "the Fonz" ever shown actually riding a motorcycle, but he could be seen on the bike in the opening credits and his love for his motorcycle was a prominent part of the story line in a few episodes.

## *CHIPS* (1977–1983)

Most metropolitan police departments have a motorcycle division, and many non-motorcycle police officers ride motorcycles in their spare time, so it is not surprising that a few of the riders in this study mentioned *CHIPS* as one of their favorite television shows depicting motorcycling/motorcyclists. Despite being about California Highway Patrol officers (hence the title), one of the officers, Francis "Ponch" Poncherello (portrayed by Erik Estrada), was somewhat of a "bad boy," having been place on probation for repeated policy violations. This explained why he was forced to ride with his straight-laced partner Jon Baker (played by Larry Wilcox), since in real life, California Highway Patrol usually ride alone. Unlike *Then Came Bronson* and *Happy Days*, motorcycle riding was a central theme of *CHIPS* and was prominently featured in virtually every episode of the series. Although stunt doubles often filmed some of the more exciting chases and/or accident scenes, Estrada and Wilcox did much of their own riding in the show. For a short time, the series co-starred Brianne Leary (daughter of Timothy Leary), who rode motorcycles in real life, as a female motorcycle officer trainee. Undoubtedly many viewers assumed that the two patrol officers rode Harley-Davidsons, but they actually rode police-equipped Kawasaki motorcycles. The motorcycles were such an integral part of the television series that, along with action figures of the two main characters, a series of die cast model motorcycles was also produced and sold.

## *Street Hawk* (1985)

A short-lived television series of which I was totally unaware, but some other riders seemed to like, was *Street Hawk*. The series featured actor Rex Smith as a former dirt-bike racer turned police officer who was chosen to test a futuristic, top-secret, computerized, all-terrain attack motorcycle capable of speeds in excess of 300 miles per hour. The show, featuring a variety of models of modified Honda motorcycles, lasted only one season (thirteen episodes), but evidently developed a small following among motorcycle enthusiasts.

## Renegade (1992–1997)

*Renegade* starred Lorenzo Lamas, who played the role of a cop falsely accused of being crooked. As a result, Lamas' character, Reno Raines, became a bounty hunter who rode cross country on a customized motorcycle chasing bad guys, rescuing women, and attempting to clear his reputation. Each episode began with a voiceover that declared "an outlaw chasing outlaws," a theme that simultaneously promoted and violated stereotypical images of motorcyclists. The series was created and produced by Stephen J. Cannell, who subsequently has written and produced a number of television hit series. Cannell even appeared in several episodes of *Renegade* in a recurring role of a crooked cop. An avid motorcyclist in his off-camera life, Lamas did almost all of his own riding in the television series. Also off-screen, Lamas designed and sold customized motorcycles as well as motorcycle parts and apparel.

This real-life motorcycle police officer will probably experience less excitement and see less action in a year than fictional officers "Ponch" Poncherelli and Jon Baker did on one episode of the television series *CHIPS.*

## *House* (2004–present)

This one surprised me the most. Having watched a couple of seasons of the television series, I was aware that Dr. House (portrayed by Hugh Laurie) rode a sport bike in a few of the episodes and regularly could be seen sporting a leather motorcycle jacket. One episode even featured Dr. House involved in a motorcycle accident that necessitated brief hospitalization. Nevertheless, I was surprised when several of the riders interviewed for this study mentioned *House* as one of their favorite television shows that portrayed motorcycling. The series takes place almost entirely in a hospital setting, and the central theme of every episode is Dr. House's uncanny ability to diagnose rare medical maladies when other doctors remain puzzled or misdiagnose them. A major aspect of Hugh Laurie's character is his nonconformist "bad boy" image which is no doubt augmented by his riding a motorcycle, but it is interesting that he rides a sport bike on the show and not a "bad boy" image, cruiser or chopper. Dr. House limps badly, usually walking with a cane, and some motorcyclists may assume the leg injury was due to a motorcycle accident, but the injury was explained early in the series as being a result of a misdiagnosed problem with his leg.

## *Sons of Anarchy* (2008–present)

Probably television's most prominent 21st century contribution to the biker genre can be found in the popular FX series, *Sons of Anarchy* (2008–present), and there was no surprise when well over half (144, 64.3 percent) of the interviewees in this research named it as their favorite show depicting bikers, motorcycles, or motorcyclists. *Sons of Anarchy* portrays a one-percenter motorcycle club that hides behind a legal automotive repair business and a semi-legal pornography enterprise to run illegal weapons and traffic illegal drugs. Violence, sex, and profanity are mainstays of the series, but it also endeavors to humanize the motorcycle club members by showing their loyalty to club, family, hometown, and some fairly traditional American values (freedom, independence, and even honesty and integrity). The show uses dark comedy as well to reveal the bikers' numerous foibles and vulnerabilities. Seemingly patriarchal, chauvinistic, and sometimes even misogynistic, as episodes unfold, it is revealed that the true power to be feared and respected by club members is the club president's wife Jemma, played by Katey Sagal.[1] Despite their outward macho posturing and seemingly hedonistic nature, during one season the club members used the entire proceeds from all their legal and illegal enterprises to finance the rescue of one member's kidnapped infant son — Jemma's grandson (seen in most episodes wearing a baby blue sleeper and stocking cap sporting the Sons of Anarchy's logo). Clearly more about the stereotypical biker lifestyle than about riding motorcycles, and even also clearly more fiction than fact, *Sons of Anarchy* is very popular among "new bikers" and motorcyclists alike, and must have some appeal to the general public as it has survived for four seasons to this point. Perhaps testimony to the popularity of a show like *Sons of Anarchy* and the renewed general appeal of motorcycles can be found in a cartoon spoof that aired on an episode of the popular animated series *South Park*. Numerous riders in this study, especially riders of metric motorcycles and sport bikes, referred to the spoof as being one of their all-time favorite shows related to motorcycling.

### The *South Park* Spoof

In an episode entitled "The F-word," originally aired on Comedy Central November 4, 2009, the boys of *South Park* attempt to change the official definition of the word "fag" from an anti-gay slur to a derogatory term describing loud and obnoxious bikers. In the episode, one of the series regulars, Cartman, confronts the bikers (obviously Harley-Davidson riders), telling them that they are "insecure losers who ride loud motorcycles to draw attention to themselves." While the episode is more about language and its malleable uses and ever-changing meanings, the episode went viral when placed on *YouTube* and gained instant widespread popularity among non–Harley riders.

Undoubtedly there are other television series that have featured motorcycles or motorcyclists in one way or another, but they did not receive enough mention from the riders in this study to warrant inclusion. In addition to the aforementioned television series, however, riders named several "reality programs" that featured motorcycles and motorcyclists. Following, in no particular order, are some of the programs most frequently cited.

## Motorcycles and Reality Television

Along with the fictional portrayal of television bikers and motorcyclists, several reality-based television programs focus on real-life riders and their bikes. *American Chopper*, *West Coast Choppers*, *American Thunder*, and *Biker Build-off* all focus on custom motorcycles, while *Throttle Junkies* looks at three distinct genres of motorcycle manufacturing: custom choppers, high-performance "crotch rockets," and off-road motocross bikes. All of these television programs as well as a few others were mentioned by interviewees in this study. Perhaps some of the best known and most popular among motorcycle-related reality programs and those most frequently mentioned by riders in this study (in no particular order) are/were *American Chopper*, *Motorcycle Mania*, *Monster Garage*, and *Full-Throttle Saloon*.

The popular television series *Sons of Anarchy* advertised here on the main street of Sturgis depicts one-percenter bikers committed to the biker lifestyle and criminal activities. Notice that none of the motorcyclists in the photograph look like they fit into the one-percenter or hardcore "biker" category.

## *American Chopper* (2003–present)

Few members of the general public, much less motorcycle riders, have not viewed at least one episode and even fewer have never heard of *American Chopper*. This reality program features Paul Teutul (known as Paul Sr.) and his son Paul Jr. (usually referred to as Paulie or just Junior), owners of Orange County Choppers in New York State. This father and son duo argue, fuss, and feud while turning out unbelievably crafted custom motorcycles on very short deadlines. The father/son feuding eventually led to a split between the two, a highly publicized lawsuit and a new television series featuring competition between father and son shops entitled *American Chopper: Senior versus Junior*. The widespread popularity of *American Chopper* spawned posters, DVDs, and even video games, and made celebrities out of its two main stars, as well as younger son/brother, Mikey. The Teutuls have appeared on late night talk shows and other television programs as well as made numerous personal appearances at motorcycle rallies, bike shows, and other motorcycle-related events. Other cast members also sprang to fame as *American Chopper* created a spin-off reality program, *Throttle Junkies*, when two of the motorcycle builders (Vinnie and Cody) left to open their own shop and develop their own television show in 2010. As mentioned in chapter 7, some people contend that the motorcycles in the movie *Easy Rider* may have served as inspiration for *American Chopper*. Whatever the inspiration, the $100,000-plus motorcycles on this reality show are far from the reality of motorcycles ridden by most American bikers or motorcycle enthusiasts.

## *Motorcycle Mania, Monster Garage* and *West Coast Choppers*

Jesse James opened *West Coast Choppers* in his mother's garage in 1992 and went on to become an American celebrity when the Discovery Channel made him the focus of a television documentary entitled *Motorcycle Mania* (1992). Interest in that program led to the development of another television show, *Monster Garage*, on which James and his colleagues built customized choppers on short deadline. The "reality" of Jesse James' motorcycling experiences include alleged associations with the Hell's Angels and other one-percenter clubs and his penchant for customized motorcycles ranging in value from $150,000 to half a million dollars—hardly the reality of today's motorcyclists. Several interviewees mentioned Jesse James and his television program, but it paled in comparison to the number who cited *American Choppers*. Today, it seems James may be best known for his marriage to and later highly-publicized divorce from Sandra Bullock as well as his disputed lineage which alleges that he is the great grandson of the legendary outlaw with the same name (*People*, 2010).

## *Full-Throttle Saloon*

In 2009, truTV aired seven episodes of *Full-Throttle Saloon*, which provided an inside look at one of the most popular bars in Sturgis, South Dakota. The popularity of the program prompted another season the following year, and again in 2011. Only open for ten days out of the year during the legendary Sturgis Bike Week, *Full-Throttle Saloon* claims to be the largest indoor-outdoor biker bar in the world (FTS, 2011). Located on 30-plus acres, the saloon includes dozens of bars, numerous restaurants, several stages with a main stage that features live concerts with big-name celebrities, a burn-out pit (as well as a garage that sells and mounts new tires), a tattoo parlor, zip lines, a wrestling ring, dozens of stores that sell all types of motorcycle-related merchandise, as well as hundreds of cabins for rent and parking for thousands of motorcycles. One of the main attractions for the Full-Throttle is the popular

"Angieland," a tribute to the owner's girlfriend and her famous derriere that the Full-Throttle Saloon website claims is "the most photographed tush in the world" (FTS, 2011). Angieland features the Flaunt Dancers, who perform a burlesque-type show nightly and pose for photos in skimpy clothing with motorcyclists for tips. Well over half of the motorcyclists interviewed in this study (159, 71.0 percent) indicated *Full-Throttle Saloon* was one of their favorite "biker" television programs, and several indicated they had been to the establishment in Sturgis. I have visited Full-Throttle Saloon during the Sturgis rally and even conducted a few interviews there. It is indeed a remarkable facility and probably worthy of its own television show. While it promotes the biker image, in reality, its crowd is primarily "new bikers" and motorcyclists by my classification scheme.

## Documentaries and Motorcycle Racing

From time to time the *National Geographic* channel or some other cable outlet airs a documentary on the Sturgis rally, Daytona Bike Week, Biketoberfest, cross-country motorcycle adventures, or some other aspect of motorcycling. Ewan McGregor and long-time friend Charlie Boorman have documented two monumental cross-continent rides on BMW motorcycles in *Long Way Round* and *Long Way Down* that were serialized on cable networks and sold in DVD sets. In *Long Way Round* (2004) the pair began their 115-day, 20,000-mile motorcycling adventure in jolly old England and proceeded across Europe, the Ukraine, Russia, Kazakhstan and Mongolia, where they rode the infamous Road of Bones through Siberia, over to Alaska, through Canada, down into the United States and finished in New York City. Supported by a small documentary film crew, McGregor and Boorman fulfilled life-long dreams and fantasies of motorcycle enthusiasts the world over, challenging their minds, bodies, and machines to the ultimate limits. Three years later, the pair filmed *Long Way Down* (2007), which documented their 15,000-plus-mile journey across 18 countries that began at the northern-most tip of Scotland and ended some 84 days later at the southern-most tip of Capetown, South Africa. The popularity of these two documentaries (now available on DVD), among both motorcyclists and non-riders has prompted much speculation about a rumored third trip that would start at the base of South America and end in Canada.

Several other documentaries, far too numerous to mention, have also aired on a wide array of television and cable networks. Stock car racing is North America's number one spectator sport and although quite a bit further behind, motorcycling is increasing in popularity every year (Eitzen and Sage, 2011). Several different types of motorcycle races appear on television, including road racing, motocross, supercross, endure, cross-country and others.

Avid motorcycle enthusiasts cheer both for their favorite racers and their favorite make of motorcycles. While Harley-Davidson may capture the bulk of cruiser and touring bike sales in the United States, the Japanese motorcycles, Honda, Kawasaki, and Suzuki, dominate the racing world.

As interest and participation in motorcycling grow, more television programs featuring motorcycles and motorcyclists are beginning to appear. One obvious trend is that the strategic placement of motorcycles as visual props is becoming much more common in all types of television programs.

## Motorcycles as Props

You do not have to be a sociological researcher or a motorcycle rider to be aware that the fifth season of *Sunday Night Football* began each airing with a black-leather-clad Faith Hill dismounting a motorcycle, removing a black helmet and singing the show's popular theme song. While it could be argued that football fans and motorcyclists may share some common testosterone-related characteristics, there is little doubt that the motorcycle in this case is nothing more than a sexy visual prop — something that is quite common on television.

### In Television Programs

Avid television viewers need not be terribly astute or even remotely interested in motorcycles to notice the high number of scenes in which motorcycles appear in non-motorcycle-related television programs. From weekly sitcoms to police dramas, motorcycles are seen parked in front of restaurants, driving down alleyways, and strategically placed in the background for visual effects, much like television extras or scenery. In more direct fashion, more characters in television programs can be seen riding motorcycles although that fact has little or nothing to do with the plot of the show. For example, the popular television series *Parenthood* focuses on the fictional Braverman family led by Patriarch Zeke (played by Craig T. Nelson) and wife Camille (portrayed by Bonnie Bedelia) who have raised grown children all of whom have now become parents in their own right. One of those grown children, Crosby (played by Dax Shepard) is the "black sheep" of the family who unknowingly fathered an illegitimate child who he did not meet until several years later. While the other adult children/parents have stable careers and home lives, Crosby works in the unpredictable pop music industry, lives on a houseboat, perpetually makes bad decisions, and, you guessed it, rides a motorcycle. Shepard, who plays the part of Crosby, lists motorcycling as one of his hobbies in real life, but is rarely seen on the motorcycle. Nevertheless, in numerous scenes the bike is prominently displayed, or his character is seen entering or leaving clad in a leather jacket with helmet in hand. In one episode, Crosby drops by his ex-girlfriend's place on his motorcycle to pick up his son and take him for the weekend, but the boy's mother protests that motorcycles are too dangerous, and that this act is one more example of Crosby's lack of maturity and good judgment.

In the first couple of seasons of the television series *Castle*, viewers learn that Detective Kate Beckett's elusive boyfriend rides a motorcycle, adding to the mysteriousness of her character and the frustration of would-be suitor, Eric Castle. In a few episodes Beckett is seen mounting the back of the bike behind her leather-clad boyfriend. In later episodes, after she has broken up with the boyfriend, Beckett is often seen leaving wearing leather and carrying a motorcycle helmet, implying that she now has become a rider herself, although the bike itself is not shown.

The short-lived medical drama *Off the Map* premiered in 2011 with star Martin Henderson playing a sexy "bad boy" doctor in a remote South American village. His character, Dr. Ben Keeton, was portrayed as a motorcycle riding skilled surgeon and humanitarian who administered a clinic for locals and performed medical miracles in the jungle, but had little use for rules, regulations, and laws. In the popular series *Lie to Me*, British actor Tim Roth plays Dr. Cal Lightman, an eccentric and quirky expert on body language and non-verbal communication who runs a firm that consults with a wide variety of law enforcement agencies and private firms who have made him wealthy by cashing in on his skills. In one episode, we learn that a young boy and his mother's boyfriend have established a relationship based on restoring a classic motorcycle, something that Lightman implied had always been of interest to him. A 2011 television drama, *Person of Interest*, features an ex-special forces soldier trained to kill who in a few episodes is seen wearing black leather and a black helmet with dark face shield riding an all black motorcycle. A wide variety of other mainstream television shows, far too numerous to mention, have also strategically placed motorcycles in camera view or had either main or peripheral characters ride them.

### For Politicians and Celebrities

A 2008 vice-presidential candidate and 2012 high-profile non-presidential candidate, Sarah Palin, made quite a media splash when she roared into Washington D.C. riding on the passenger pillion of a Harley-Davidson, clad in black leather riding gear, half-helmet, and a pair of aviator/motorcycle sunglasses on Memorial Day weekend, 2011. Ms. Palin was not the first, and certainly will not be the last politician, to use a motorcycle as a photo-op prop. California's ex-governor and avid motorcycle rider

Arnold Schwarzenneger frequently posed on one of his bikes, and Indiana Governor Mitch Daniels, who has ridden for over thirty years often leads rides through his state. Utah governor Jon Huntsman has been photographed on his bike numerous times. GOP consultant Rick Wilson points out that motorcycles are an important part of American culture and are particularly popular in the "red (Republican) states" (Schultheis, 2011). Motorcycles are not confined to Republican politicians, however, as New York governor Andrew Cuomo and former West Virginia Governor now Senator Joe Manchin have also been spotted riding cruisers. Colorado Senator Ben "Nighthorse" Campbell was an avid rider before entering politics, and 2004 Democratic presidential candidate John Kerry rode his motorcycle onto the stage at the *Tonight Show* as host Jay Leno (also an avid motorcyclist) teased him about giving boring speeches. Wilson contends that "motorcycles symbolize masculinity and fearlessness," a sentiment shared by former Democratic Governors Association' Executive Director Nathan Daschle, who added, "It gives a real 'everyday guy' kind of feel ... it's kind of the anti-limousine" (Schultheis, 2011). Arizona Representative Gabrielle (Gabby) Giffords, survivor of an assassination attempt in 2011, also a longtime rider, proved that motorcycles and fearlessness are not just for men.

In the cases of Schwarzenneger, Daniels, Giffords and a few others, motorcycles were a meaningful part of their lives before they entered politics. Conversely, despite her "outdoorsy" image, Sarah Palin seemingly took to motorcycling (at least riding 2-up) rather suddenly to capture media attention and emphasize her appeal to blue-collar voters while "polishing a carefully crafted public image" (Wasef, 2011). Palin may have taken a cue from her former running mate, non-motorcyclist John McCain, who attended the Sturgis rally in 2008 while pursuing the office of president of the United States (Wasef, 2008).

## In Commercials for Other Products

If there is some doubt as to the effectiveness of using motorcycles to gain votes, there is none about using them to sell products. The 21st century has seen unprecedented use of bikers, motorcyclists, and motorcycles to advertise everything from designer shoes and hair care products to mobile phone service, fast food, soft drinks, automobiles, and insurance.

Television advertisers, quick to capitalize on popular fads and social movements, are also keenly aware of the rebirth of the popularity of motorcycling and have created commercials to appeal to both hardcore bikers and motorcyclists. America's largest and best known sandwich restaurant launched a series of commercials in 2010 that featured scenes of bikers riding across open desert (reminiscent of scenes from *Easy Rider* and *Wild Hogs*), only to stop at one of the chain's restaurants with the voice-over tagline, "Ride hard and eat fresh." In another television advertisement, a lone tattooed biker sits on a rock in the scorching desert proclaiming that there's a place where it's so hot that rattlesnakes explode. A band of bikers roar across that stark desert when suddenly an "oasis" appears—a familiar sandwich restaurant— as the biker proclaims, "But we go because ya gotta eat bold," and a narrator voices over a promotion for fiery foot-long sandwiches. Other popular fast food chains quickly followed suit, featuring motorcyclists in commercials, and several soft drink companies have used bikers and/or motorcyclists in their television advertisements. For example, most motorcycle aficionados recognized *American Chopper*'s Paul Teutul Sr. as the intimidating biker in a popular Dr. Pepper commercial.

Few people associate bikers or motorcyclists with designer shoes, but a popular 2010 television commercial did just that. A young, hip-looking man is seen sitting on a motorcycle on the side of a deserted road when a tough, grizzled-looking biker pulls up beside him and looks him up and down in an intimidating way. A worried look appears on the young motorcyclist's face, but quickly disappears when the biker looks down at the motorcyclist's feet and asks, "Where'd you get those shoes?" the tagline for a famous designer shoe company.

Another product rarely associated with bikers or motorcycling is women's shampoo, but Herbal Essence ran a commercial featuring a beautiful female biker dismounting a cruiser, stripping off her leathers, removing her helmet, and then taking an outdoor shower. She emerges from the shower shaking her long luxurious brunette tresses and tosses the shampoo bottle to a grizzly-looking male biker clad in similar leathers. Moments later he emerges from the same shower shaking his head to reveal a glorious mane almost identical to the female biker's.

Perhaps two of the more interesting television commercials reflecting the revived popularity of motorcycles aimed squarely at Baby Boomer consumers is one by Cadillac and another for United Healthcare. The Cadillac commercial uses the theme "put the thrill back in driving" which juxtaposes video of a fifty-plus-year-old male riding a motorcycle at high speed next to shots of him driving a new Cadillac sport coupe. Camera shots alternate back and forth from the man on the motorcycle to him in the car clearly suggesting that driving the new Cadillac is every bit as exciting as riding a motorcycle. United Healthcare features a 60-plus-year-old male on a motorcycle who indicates that he received two prescriptions that could have had deadly interactions, but his life was saved by his United Healthcare pharmacist who caught the error. He then remounts his bike and proclaims, "I want to leave this life exhausted."

Finally, insurance companies, especially those that specialize in under-

**This tricked-out trike was built by a motorcyclist who was inspired by some of the customized bikes he saw on reality television shows.**

writing motorcycle policies, have flooded the television airwaves with commercials for their products. Geico ran several advertisements with the cavemen riding sport bikes, and Progressive countered with their ever-popular character Flo riding a cruiser alongside a male biker who proclaimed, "This is why we do this," and then cited freedom, excitement, and inexpensive annual premiums. Still another major insurance company regularly features motorcyclists in its commercials, and even refers to the need for riders to protect themselves from automobile drivers and "gremlins" that threaten their safety.

## Advertising Motorcycles and Selling a Lifestyle

Perhaps more interesting and telling than the use of motorcycles to sell other products are the television commercials advertising motorcycles themselves. Since at least the 1960s, motorcycle manufacturers have presented their products to television viewers in a variety of ways. In almost every case, the manufacturers appeared to be selling more than just a machine.

In chapter 1, when differentiating bikers from motorcyclists, I discussed the massive advertising promotion launched by Honda motorcycles under the theme of "you meet the nicest people on a Honda." In that campaign, print ads appeared in newspapers and popular magazines, and television commercials brought those photographs and posters to life with clean-cut middle-class actors portraying family members riding scooters and cycles to work as well as entire families riding motorcycles in parks, through town, and across the countryside for leisure and recreation. Sales of Honda motorcycles skyrocketed. In 1964, riding high on the success of the print ad campaigns, Honda became a sponsor for that year's Academy Awards television broadcast. The program was seen by millions of television viewers in the United States. Prior to that time, no foreign company, much less one that manufactured motorcycles, had ever had such massive television exposure. Today, advertising students at colleges and universities around the world study the marketing genius of the combination of print and television advertisements based on Honda's "you meet the nicest people..." (Rau, 2007).

Learning from its competitor's success, Kawasaki motorcycles began its own massive television advertising campaign in the 1970s using a catchy jingle based on the slogan, "Kawasaki lets the good times roll." These television commercials featured elementary school–aged children, teenagers, young adults, and middle-aged people riding dirt bikes, sport bikes, and a variety of street bikes. Motorcycling, at least metric-style, was clearly portrayed as a wholesome and fun activity.

Harley-Davidson, long associated with hardcore bikers and a bad boy image, was America's sole remaining motorcycle manufacturer. Facing potential bankruptcy, Harley-Davidson was slow to respond to the Japanese motorcycle television commercials, either assuming that its status and reputation was well-established, or that reliance on American patriotism would be enough to keep them afloat. That is not to say that Harley-Davidson did no advertising. On the contrary, almost since its inception, Harley-Davidson had run print advertising in newspapers and popular bicycling and motorcycling magazines, but most of its advertisements were aimed at people who were already bicycling or motorcycling enthusiasts as opposed to the Honda and Kawasaki television commercials, which were clearly aimed at attracting new customers from the non-riding public. During the 1960s, confronted with stiff competition from the Japanese bikes, and facing possible bankruptcy or hostile takeover, Harley-Davidson merged with American Metal Foundries (AMF) to remain solvent. Over the next decade, Harley-Davidson, the most popular motorcycle in the United States and in parts of Europe, struggled to maintain its identity — a battle that some contend was lost (Saladini and Szymezak, 1997). Realizing the almost certain demise of the legendary Harley motorcycle, a group of company executives arranged to buy back the entire operation. Near bankruptcy, Harley-Davidson created several new lighter and lower-priced motorcycle designs, and bolstered by a new tariff imposed on Japanese motorcycles over 700cc in size, launched a massive advertising and marketing campaign to win back disgruntled riders who had moved on to other brands. More importantly, Harley's new advertisements were geared to attract new customers from demographic categories that largely had been ignored by the company in the past: women, and younger middle-class and upper-middle-class males. Meanwhile, the company worked diligently to not lose any of its original market — one-percenters, hardcore bikers, and blue collar riders who maintain almost cult-like loyalty to the Harley-Davidson brand.

Today, Harley-Davidson regularly runs television commercials. Some are aimed at recruiting mechanics and other skilled workers into the industry, but most are directed toward consumers. Either way, virtually all of the advertisements emphasize that Harley-Davidson is more than just a motorcycle, it is a lifestyle. Words like "freedom," "excitement," and "lifestyle" dominate most of the television advertisements. Although many of the television commercials are aimed at women and middle-class Baby Boomers, Harley manages to maintain its non-conformist bad boy image in most of its commercials with phrases like "you know you want to," and "give in to the temptation." In one television commercial, an attractive female dressed in black tank-top, black pants, and black boots is shown hitchhiking, holding a sign that reads "Freedom or bust." Male motorcyclists stream past her paying absolutely no attention. Finally, in desperation, she removes her top and tries again. A Harley rider goes speeding past, then suddenly locks up his brakes, and waits patiently as the young topless woman scurries to the bike and mounts the pillion seat; he speeds off as she tosses the top and the sign back over her head. In 2007, for a seasonal commercial, Harley-Davidson showed "Biker Claus" riding in a sleigh pulled by eight Harley-Davidson motorcycles. Santa kicks in the door of a house as a mean-looking Doberman Pinscher cowers down by the Christmas tree. Santa begins removing chrome exhaust pipes, shock absorbers, and other motorcycle paraphernalia from his sack and putting them under the tree. Then, he pulls out a list with the word "Naughty" at the top and checks off a name. The commercial ends with the question, "How bad have you been this year?"

Regardless of type, brand, or style, television audiences are becoming accustomed to seeing motorcycles in television series, in reality shows, as props, and in commercials for all types of products. In the following chapter, we discover that just as modern technology (e.g., television) has discovered motorcycles and motorcyclists, two-wheeled riders have discovered and fallen in love with a wide range of modern technologies.

# CHAPTER 9

# Motorcyclists, the Internet and Other Technologies

ME: Do you mind if I take your photo?

RIDER: Why would you want to do that?

ME: Because I don't think I've ever seen a person sitting on a motorcycle using a laptop. I think it makes for an interesting photograph.

RIDER: I broke the belt on my chaps a few miles back, so I went online to my message board asking if anybody knew of a really good deal on chaps right now. A couple of guys told me a place that was having a clearance sale, so I just ordered a new pair. I'm having them delivered to my sister's house and hopefully they will get there in a couple of days, about the same time I do.

ME: No judgment; I understand completely. I just wondered if I could take your picture. You know you don't see a guy on a bike using a laptop every day. Do you usually bring it along on rides?

RIDER: Not always, but I'm in real estate, and sometimes I have to work while I'm on the road. Plus, I like to read a couple of my favorite message boards and keep up with some of my riding buddies through e-mails and chat rooms. I can use my phone, but it's just as easy to put this in a saddlebag and bring it along on long trips away from the home and office.

ME: Makes sense. Mind if I take your photo?

RIDER: I'd rather you didn't. Now that you've brought it up, I feel kind of silly. Guess I've totally ruined the biker image, huh?

ME: Not really. I'm guessing you're more of a motorcyclist than a biker anyway, and as far as that goes, I wouldn't be too surprised to see a hardcore biker using a laptop these days.

RIDER: Biker? Motorcyclist? What's the difference?

ME: If you have time, how about I buy you a cup of coffee and we visit? You might be interested in a book project I'm working on.

RIDER: Sure. You're writing a book? Now I know I don't want my picture taken. Bad enough you saw me doing this. Don't want the whole world to know.

ME: No problem. No photos, let's just talk.

Laptops, smart phones, and motorcycles? Sure, why not? As with almost every aspect of American culture, new technologies and the World Wide

Web's influence permeate the motorcycle subculture. Motorcyclists shop for aftermarket parts, riding apparel, insurance, and even their motorcycles online. In addition to specialized sites like Cycle Trader and Motorcycle Trader, that deal exclusively with motorcycles, ebay, Craigslist, and a host of other websites have special categories for motorcycles, parts, and services exclusively aimed at motorcyclists. Every major manufacturer, dealer, parts supplier, and motorcycle-related retailer knows that they must advertise as well as make their products and services available online if they want to be competitive in today's marketplace. Moreover, old-fashioned gang fights and "rumbles" of the 1950s and '60s have been replaced with Internet blogs, chat rooms, and message boards where riders of various brands of motorcycles (especially American-made versus Japanese bikes) chide, disparage, and "beat up" one another. As mentioned in chapter 7, in the classic movie *Easy Rider,* to symbolize their newfound freedom, one of the main characters threw away his Rolex wristwatch before embarking on a cross-country motorcycle journey. Thirty years later, the characters in *Wild Hogs* tossed their mobile phones for the same reason. Today, motorcyclists are far more likely to make sure they bring along their mobile phones, MP3 players, laptops, GPS units, and other high-tech devices than to discard them before mounting their bikes. The times they are a changin'.

# Motorcyclists and the Internet

Motorcyclists, like most other Americans, are no strangers to the World Wide Web. They buy, sell, and trade motorcycles and related parts and equipment, advertise rallies and shows, meet, greet, and chat on the Internet. In the motorcycle subculture, greasy garages, smoke-filled bars, and bike shops have, in large part, been replaced by the more sterile environment and limitless bounds of cyberspace.

## *Buying, Selling and Trading*

Every major motorcycle manufacturer maintains a website where potential customers or mere browsers can access information about, photographs of, and specifications for their entire line of products. In addition to details about the various models of motorcycles available, visitors to the website can usually "build or customize their own bike," get a price quote, make e-mail or telephone contact with a salesperson or technician, find names and contact information, and print out directions to the nearest dealers in their area. Whereas hardcore bikers may still tend to congregate in biker bars, garages, and repair shops, motorcyclists are more likely to come together in cyberspace than traditional biker hangouts.

In addition to finding and even purchasing new motorcycles online, a wide array of websites provide venues for people or dealers to advertise and sell used bikes. Most of the riders interviewed in this study who had purchased new motorcycles had done so by visiting local dealerships, but over half of the interviewees (119, 53.1 percent) indicated they had "shopped" for new bikes online at some time, whether they had actually made a purchase or not. Even some who purchased a new motorcycle from a dealership did so in a somewhat unconventional way. A rider in Texas told me that he had been unable to find the specific model of BMW he wanted anywhere in his area, but located a dealership in Kansas on the Internet that had two of them. After calling to confirm that the dealership still had the bikes, he purchased a one-way plane ticket to the airport nearest the dealer's town, rented a car one-way to the dealership, made the purchase, and then rode the motorcycle some 500-plus miles home. When I expressed some surprise as to the way he acquired his bike, he responded,

> Hey, I may never buy a bike any other way from now on. I saw actual photos of the bike online, talked with both the owner and the sales manager of the dealership, printed out all the specs, visited a place I had never been before, and gave the bike the most thorough test ride possible before I ever parked it in my garage.

Many more riders (130, 58.0 percent) said they purchased their bikes used, and the majority of them (99) said they found their used motorcycle on the Internet. One Nevada rider confided to me,

> I may have done something really stupid. I found a used Hayabusa [a high-performance Suzuki motorcycle] on ebay. There was no reserve and the bid was ridiculously low, so I thought, what the heck, and put in a bid. About 30 minutes before the auction ended, the bid started moving up, but it still was a really good deal, so I kept bidding. Eventually, I won the auction for what was more than I originally planned on spending, but it was still a really good deal. Of course, after the whole thing's over, I notice the bike is located in Canada! Turns out, with shipping, and other charges, I probably could've bought a similar bike locally for about the same money. And that was over a week ago and I still haven't seen the bike, so I may have bought a whole lot of nothing.

About six months later, I ran into that same rider, and after we talked a bit, I asked about the Hayabusa purchase. "Turned out great," he replied. "Maybe the best bike I've ever bought, and the best and easiest deal I've ever made."

Admittedly, most purchasers of used motorcycles still probably do it the old-fashioned way, looking through advertisements, contacting current owners, taking a test ride, and negotiating a deal. But even those transactions have changed as motorcycle advertisements more often appear online than in newspapers, and many sellers and buyers prefer to use PayPal or other electronic means for payment transactions as opposed to writing and accepting personal checks. Moreover, a great deal of buying, selling, and trading takes place through online message boards, motorcycle forums, and chat rooms.

## Forums, Message Boards and Chat Rooms

For the past several years, I have been a member of a riders' association that sponsors 12 separate message boards just for riders of my particular make and model of cruiser motorcycle. Additionally, it sponsors 53 state or regional message boards, and one message board which is solely devoted to posts comparing and contrasting Hondas to Harley-Davidsons with entries ranging from jokes and good-natured "barbs," to nasty jibes, flaming diatribes, and all-out threats of physical bodily harm (which are prohibited by the board's rules, but manage to make their way onto the board, nevertheless). I also am a member of another forum dedicated solely to riders of one particular make and model of sport bike. As a member of that group, I have access to an additional 12 forums devoted to riders of different models of the same manufacturer's bikes as well as two classified advertisement boards, and three different forums for non-motorcycle-related topics. There are at least 18 different forums dedicated to Victory riders, Harley-Davidson's largest American-made motorcycle competitor, but that figure pales to the number of boards and forums created for riders of Harley-Davidsons. Similarly, online forums, chat rooms, classifieds, and technical websites can be found for riders of Kawasaki, Suzuki, Yamaha, BMW, Ducati, and almost every other make and model of motorcycle in the world. Other motorcycle-related message boards abound and it would be next to impossible to determine how many motorcycle and motorcycle-related websites exist as new ones spring up almost every single day and others fade away.

Through these forums, message boards, and chat rooms, members become "acquainted," and swap mechanical tips, discuss modifications and repairs to particular makes and models of motorcycles, and announce upcoming rides, rallies, and events, as well as buy and sell motorcycles and parts. Additionally, the "brotherhood " comes to life on these boards as members post when fellow riders have been injured in accidents, had a bike stolen or damaged, or otherwise have suffered some personal hardship or tragedy. In these cases, it is common for fellow riders to donate money, send free replacement parts, or offer up prayers, condolences, and well wishes for their "brethren" who are experiencing difficult times. Conversely, if a member posts that he/she has been cheated by a dealer, an online company, or a fellow member of the board, the information spreads like wildfire, prompting everything from chastisement and denouncements to boycotts of companies and removal of members' privileges to participate on the message board. The intensity of this type of networking in cyberspace can be found in a plea made by one member who was accused by another of not sending a part after the former had paid him the requested amount, and a rash of messages appeared condemning the seller. Finally, the accused party responded: "Hey guys, it was not my fault. I shipped the part, but it must have got lost [sic]. You guys all know me. I would never cheat anybody. All I got is my integrity on this board and I ain't about to sacrifice that for a lousy 35 bucks."

Nevertheless, after several board members intervened, and several posts went back and forth in which the seller claimed he had sent the part by UPS but was not given a tracking number, the readers unofficially "ruled" that the seller must refund the buyer his $35 and make a public apology, or lose his posting and selling privileges on the board. Within 24 hours, a public apology appeared along with a statement that the money had been refunded. When the aggrieved party acknowledged that the money had been reinstated in his online account, all was forgiven, and board members determined that justice had prevailed. Much faster than small claims court and none of the hassle.

Symbolically, these forums, message boards and chat rooms serve to establish social status within the online motorcycle subculture. For example, status and credibility are often linked to how long a rider has been a member and/or how many posts an individual has made on the site (information usually included in a member's profile). For example, in one instance, a member complained that he had sold a set of saddlebags to another member for $75 and that over three weeks had gone by since he had sent the bags and he had not yet received payment. Immediately another member posted the response: "How many posts did the other member have? I won't do business with anybody on the board unless they have at least 50 or more posts." Others joined in, supplying the varying number of posts, 25, 30, or in some cases 100, before they "trusted" another member enough to send money or items to them. One board of which I am a member distinguishes between "members" (fewer than 100 posts) and "senior members" (100 or more posts). On that board, several participants have indicated that they will only transact business with "senior members." On another board, there was a fairly lengthy thread about the need to re-jet a carburetor when certain aftermarket pipes were added to a particular model of motorcycle. After well over 50 posts were made with disagreeing opinions, one member finally "decided" the issue by posting: "There seems to be a lot of disagreement over this, but I'm going with _____. He has over 1,200 posts on this board, and I've never known him to be wrong on a technical question yet."

Most online forums, message boards and chat rooms have a highly respected member who serves as moderator, monitors the board, and sometimes resolves disputes. There are usually posted "rules," regulations, and guidelines that outline appropriate usage of the board, and the monitor is charged with enforcing them. Often, these rules are tested to the point of violation, and although minor infractions are usually tolerated, flagrant violations often result in some type of informal or formal sanction — the most severe of which is being banned from using that particular online venue — a form of ostracism that most users want to avoid. Nevertheless, occasionally a post such as the following can be found:

> Newbie here. Just wanted to say hello. I was recently kicked off the _____ board and decided to try posting over here instead. I guess I deserved to be banished because a couple of my posts turned into flames, but I promise to be better behaved over here if you guys will have me.

This message drew several positive responses welcoming the new member until one person asked about the nature of the offense committed on the other board. The original poster responded that he had entered into a couple of innocent disagreements with an individual member on the other board and that "everybody on the board ganged up on [him]." Soon other members of the new board posted several queries and began to "take sides" over the issue that resulted in banishment from the other board. Before long, the new member to the board became angry and posted a flaming diatribe laced with profanities ending with the exclamation, "You motherfuckers are no better than the assholes on the other board!" Within an hour that post was removed and the "newbie" to the board was not heard from again — presumably also banished by that board's moderator, who posted a reminder to all members that "this site is a public forum intended to be 'family friendly'" and that posts "containing profanity and/or intentionally inflammatory rhetoric will be removed and may result in offenders losing their posting priviledges [sic]." Similarly, while many suggestive and provocative photos and avatars are allowed, nudity, vulgarity, and obscenity (as determined by the moderator) are quickly removed usually with an accompanying warning that these violate the mutually agreed upon norms of the board.

## Promoting "Brotherhood" Online

Websites can also promote brotherhood among motorcyclists and various riding groups by uniting subgroups within the motorcycle subculture. For example, there is a global bikers network with the slogan "where cyberspace meets the open road," designed to provide a place where riders from around the world can post photos, plan trips, and "meet and greet" fellow riders. As noted in chapter 4, there is a Brotherhood of Gray Beard Bikers for older motorcyclists, and a Brotherhood of Old Bikers who use the acronym BOOBS, and several websites operate under the heading "Brotherhood of Bikers" which is a motorcycle "club" whose motto is "Striving Toward a Better Biker Image."

Most motorcycle-related organizations (see chapters 4 and 6), all the major rallies (chapter 6), and most of the sponsors of bike shows operate websites where they announce upcoming events, advertise and sell items, and provide networking opportunities for their members or others interested in

**Alan Buttell, lifelong motorcycle enthusiast and successful attorney, checks the internet to find the nearest restaurant.**

their activities and events. Chapter 3 covered the strong sense of brotherhood among motorcyclists and alluded to other ways in which computers and technology contribute to that phenomenon. In addition to promoting brotherhood, these sites also serve as a form of boundary maintenance.

Almost every subculture develops an argot, or special language, that is part of the popular lexicon of members, but often has different meanings or no meaning at all for non-members. If you have ever been in a hospital or a physician's examination room and listened to two or more doctors or nurses discuss your diagnosis or prognosis, you are well aware of the fact that medical professionals speak a different language than the rest of us. You may be tempted to get your will in order and arrange burial plans when you hear a doctor tell the nurse that you suffer from nasopharyngitis or acute viral rhinopharyngitis, but will be relieved to discover that both of those diagnoses mean you simply have a common cold. Similarly, when your CPA tells you he needs all of your W-2s and 1099s in order to complete your 1040, you may be surprised to learn that he or she just needs your reported earned income statements. Motorcyclists also develop numerous ways of including and excluding others, including language (see glossary at the end of the book), as well as Internet websites, various forums, and chat rooms. Although anybody can visit these websites, and might even participate in some of the discussions or online chats for a brief time, unless they are familiar with motorcycles, the jargon, and a wide array of other meaningful symbols and accoutrements that surround motorcycling, they will soon be identified as non-riders or "trolls."

This is not meant to imply that non-riders are unwelcome or shunned by motorcyclists. Rather, it simply illustrates that subcultures have certain traits, characteristics, customs, values, and traditions that set them apart from others. Therefore, in order to maintain their distinctive identity, there must be some types of boundaries that help delineate them from larger culture and non-members. While these boundaries may be permeable, they exist nevertheless. Distinctive dress, paraphernalia, and the motorcycle itself, as well as the meaningful symbols and values discussed in chapter 3, help create and maintain these social boundaries in everyday life. Although these distinctions are less discernible over the Internet, they and other distinctive characteristics may ultimately come into play even when the interaction takes place in cyberspace.

## Other Forms of Technomedia[1]

Growing up in the 1950s and 1960s, I was no stranger to modern technological inventions. After all, our home had electricity, running water, an indoor toilet (one), and a telephone (albeit we shared a party line with 3 other families). Even more impressive, we were among the first in our neighborhood to purchase a television — a huge wooden box with a 12-inch screen that after a few minutes of warming up and adjusting of "rabbit ears" could pick up each of the three major networks during the 5–6 hours of the day that they broadcast programming. The rest of the time, we could either stare at the blank screen or look at a black and white (mostly gray) test pattern that allowed us to adjust both the vertical and horizontal hold buttons in order to keep the picture from endlessly flopping up and down or across the screen.

In elementary school, I remember reading in *The Weekly Reader* that scientists had invented computers and robots that could solve mathematical problems, play chess, and even talk (more or less). While that seemed more like science fiction than actual science to me at the time, I never dreamed that one day I would own a home not only replete with electricity and running water, but three bathrooms, abandoned phone outlets in every room, and four television sets programmed by satellites—one plasma, two LCD, and one LED. The abandoned phone landlines, of course, a result of the credit-card-sized smart phones/computers my wife and I carry everywhere. These devices not only serve as a telephones, but also solve mathematical problems, play chess (and hundreds if not thousands of other games), talk to us, play music, send and receive e-mails and text messages, take both photographs and videos, and perhaps most importantly, connect us directly to the World Wide Web. Conveniently, they even have adapters that allow us to plug them into an automobile or motorcycle to act as a radio, MP3 player, or GPS navigation system — things increasingly becoming viewed by some riders (not me) as motorcycling necessities.

## *iPads, Mobile Phones, Radios, CD Players, and MP3s*

Most motorcyclists are well acquainted with modern technologies, and motorcycle manufacturers have incorporated many of them into their bikes. The "dashboards" (a word that up until a couple of decades ago was never even associated with motorcycles) of most touring bikes today resemble high-end automobiles or even space shuttles more than their two-wheeled predecessors.

Because of their affinity for and heavy reliance on the Internet, some riders carry a laptop computer or the smaller and more convenient ipad or other "smart" tablet along on rides. Of the 224 riders interviewed for this research, only 3 regularly carried a laptop or ipad, but only a few years ago even that small number would have been stunning. In the near future, I suspect the number of computer-equipped riders will greatly increase, and if we consider the smart phone a computer (which it is), then the figure rises dramatically.

Cell phones and smart phones in the motorcycling subculture, as with larger culture, proliferate. Only two of the people I interviewed in this research, a 78-year-old Harley rider and his 70-plus-year-old wife, did not carry a cell phone when they rode. Meanwhile, their touring bike was equipped with a CB radio, an intercom system, an AM/FM stereo and although they did not use them, a CD player and a connection for an MP3 player. Almost every middle-aged or older rider, if asked about carrying a cell phone, cited either convenience or safety as major reasons for them. For example, one female rider told me,

> I can't imagine riding without taking my cell phone with me. It's so convenient. I can check in with friends or family, look up restaurants or gas stations, and, while I've never had to so far, knock on wood [for some reason, she knocked on her gas tank], if I broke down or got stranded, I could call somebody for help.

Male riders tended to say similar things. I stopped asking younger riders (the under 40 crowd) about carrying cell phones, after the first two or three gave me such strange looks that I realized I might just as well have asked them why they brought along their arms or legs.

Radios, CD players, and MP3 players are far less common among riders than cell phones, but over the years, I have seen increasing numbers of all three. Again, many of the high-end cruisers and touring bikes are including them as either standard or optional equipment, hence increasing their usage. Even though these amenities are difficult to justify as "necessities," they can make long rides more enjoyable, at least for some. Personally, I, like many riders, enjoy the solitude associated with motorcycling, and would find listening to a radio or other device distracting. My wife and I were looking at a fully decked-out touring bike at one dealership when the salesperson showed my wife the intercom hookup in the armrest of the passenger pillion, which he more accurately called the "passenger seat," since it resembled a living room recliner. "Now, you and your husband can talk to each other when you ride." Without hesitation, my wife responded, "Are you kidding me? One of the things I love about the motorcycle is that I can just relax and get caught up in the moment and not have to listen to him." I guess my wife is a motorcycling purist. At least that is the way I prefer to define the situation.

## GPS, LoJack and More

Other technological devices available to motorcyclists are perhaps more functional, and hence easier to justify or rationalize as desirable or even as "necessities." Antilock brakes, adjustable shocks, and other optional or sometimes standard equipment are linked to increased safety. Navigational systems and security systems, on the other hand, help safeguard the motorcycle against theft and may result in insurance discounts and other potential benefits.

Just as GPS and other navigational systems have become increasingly available and popular in automobiles, they are becoming more commonplace in the world of motorcycling. While I cannot imagine hardcore bikers or one-percenters equipping their choppers and hogs with such "frivolous" devices (although I'm willing to bet that even most of them now carry cell phones), today's motorcyclists are more likely to see them as viable and even pragmatic options. Despite the popular motorcycling adage that "it's not the destination, but the journey that matters," one of the more popular technological devices with motorcyclists is GPS (global positioning system). These satellite-based navigational systems help motorcyclists plan trips, locate fueling stations, motels, and restaurants, as well as find their way along two-lane highways and unmarked roads, popular with many riders who want to avoid interstate highways and other high-traffic routes. If kept updated, these devices alert riders to areas of road construction, accidents, and other traffic delays and suggest alternate travel routes so that motorcyclists can avoid delays and potentially dangerous situations. More than one interviewee has echoed the sentiment of the rider who told me, "I can't even count how many times my GPS has saved my butt." More than once, I have been stranded out on rural roads, low on fuel, and wondering how I was going to find my way back to civilization. Nevertheless, there are still a number of riders who, like me, concur with the rider who commented: "I can't believe all the whistles and bells they're putting on bikes these days. I never even had a fuel gauge on a bike until I bought this one. Radios, intercoms, and even GPS — how ridiculous! Hell, half the fun of riding a bike is getting lost."

Although most cruisers and touring motorcycles weigh well in excess of 500 pounds, some even over half a ton, they are fairly easily loaded onto trailers or trucks in minimal time and with minimal equipment. Consequently, stealing a bike is not that difficult. Motorcyclists rarely worry about other riders stealing their bikes and rarely lock them at shows, rallies, or other places where motorcyclists congregate. Out on the streets, in parking lots, and even at home, however, motorcyclists usually lock their bikes and take other precautions to keep them from being stolen. Some riders add LoJack or other high-tech devices in order to deter theft or help locate their bikes if stolen. As with automobiles, most insurance companies offer a discount if motorcycles are equipped with anti-theft or locator devices, and many cruiser and touring motorcycles today come with such amenities as standard or optional equipment.

# Baby Boomers, Technology and Redefining Motorcycling

Baby Boomers have had dramatic impact on every basic social institution in the United States from the family and education to sports, entertainment, religion, government, and economics. It should come as no surprise that they also have transformed the world of motorcycling. As noted in earlier chapters, Baby Boomers represent the largest and fastest growing segment of purchasers and riders of motorcycles. While a small minority in this age group comprise part of the one-percenter contingency, and some others are barely distinguishable from their hardcore biker counterparts, the majority of Baby Boomers who ride are middle- and upper-middle-class, highly educated motorcycle enthusiasts who simply love to own and ride motorcycles. Because of their sheer numbers combined with their relative affluence, Baby Boomers have expanded the demand for motorcycles and helped drive up their prices (Box, 2007; National Safety Council, 2007).

Moreover, Baby Boomers have tended to embrace technology and enjoy creature comforts. These facts revolutionized and redefined what once were considered luxuries in homes as now being necessities: central heat and air, separate bedrooms for all family members, two or more bathrooms in every home, walk-in closets, master suites, and two-, three-, and four-car garages equipped with climate control and automatic door openers synchronized with remote controls in their automobiles. Those automobiles even further reflect Baby Boomer values and emphasis on gadgets, creature comfort, power, and speed. Most Baby Boomers own more than one automobile and their cars are as much an expression of themselves and their careers as they are considered a means of transportation. Their automobiles also express many of the paradoxes of Baby Boomer values. Although many Boomers' parents pledged loyalty to American-made models like Ford, Chevy, and Chrysler, their offspring were among the first to switch to foreign-made models and helped propel Toyota, Honda, and Volkswagen to industry leaders in both manufacture and sales in the United States. While espousing such green qualities as lower emissions and higher fuel economy, Baby Boomers also demand modern styling, muscle-car power, and sports-car maneuverability combined with separate climate controls and entertainment centers for all passengers. Modern navigation equipment, voice-activated controls, and a host of other technological bells and whistles are viewed by many drivers as standard equipment. All of these accoutrements must be accompanied by antilock brakes; positrac suspension; collapsible fenders and bumpers; front, side, and rear airbags; and all of the state-of-the-art safety features available. Along with a multitude of other factors, these expectations have led to the average automobile purchased by today's Baby Boomer costing more than the homes they were raised in, and the first house they purchased for themselves.[2]

Not surprisingly, Baby Boomers' preferences in motorcycles run parallel to their tastes in automobiles. While touting the virtues of "American-made" Harley-Davidson, the Baby Boomers were quick to embrace the Japanese and German motorcycle imports. Many older and hardcore riders tout the simplicity of classic American made bikes with their rigid frames, lack of shock absorption, vibrating motors, sparseness of controls and gauges, and almost total absence of creature comforts. Contrast that to today's ultimate touring motorcycles, both American- and foreign-made, that feature powerful engines, smooth transmissions with overdrive, cruise control, antilock braking systems, reserve fuel tanks, heated seats and grips, navigation equipment, CD players and MP3 connections, and a host of other amenities.[3] At a rally in Texas, I was talking with the rider of a brand-new Honda Goldwing that included all the aforementioned accessories along with a few others and stickered at just under $30,000. I joked, "I love the Goldwing, but I'm not sure that you're still riding a motorcycle — it's really more of a Honda Civic on two wheels." The rider bristled and replied indignantly, "Civic, hell, this is at least an Accord! In fact, I'd compare it more to a top-of-the-line Acura."

At rallies and other motorcycle events it is common to see couples riding two-up on 1,000-plus-pound touring bikes pulling trailers with pop-up campers. Many others have converted their touring bikes into three-wheelers (trikes) that include plush leather seats, trunks, and most of the amenities of a compact luxury car. More than one company manufactures three-wheeled bikes that have two wheels in front and one in the back. And at Sturgis, Honda displayed a four-wheeled Goldwing with a price tag of a little over $40,000! I asked the vendor what differentiates a motorcycle from a car, and without blinking he responded, "The handlebars—if it had a steering wheel and a removable top, it would be a convertible." Evidently, that is not the criteria, however, because a couple of hundred feet away I encountered a three-wheeled custom-made T-Rex complete with a steering wheel and fiberglass top that stickered at $80,000. I asked that vendor what made the T-Rex a motorcycle and not a car, and he replied, "Because it doesn't have four wheels."

This futuristic-looking three-wheeled Can-Am Spyder has prompted more than a few long-time riders to ask "What is a motorcycle?" Motorcycle shows and rallies now feature two-wheeled, three-wheeled and four-wheeled vehicles complete with virtually every amenity available in luxury automobiles.

Such technological innovations prompt discussions and sometimes even arguments over just what constitutes a motorcycle (Rau, 2010b). Magazine articles and letters to editors often debate whether trikes are motorcycles or should be categorized as some other type of motorized vehicle, prompting one rider to respond, "Trikes aren't bikes." Motorcycles have two wheels; if it has more than that, it is either a car or a "semi-car" (Jacobsen, 2011:4). In most states, for vehicle registration and license purposes, three-wheeled motor-powered vehicles designed for street use and two-wheeled motorcycles that have been converted to three wheeled vehicles are considered "motorcycles." While I guess the word "bike" technically refers to two wheels,[4] at rallies, shows, and other gatherings of motorcyclists, I've seen two-wheeled, three-wheeled, four-wheeled, and even five and six-wheeled contraptions that all passed for motorcycles, at least as far as the rider was concerned.

Whatever the agreed upon or disputed definition, everybody agrees that today's motorcycles are a far cry from their motorized bicycle predecessors. One male Baby Boomer rider in his early 60s who had begun riding at age twelve more or less summarized for his entire age group:

> When I first started riding, I didn't want anything on a bike whatsoever — no windshield, no bags, nothing. I loved the simplicity of motorcycles. Then, as I got a little older I realized how convenient a pair of saddlebags could be, so I bought a throw-over pair, so I could have them when I wanted them, but leave 'em at home when I didn't. Then, I decided I needed a windshield. You know, protection from wind, rain, rocks. Of course, it wasn't long until I added highway pegs for comfort on long trips. Then a tank bib with storage compartment. Now look at this thing [he pointed to his fully-equipped touring bike]. It's got more damn whistles and bells than my wife's car ... which I guess is only fitting since it cost more!

We know that today's motorcyclists ride vastly different machines equipped with a wide array of amenities as compared to their predecessors. We also know that motorcyclists view their bikes and the riding experience differently than one-percenters and hardcore bikers. A remaining question, however, is what motivates today's motorcyclists to engage in such a possibly stigmatizing and potentially dangerous activity.

CHAPTER 10

# Why Motorcyclists Ride: Motorcycling and Life on the Edge

"What is the matter with you — do you have a death wish?"
"No, as a matter of fact, I have a life wish!"

I have had that brief conversation more times than I can count. The paradoxical nature of motorcyclists is striking. Motorcyclists are simultaneously deviants yet conformists, risk-taking yet safety conscious, individualists yet an integral part of a large subculture and mainstream society, feminists yet sex objects, loners yet part of a brotherhood, seeking freedom but bound by constraints, and we reflect several longstanding motorcycling traditions while creating something almost entirely new. The most interesting question about American motorcyclists may be why well-educated, middle- and upper-middle-class people who are highly invested in mainstream society with careers, families, mortgages, and many other important commitments and responsibilities risk everything, including their lives, for a few minutes, hours, days, or weekends of fun, enjoyment, and exhilaration. The answers to that question, and more specifically the question "Why do you ride?" are both sociologically complex and yet remarkably simple. Probably the best way to approach those questions is to start by letting motorcyclists answer them in their own words.

## In Their Own Words

Despite wide variation in answers to "why do you ride?" some distinctive patterns emerged that allow responses to be grouped into one or more of the following categories: (1) something inherent in the individual, or what many motorcyclists describe as being "born to ride"; (2) fun, excitement, and exhilaration; (3) freedom; (4) transcendentalism; and (5) the challenge. As acknowledged in chapter 1, creating any typology, especially regarding human behavior, is risky, and as always the categories are not necessarily exhaustive or mutually exclusive. Nevertheless, for descriptive and analytical purposes, these categories can be quite useful.

## Born to Ride?

When asked "What is your primary motivation for riding?" or more simply, "Why do you ride?" slightly more than ten percent (26, 11.6 percent) responded in a way that reflected some inherent characteristic that implied they were "born to ride." For example, one male rider in his mid-fifties responded, "Why do I ride? You might as well ask me why I breathe." Another 40-something male answered, "I can't help it; I have to." A male rider in his early sixties said,

> Geez, I can't remember ever not riding. I started as a little kid going from tricycle to bicycle, and then bicycle to scooter. I was riding full-fledged motorcycles just out of grade school. It seems like riding motorcycles is just something that came naturally to me. My dad said I never even had training wheels on my first bicycle. At about age 3 or so I just jumped on my sister's bike and took off. I can remember in kindergarten riding my Schwinn and twisting the handlebar grip while making revving noises. As soon as I could get on something with a motor, I did. Been riding ever since.

One of my favorite responses came from a fellow Baby Boomer who replied, "Wanting to ride is natural — just ask a dog why he sticks his head out of a car window." Another male rider minced no words and was without doubt was among the easiest of all interviewees to place in one of the five categories. When I asked him why he rides, without hesitation, he responded, "I was born to ride, pure and simple."

## Fun, Excitement, and Exhilaration

Perhaps one of the most direct and simple answers to why motorcyclists ride might also be the most obvious: riding is fun. It doesn't take a Ph.D. in sociology or several years of research to figure that one out, but it also should not be dismissed from an academic or intellectual standpoint. Research on crime and delinquency has found that deviant behavior "has a sensual, magical, creative appeal that is lacking in most conventional, law-abiding acts" (Katz, 1996:4) and that many juveniles experience an "unparalleled adrenalin rush and emotional high connected with the risk of their illegal activities" (Thompson and Bynum, 2010:192). These explanations attribute crime and

Many riders contend that they were "born to ride." While that explanation may not be sociologically sound, some youngsters seem to take to motorcycles like ducks to water.

delinquency to "short-run hedonism" that is often outgrown and tends to desist through the maturation process. But does the need for an adrenalin rush or emotional high dissipate with maturation, or does the manner in which those needs are fulfilled change over time? According to two researchers, "all riders are adrenaline junkies and risk takers to one extent or another" (Veno and Winterhalder, 2009:55).

Time and again, I heard the same refrains from motorcyclists: "Because it's fun," "The most fun thing I do," or more crudely put, "Are you shittin' me? If you ride, you know how much fun it is." Over half of the respondents in this study (127, 56.7 percent) included the word "fun" in their responses to why they ride.

Another word that appeared just as often was "excitement." Numerous quotes from riders used in previous chapters have included the word "excitement" and chapter 3 focused on excitement as being a traditional biker value that retains meaning for motorcyclists today. One female rider told me, "Riding my bike is pure excitement.... I absolutely love it!" A young male rider echoed that sentiment saying, "I thought driving a car was fun and exciting when I first got my license, but when I rode my first motorcycle I discovered what excitement was all about." A 55-year-old accountant and sport bike rider confessed,

I may have the most boring job on the planet. I sit at my desk 40 hours a week crunching numbers, but when I get on my bike, a whole new world opens up to me. I'm a numbers guy, and I can't tell you how exciting it is to look down and see a speedometer registering 100, 110, or 120. A lot of times I ride my bike to work, just so at the end of a boring day I can feel a little excitement on the way home.

As a long-time rider, I've come to appreciate motorcycle rides that offer little or no excitement because many of the things that make a ride exciting are also the things that make it potentially dangerous. Speed is indeed exciting, but not surprisingly, things happen much more quickly at high speeds and reaction times and potential responses for avoiding trouble diminish proportionately. Nevertheless, I concur with all those riders who indicated that excitement is part of the allure of motorcycling, although I think that exhilaration may be a more accurate descriptor of the feeling that motivates many riders.

Perhaps exhilaration is simply a synonym for excitement, but it also seems to imply a more affirmative connotation than excitement, which can have both positive and negative meanings. Exhilaration is that feeling of elation that borders on euphoria. One female rider explained,

Riding my bike is like having an orgasm. I don't mean it's literally sexually satisfying although I know some women say that it is. But what I mean is that for me it's a high. I've never been into the drug scene and I hate the feeling I get when I drink too much. For me, riding is exhilarating. It lifts me up when I'm down. It makes me happy. It's hard to describe the feeling, except to say it's all good.

## The Freedom Factor

If I heard the word "freedom" from one interviewee, I must have heard it from at least two hundred of them as being one of the primary motivations for riding. In fact, it was included in so many responses from riders that it seemed almost obligatory. In chapter 3, I alluded to popular song lyrics that implied freedom was basically a synonym for not having anything of value," and pointed out that members of today's motorcycling subculture have plenty at stake. As one study noted, motorcyclists are as much a "subculture of consumption" as they are a subculture of motorcycle riders (Schouten and McAlexander, 1995). Much like the riders portrayed in *Wild Hogs*, however, they may be willing to risk their marriages, their middle-class lifestyles, and even their lives, for what they may have to gain—*freedom*—freedom from their jobs, family responsibilities, and other routine demands.

As with almost everything in life, freedom is relative. One-percenters and hardcore bikers may be seeking freedom from almost all of larger society's constraints ranging from the mundane civilies of everyday social interaction to freedom from obeying laws against illegal drugs, weapons, violence, and even murder. Conversely, most motorcyclists are far more conforming in their everyday lives and are more likely seeking temporary freedom from mundane jobs, family responsibilities, and the "cages" they typically use for transportation. Still, ask any motorcycle rider from one-percenter club member to an elementary school teacher who rides a moped to work why they ride and you are very likely to hear the response of "freedom."

A variety of other leisure and recreational activities may provide similar freedom, but Laurendeau and Van Brunschot (2006:174) suggest that motorcycling may be far more "freeing" than many other risk-taking activities. For example, unlike mountain climbing, skydiving or scuba diving, motorcyclists can choose when, where, and with whom to ride their bikes. Mountain climbing, skydiving, and scuba diving, on the other hand, are comparatively encumbered, requiring certain geography or topography, special planes or boats, spotters, pilots or navigators, and certain areas designated as being appropriate for those activities. Still all these activities provide a sense of freedom that some practitioners describe as being a form of natural "high."

### Transcendentalism: Motorcycling as Zen

Fun, excitement, exhilaration, and freedom sometimes translate into a more powerful feeling of transcendentalism. In Pirsig's *Zen and the Art of Motorcycling* (1974), the main character's alter ego, Phaedrus, struggles with what he sees as two diametrically opposed viewpoints of life: romanticism and rationality. A cross-country motorcycle ride metaphorically illustrates these two contrasting viewpoints and the conundrum faced by riders who simultaneously "live in the moment" but also must plan ahead, prepare for uncertainties, and suffer the consequences of not paying attention to details. In the author's note to this fictional work, Pirsig (1974:i) explains that, despite its title, the book "should in no way be associated with ... Zen Buddhism," and that "it's not very factual on motorcycles, either." Nevertheless, almost every motorcycle rider can relate to his thesis. Whether the book relates to Zen Buddhism or not, Pirsig's descriptions of riding and the characters' relationships to their motorcycles ring fairly authentic. Riding a motorcycle can be so relaxing and pleasurable that the rider often feels a sensation of being mesmerized or almost hypnotized.

Perry King, star of former television series *Riptide* and *Melrose Place*, who has ridden motorcycles since the age of 15, commented in his early sixties that "riding a motorcycle is like meditating.... You become peaceful, centered, and deeply happy. It has helped me keep my sanity my whole life" (Nichols, 2011:54). Time and again, I heard similar statements from riders interviewed for this study. A female rider in her early thirties noted, "I lose myself when

I ride.... It's a real stress reliever." A male rider in his early forties said, "If I come home feeling tense or angry, I simply hop on my bike, ride a few miles and feel like I've taken a tranquilizer." A forty-something male rider I interviewed summarized, "I forget everything when I ride. No worries about the job, my marriage, the mortgage, the kids, taxes, nothing. I just get on the bike and feel the tension melt away."

In an almost eerie response, one of the riders in this study described riding in the following way:

> When I ride, I get in this *zone*. It's almost a mystical state. I would describe it as almost an out-of-body experience where I feel like I'm hovering over the motorcycle looking down on me riding it. I assume most riders will know what I mean, and most people that have never been on a bike won't have a clue.

My guess is almost every motorcyclist can relate to those feelings and many non-riders reading those words are rolling their eyes and wondering what in the world he is talking about. In the foreword to Stephen Thompson's (2008:ii) *Bodies in Motion: Evolution and Experience in Motorcycling*, this transcendence is described as "a state of awareness in which the passage of time seems to slow and one feels more connected to some kind of universal consciousness ... [that] usually leaves the rider calmer, more focused and in a notably refreshed state."

Although the Zen-like qualities of motorcycling are quite pleasant, riders must be careful about the transcendental aspects of riding because of the potential dangers. *Tonight Show* host and longtime motorcyclist Jay Leno points out, "Riding a motorcycle forces me to stay alert. Whenever I see a motorcyclist with headphones on, I think: Whadda you, crazy? You have to use all your senses, all your instincts, on a motorcycle" (Nichols, 2011:56).

I know many riders, myself included, who have settled into that comfort zone while riding, especially out in the countryside, only to be suddenly jerked back to reality by an animal darting across the road or rounding a bend to find a slow-moving tractor, an overturned load of lumber, or some other debris or hazard. One of my most enchanting experiences on a motorcycle occurred during an organized ride out in the country only a few miles from my home. There were approximately thirty of us riding in staggered formation on a meandering narrow country road at speeds between thirty to fifty miles per hour. Riding near the end of the pack, at one point I glanced up to see what appeared to be a very large hawk gliding out from a tree-covered area. The bird soared over the road about forty feet off the ground and then disappeared back behind the trees. Hawks are quite common in northeast Texas and I have rarely taken a ride in that area without seeing at least one, and usually several. Moments later the large bird reappeared and I discovered that it was actually a bald eagle with a wingspan of approximately five to six feet, now gliding only twenty-five feet or so off the ground less than a hundred yards in front of me. The sight was absolutely awe-inspiring. Eagles are fairly rare in that particular part of the country, and I had never seen one in the wild so up close and personal. I could not take my eyes off the majestic creature as I pointed toward it so that the three or four riders behind me would not miss the bird. Just as quickly as it appeared the eagle soared back out of sight behind the trees and I was aware that I was rapidly approaching a sharp curve covered in loose gravel apparently lost from a truck that must have tried to take the curve a bit too fast — something I was inadvertently now doing on a motorcycle. My front tire skidded to the side a bit as I counter-steered to maintain control as I rolled off the throttle and almost willed the motorcycle to stay semi-upright and regain traction while coming out of the apex of the curve. Years of riding experience, quick reflexes, and a whole lot of luck helped me avoid a potentially nasty spill. Just that quickly, the sublime can turn into the ridiculous as cold hard reality sets in.

The reality of riding can be both pleasant and harsh, as almost every motorcyclist knows. When asked why he rides, a 59-year-old attorney who has ridden since he was a teenager replied,

> Motorcycling is *real*. Everything else in my life seems unreal or controlled in a lot of ways. In the courtroom, the entire setting is contrived with prescribed roles and rules of conduct. A trial is a performance. My house, office, and car are all climate-controlled — heated in the winter and air-conditioned in the summer — a perfect 72 degrees year-round. On my bike it's freezing cold in the winter and hotter than hell in the summer, the way it should be. When I'm riding I smell the odor of roadkill one minute and the sweet scent of wildflowers the next. I don't like windshields, fairings, or any of that other bullshit that separates me from the reality of riding. I like the feel of the wind, the grit of the earth when it hits you at 70 miles per hour, and even the wet of the rain. There's something very reassuring about the reality experienced when riding a motorcycle.

## The Challenge

Another recurring word in many of the responses to the question "Why do you ride?" was "challenge." A 74-year-old former dirt bike and off-road racer told me:

> I ride for the challenge — pure and simple. Always have. That's why I always preferred off-road riding. It's you, the machine, and nature. I loved racing, but never viewed it as me against the other racers as much as me against the terrain, me against the desert, or me against the elements. Today, I only ride on the streets, but hell, that's a challenge, too. Now, it's me against the idiots in cages.

A female rider in her forties said that she had always liked the challenge of competing against her brothers, and now views riding motorcycles as "just another challenge." When asked to elaborate, she said she meant *challenge* both figuratively and literally, surmising that her riding a bike not only challenges gender stereotypes but also challenges her physically and mentally.

With the exception of "born to ride" all of these categories of motivations provided by motorcyclists for why they ride can be incorporated into some basic sociological explanations for the rise in popularity of motorcycling in the United States. Although all of these sociological explanations are plausible, none is solely sufficient. It is probably important to look at all of them in conjunction to develop the most thorough possible explanation.

# Sociological Explanations

Sociologists have long been interested in human behavior, especially when it occurs in groups. Moreover, when groups of people participate in a particular activity in such a way as to form a unique subculture replete with values, attitudes, beliefs, norms, and meaningful symbols that distinguish them from other subcultures and the larger culture, they are of particular interest. In analyzing any subculture sociologists tend to look at four predictable sociological variables for patterns and trends of analysis: age, race, sex, and social class. It is no surprise that these variables emerge as important in helping explain the emergence of a motorcycling subculture comprised in large part by middle-aged and older white males primarily from the middle and upper-middle classes. How these variables interrelate may provide valuable insight into the phenomenon of an increasingly growing popularity of motorcycling in the United States.

## *"Vulgarization" of the Middle Class?*

Why are so many middle-class and upper-middle-class people now riding motorcycles? One possible answer might involve what some sociologists call the trend toward *vulgarization* of the middle class—a growing phenomenon where highly educated, middle-class Americans increasingly participate in so-called unsophisticated activities, especially sports, that used to be primarily the domain of the working or lower classes, such as boxing, hockey, NASCAR, professional wrestling, bowling, and perhaps riding motorcycles (Eitzen and Sage, 2011). Some support for that contention can be found in some of my observations and interviews. For example, one rider, a building contractor, commented:

> I like riding because I meet some of the most *real* people on motorcycles. None of the put-on and BS that you get from people at work and at so-called *classier* places like museums, horse races, and other places. It seems to me that bikers are the salt of the earth—just normal people, rich or poor, or whatever.

Another rider who practiced law noted,

> Growing up, my parents always looked down on people who rode motorcycles. They saw them as lower class. When I begged for a motorcycle, my father [also an attorney] used to always say, "Son, the type of people who ride motorcycles are the same kind who like to swill beer and go to boxing matches and cock-fights. That's not us. We drink wine, go to the country club, and play golf." Funny thing is that other stuff always sounded like more fun to me, and to this day, I much prefer beer to wine and boxing to golf — not to do, but to watch. And, I own four motorcycles worth about 15 grand each, so if that's lower class, then so be it.

Nevertheless, although many of the riders I observed and interviewed also liked many of the so-called "proletariat sports" (boxing or ultimate fighting, wrestling, auto racing, and others), I am not convinced that the vulgarization of the middle class has a great deal of explanatory power. One might just as readily argue that those activities, once inexpensive and requiring little formal education or training, have increasingly become more expensive, more technological, and hence, more appealing to educated members of the middle and upper-middle classes. Vulgarization of the middle class? Maybe. Sophistication of lower-class leisure activities? Maybe. Other sociological factors seem to be at work.

## Temporary Deviance

One factor may be that people, especially those in the middle and upper-middle class who conform to normative expectations throughout their routine daily activities, may feel compelled at times to kick up their heels and blow off a little steam by participating in some form of temporary norm-violating behavior. Sociologists have long differentiated between primary deviance and secondary deviance, the former of which is often temporary or transitory and does not significantly damage an individual's personal and social identity as a conformist (Lemert, 1951). Mardi Gras, Halloween, costume parties, and sometimes even vacations provide socially acceptable respites from our conformity to routine activities. Motorcycling may serve a similar function.

Motorcyclists may be participating in what could be considered "time out" deviance in which the vast majority of their lives is spent in conforming roles, but on occasion, they violate societal expectations associated with their age, social class, and otherwise fairly staid everyday lives. In these cases of temporary deviation, the deviance is acceptable and often "acts as a safety valve by channeling the 'self expression impulse,' and 'sustaining a high degree of uniformity within groups'" (Bryant, 1990:32). For example, one of the male riders who worked as an insurance underwriter voiced this "safety valve" concept when he said,

Sometimes on my job I get so fed up with my boss, the rules, and the whole situation that I just feel like I'm going to explode. I've been there over twenty years and every little thing is done according to policy or actuarial tables, or some corporate mandate. There are no exceptions, no room for discretion, and no room for individuality in what I do. I can literally feel the pressure build, and then I go out and get on my bike, and I feel my blood pressure go down. I fire it up and a sense of calm comes over me. Thirty minutes of riding can undo the damage done by eight hours of work. [Laughs.] I don't mean this to sound as bad as it's going to, but I sometimes think if these guys that "go postal" on their jobs rode motorcycles, there would be a lot less of that kind of violence.

In a popular motorcycle magazine's regular column entitled "Mental Motorcycling," a writer and rider discusses the bad boy image associated with motorcycling and why today's motorcyclists often opt for buying black motorcycles, adding loud pipes, and riding ominous-looking, intimidating machines:

When we have to be "good" so much of the time — paying bills promptly, pleasing bosses, being dutiful spouses and parents, maintaining our lawns to neighborhood association guidelines, etc. — it's only natural that we'd want some way of feeling more powerfully autonomous. We need to feel *bad*.... Enter the demon styling of a hyperbike, or the menacing thunder of an outlaw cruiser. These are opposites of fearful compliance, and so are we by association [Barnes, 2011:27].

The temporary deviance of weekend riding, though gratifying, does not a bad boy make, however. As one sociologist noted, acceptable deviance provides both individuals and groups a "false sense of freedom, while ensuring that the 'rules' are followed" (Harman, 1990:75). A far cry from their one-percenter and hardcore biker counterparts, motorcyclists tend to follow one set of "rules" even while temporarily violating another.

This idea of riding serving as a safety valve or a way to blow off steam is closely related to the concept of motorcycling as Zen discussed earlier. The fact that such large numbers of Baby Boomers are taking up the activity may also suggest that it may be related to a transitional period in life where people pursue new statuses and roles, some of which serve to redefine their social identities and provide new meaning in their lives.

## Midlife Crisis and Facing Mortality

In the mid–1970s, Gail Sheehy (1976) wrote a best-selling book entitled *Passages: Predictable Crises of Adult Life*. In it, she contended that sometime around ages 35 to 45 people begin to experience changes in their "sense of aliveness" and begin to see the "dark at the end of the tunnel" (Sheehy, 1976:350–354). Consequently, middle-aged people (both male and female) begin to question their lives and experience what is often called a midlife crisis. For some, this results in resignation that they are growing old and that their best years for the most part lies behind them; for others, it becomes a time of refreshment, re-evaluation, and embarking on meaningful activities to make the remainder of their life more gratifying and worthwhile. More simply, the attraction of riding motorcycles, especially among middle-aged, middle-class participants (the fastest-growing segment of the motorcycle subculture), may be related to the so-called midlife crisis experienced by those entering their "forlorn forties" or "refreshed/resigned" fifties, looking for new meaning in life, excitement, and simply something different (Sheehy, 1976;1993). One male rider in his mid–50s verbalized this phenomenon when, at a rally, he proclaimed, "Come look at my midlife crisis present to myself," as he walked over and pointed to a brand-new, fully loaded touring bike. Another rider once told me in only a half-joking manner, "I'm too big a coward to cheat on my wife, so when I started experiencing the whole midlife crisis thing, I went out and bought a motorcycle. I figure in the long run it's cheaper, and a helluva lot safer."

For women, especially Baby Boomers who witnessed, participated in, and experienced the feminist movement, this may include the challenge of actively participating in a male-dominated activity and breaking the constraints of traditional gender roles while maintaining a sense of feminine identity. For men, this phenomenon may be almost the exact opposite: an attempt to do something manly and recapture a feeling of masculinity in a culture and at a life stage in which traditional masculine roles have been devalued, or at least redefined. Just as Sheehy (1993) discussed the physiological, psychological, and sociological aspects of menopause for women, Jed Diamond (1998; 2010) contends that men go through similar hormonal changes that prompt not only physiological changes (e.g., lower levels of testosterone), but also psychological and sociological changes that may result in a variety of seemingly erratic behaviors as compared to their earlier personalities and lifestyles. The medical community is mixed over the actuality of menopause for either women or men, but the behavioral sciences of psychology and sociology are focusing much attention on how people respond to the changing and increasing stresses that accompany the middle stages of life. While individuals may respond to these differently, distinctive trends and patterns may be discernible. One thing seems fairly certain: as people age they tend to face their mortality.

In a culture that promotes the ideology of immortality and seems in denial about death (Becker, 1997), it is amazing how many riders in this study openly talked about the subject. Acutely aware of the dangers associated with riding motorcycles, numerous riders indicated that they had come to grips with the fact that motorcycling could be deadly. Although psychologists might contend that it is merely rationalization or cognitive dissonance, many riders

Many riders cite freedom, peace, tranquility and transcendentalism as primary motivations for riding a motorcycle. Sociological explanations suggest other factors might explain the popularity of motorcycling. Whatever the reasons, more and more Americans are taking to the roads on two wheels.

expressed the sentiment that death is one of the realities of life and that being killed on a motorcycle would be far preferable to some of the other ways that they might die. For example, one rider commented, "I know riding can be dangerous, but I watched my father die little by little from cancer. It took him over two years to go, and by the time he finally went there wasn't enough of him left to even recognize."

Another rider commented, "If I have a choice between going out in a hospital bed or nursing home with tubes running in and out of my body, or going out on a motorcycle at 100 miles per hour, I know what I prefer." A 60-year-old rider told me that when his wife confided that she worried about him getting hurt or killed while riding, he responded, "Rest assured that if I get killed on my motorcycle, I will have died happy."

Another interesting phenomenon that emerged during this research was how many motorcyclists had already had a near-death experience not related to motorcycling. Several male riders indicated that they had always wanted to ride a motorcycle, but had deferred because their wives thought it was too dangerous, or they had family responsibilities that prohibited them from taking such a risk. Then, totally unexpectedly, they had suffered some life-threatening situation during a very routine, non-risky endeavor. While attending a funeral for a former classmate, one of the other pallbearers who I had not seen since high school asked me if I still rode motorcycles. I responded in the affirmative, and he said,

> You know, you let me ride yours once, and after that I always wanted to ride one, but was about half afraid to. First, my parents wouldn't let me. Then, my wife wouldn't. I admit, I thought they were too dangerous. Then, about three years ago I suffered a heart attack sitting at my computer at work. Less than two weeks after I got out of the hospital, I bought a bike. I figured life's too short to worry about something happening to me doing something I like when I'm just as likely to die while doing something I don't.

The words had barely escaped his lips when another pallbearer concurred. "Me, too." I recalled that he had ridden a bike in junior high school, but sold it and bought a car when he turned sixteen. He went on to explain that he had loved riding when he was younger and always wanted a motorcycle as an adult, but thought it was too risky to indulge himself since he had a wife, family, mortgage, and all the rest. Then, one Saturday afternoon while mowing his lawn he felt dizzy and almost passed out. His wife rushed him to the hospital and within a few hours he had undergone quadruple bypass. He said in the recovery room, the first two questions he asked the cardiologist were: "How soon can I have sex again?" and "Will I be able to ride a motorcycle?" The doctor laughed and replied, "You must be the hundredth guy who has asked me those two questions after a heart attack." Interestingly, by the time our conversation ended, I discovered that four of the six pallbearers (including me) had suffered heart attacks in our mid–50s while carrying out some mundane daily activity. Three of the four had purchased motorcycles and started riding as a result. Two of those three had ridden when younger and then had stopped for a period of time while one had never ridden a motorcycle before the heart attack but had always wanted to and decided to start after his recovery. Perhaps this relates to the "fatalism" referred to in chapter 3; perhaps once somebody has a life-threatening experience they are more aware of their own mortality and the temporary nature of life; or maybe once people conquer their fear of dying they also overcome their fear of living.

Whatever the case, a common theme among motorcyclists regardless of age, sex, or life experiences seems to be their acknowledgment and acceptance of the risks associated with motorcycling — including permanent injury or death. This phenomenon may be at least partially explained by *edgework*, a growing research topic in sociology.

## Risk-Taking and Living on the Edge

There is an old adage that most riders have heard at least a thousand times: "There are old motorcyclists and there are bold motorcyclists, but there are no old, bold motorcyclists." In fact, several riders in this study repeated that saying, some as if they had come up with it originally. Despite its popularity and logic, the statement is not necessarily true. Over the course of my riding experience and during the research for this study I have run across a number of young, middle-aged, and old bold motorcyclists. That is, if the definition of *bold* means brave, courageous, daring, and intrepid, as suggested by most dictionaries. On the other hand, if bold is meant to imply stupid, dangerous, thrill-seeking, or careless, then with a few exceptions the adage is apropos. Although it may be a fine line, most motorcyclists understand that there is an important distinction between accepting the risks and dangers associated with riding and utter disregard for the laws of physics by pushing the envelope beyond mechanical and human capabilities in ways that violate commonsense concerns for personal and public safety. There do seem to be riders who have some type of "death wish," and for some, that desire becomes reality.

Another plausible explanation for why motorcyclists ride may be found in the literature on *edgework* — engagement in risk-taking behaviors such as mountain climbing, skydiving, scuba diving, and other extreme sports, which could be expanded to cover motorcycle riding (Lyng, 2005). Whether a one-percenter, lifelong hard-core biker, or a motorcycling enthusiast, riding a motorcycle imposes certain risks, and sliding across pavement at 70 miles per hour does not differentiate among victims. So, why take the risks?

The motorcycle subculture is comprised largely of middle-aged men and women (mostly men) who have conformed to virtually all of the values, norms, and demands of their middle-class Baby-Boomer lifestyles: education, careers, families, civic clubs, little league, and dance classes. They have raised children, cared for elderly parents, put kids through college, provided financial security for grandchildren, and have met or exceeded virtually all that society has demanded or expected of them. Lyng (2005:5) indicates, "Risk-taking experience can be understood as a radical form of escape from the institutional routines of contemporary life." Consequently, it is not difficult to understand why when the weekend rolls around, motorcyclists don their leather, strap on their helmets, straddle their expensive motorcycles, and take to the roads to challenge their riding skills, attend motorcycle shows and rallies, or to just experience the freedom, relaxation, and sense of "time out" that riding provides. Although there are more male motorcyclists than females, the edgework explanation may be just as viable for women who ride. Previous research has indicated that "some women are risk takers and get a thrill from living a life on the edge" (Veno and Winterhalder, 2009:55). As Lyng (2005:6) notes, according to "the 'weekend warrior' thesis ... participants in [risk-taking] activities are seen as seeking a temporary escape from the stultifying conditions of work life and bureaucratic institutions." This is especially true of the types of activities that can be the most consequential — those involving "the line between life and death" (Lyng, 2005:4).

Paradoxically, although risk-taking may be part of the appeal and motivation for riding, many motorcyclists tend to want to "have their cake and eat it, too." They are risk-takers, yet are safety conscious. People who take motorcycle safety courses and wear gloves, helmets, and Kevlar-lined clothing in order to ride expensive motorcycles equipped with safety features such as highway crash bars, antilock brake systems, and, in some cases, even airbags most certainly do not want to die. While the perception of danger may be an enticing if not essential element of riding, confronting and conquering the fear of that danger may be equally important. Numerous philosophers, theologians, and counselors have admonished that acknowledging and conquering fear can give a whole new meaning to life (e.g., Kushner, 2009).

# Full Circle: Bikers and Motorcyclists

This book began with an attempt to establish a classification scheme of motorcycle riders by dividing them into three major categories: Bikers, neo-bikers, and motorcyclists. Bikers were further subdivided into one-percenters and hardcore bikers. Motorcyclists were subdivided into Rolex Riders/Rich Urban Bikers (RUBS); motorcycle enthusiasts; crotch rocketeers, stunters, and racers; and dirt bike and off-road racers. Comparisons and contrasts illustrated similarities and differences among and within each of these categories. The focus of this research has been on motorcyclists—their values, meaningful symbols, interaction with one another, formal organizations, shows and rallies, depictions in motion pictures and on television, and redefinition of motorcycling through the use of technology, and why they ride.

Some motorcyclists seem to think that they were born to ride, while others indicate that they are motivated by fun, excitement, exhilaration, freedom, transcendentalism, and the challenges experienced while riding. Sociologically speaking, the increased popularity of motorcycling may be attributed to a trend toward vulgarization of the middle class, temporary deviance that acts as a safety valve, and/or the fact that one way many Baby Boomers, the largest consumer segment in the United States, are responding to their midlife crises and facing their mortality is by taking more risks and living on the edge. Motorcycling is one way to do so. Despite some of the similarities in dress and sometimes even demeanor or behavior, riding motorcycles does not make them bikers, and the difference is more than mere semantics. For motorcycle enthusiasts, riding motorcycles is *what they do, not who they are.*

## Master Status versus Status

A social status is a position that a person holds in society. Most of us have a wide variety of statuses, or a status set, that comprises our personal and social identities (Thompson and Hickey, 2011). Perhaps the most significant difference between bikers and motorcyclists is the extent to which riding a motorcycle shapes the rider's identity. Being a biker represents a commitment to a particular lifestyle and consequently becomes a person's master status—a status that dominates all others that a person holds, the one status (out of many) that defines *who they are* (Hughes and MacGill, 1952). For motorcycle enthusiasts, however, riding a motorcycle is only one of the many sources of their identity, and almost never the most important one. Although I did not interview any for this study, I would imagine that if you asked a one-percenter or hardcore biker who he is, and what he does, he would probably respond with "I'm a _____ [insert name of motorcycle club]," or perhaps more generically, say, "I'm a biker" which would answer both queries (if he responded to you at all). Conversely, ask a motorcyclist the same two questions (which I did 224 times in this research) and they will first tell you their name followed quickly by their occupation. If they are unemployed or retired, they will usually tell you so and indicate what they want to do or what they used to do. In short order, you will discover that they are butchers, bakers, or candlestick makers, as well as wives, husbands, mothers, fathers, grandmothers, grandfathers, and a host of other things equally or more important to them than being motorcyclists. If you have time, they will discuss their hobbies, which will most likely include a wide range of activities, one of which is riding a motorcycle. For example, I am a university professor, a husband, a father, and a grandfather (to name but a few of my identities) who happens to ride a motorcycle. I have never thought of myself in the reverse order. Riding a motorcycle is what I do, not who I am. This distinction is reflected in my behaviors and the social roles I fulfill, just as it is with virtually all motorcyclists.

## Role Engulfment versus Role Embracement

Social roles are the expectations that accompany social statuses. Renowned anthropologist Ralph Linton (1936) explained we *occupy* statuses, but we *play* roles. Sometimes individuals become so caught up in their master status that it becomes almost their sole identity and the accompanying role seems to "engulf" them or shape almost all of their activities and behaviors.

This is particularly true if the master status involves what could be considered as deviant, violating normative expectations (Schur, 1971). Hence, bikers tend to *be* bikers. It is not just part of their identity, it *is* their identity. Thus, being a biker means being a biker 24/7, and doing what bikers do. Looking like a biker, dressing like a biker, and acting like a biker — because he *is* a biker.

On the other hand, being a motorcyclist simply means that one of the many things that person does is ride a motorcycle. While riding a motorcycle, the motorcyclist tends to look like a motorcyclist, dress like a motorcyclist, and act like a motorcyclist — perhaps to the uninitiated even being confused for a biker. Yet, when not riding, the motorcyclist may look like a doctor, dress like a doctor, and act like a doctor, or look like a plumber, dress like a plumber, and act like a plumber. You get the point. Motorcyclists tend to embrace the role, meaning it influences their actions and is a meaningful part of their identities, but it certainly does not engulf or define them. Again, riding a motorcycle is what they do, not who they are.

# A Final Word

Motorcyclists may range in age from their teens to their nineties, but the largest segment of today's motorcyclists are Baby Boomers — a generation that is used to wanting it all and, for the most part, having it all. As noted at the beginning of this chapter and throughout the book, we are a generation whose lives and values are seemingly filled with contradictions. Motorcycling reflects many of those paradoxes. We crave fun, excitement, thrills, and danger, yet we take motorcycle safety courses, purchase expensive motorcycles with many safety features, wear helmets, don Kevlar riding gear, and take out large insurance policies on our health and lives. Motorcycling tends to be sexist and patriarchal, and perpetuates a macho environment, yet many male riders are highly educated, fairly enlightened, and egalitarian in philosophy, while many female riders, especially those who ride their own bikes, are avowed feminists. Since World War II, motorcycle riders have had a bad boy image, yet today's motorcyclists are anything but social outcasts or outlaws. Motorcycling has gone mainstream.

Wilfrid Noyce (1959) wrote that a machine is much like a desert in that people are either appalled by it or fascinated by it. Such seems to be the case with motorcycles. While a few people may be ambivalent, most seem to either hate them or love them. Similarly, the owners and riders of motorcycles seem to be closely associated with the machines. Some non-riders may ridicule motorcyclists; others might roll up their car windows,[1] hide the children, or try to avoid motorcycle riders as much as possible. No doubt, some see motorcyclists as deviants and perhaps potentially dangerous. Still others, however, look at motorcycle riders with envy. When motorcyclists stop at an intersection, children often stare out of car windows at our bikes in awe; men look at the machines longingly, and women's faces register everything from outright disgust to barely concealed lust. Almost every time I ride my motorcycle up to any filling station, convenience store, restaurant, or other public place, I am approached by at least one wide-eyed middle-aged or older male who fawns over my bike and either reminisces about riding a motorcycle in his youth or expresses his dream to ride one now or in the future. If he is a rider, he usually asks a few questions and then tells me about his bike. If accompanied by a woman, she often stands in the background rolling her eyes. Fewer women approach alone, but those who do usually either own motorcycles or ride with their husbands.

Whatever the response, there seems to be an almost mystical fascination with motorcycles and their riders. And, therein lies the answer to why motorcyclists ride. Perhaps Melissa Holbrook Pierson (1997:18) summed it up best in her book *The Perfect Vehicle*: "Riding on a motorcycle can make you feel joyous, powerful, peaceful, frightened, vulnerable, and back to happy again, perhaps in the same ten miles. It is life compressed, its own answer to the question 'Why?'"

# Glossary

**ABATE**— stands for American Bikers (or Brotherhood) Active Toward Education.

**American Motorcycle Association**— largest and one of the first organizations for motorcyclists.

**Ape Hangers**— raised handlebars that place the rider's hands at shoulder height or higher.

**Bagger**— originally referred to cruiser/touring motorcycles with permanently attached hard bags (e.g., HD Electra Glide, Honda Goldwing), but today is often used to refer to any cruiser/touring motorcycle with saddlebags.

**Biker**— hardcore motorcycle rider who is committed to the "lifestyle" and is often a member of a recognized motorcycle club (see also **hardcore biker**)

**Biker Babes**— young girls who sell beer, wash motorcycles, and compete in wet t-shirt contests at motorcycle rallies and other biker gatherings.

**Biker Brotherhood**— informal network of motorcycle riders who share a sense of camaraderie and *esprit de corps*. Includes both male and female riders.

**Biker Wave**— acknowledgment most motorcycle riders make when passing another rider. Consists of extending the left arm out from the body at or below waist level, usually showing two fingers (the index and middle finger like a horizontal peace sign).

**Bike Show**— event that features classic and contemporary motorcycles. Often held in conjunction with a rally.

**Bikes, Blues and BBQ**— first held in 2000, a relative newcomer to the motorcycle rally scene is the Bikes, Blues and BBQ (BBB) rally held every fall in the university town of Fayetteville, Arkansas.

**Bitch seat**— slang term for the passenger pillion (back seat) of a motorcycle.

**BOOBS**— Brotherhood of Old Bikers.

**Boundary Maintenance**— every subculture establishes ways to maintain identity and separate those who are a meaningful part of the subculture from those who are not.

**Brain Bucket**— motorcycle helmet.

**Cagers**— drivers of automobiles and trucks.

**Cages**—cars and trucks.

**Chrome Divas**— organization for women who ride their own bikes, ride as passengers, or simply love motorcycles.

**Chrome Whores**— male or female riders who put as much chrome as possible on their motorcycles.

**Citizen**— a motorcycle rider who is not affiliated with any club.

**Counter-steering**— steering technique where rider pushes on right handlebar to go right and pushes on left handlebar to go left (instead of turning or pulling on handlebars).

**CRAP**— stands for Cheap Rider and Proud. A group of motorcyclists who participate in an online message board that takes pride in innovative and inexpensive motorcycle modifications.

**Crash Bars**— highway bars. These bars attach to the motorcycle to protect the bike if it is dropped and, in case of an accident, they might help keep the bike from falling on and trapping the rider's legs.

**Cross-country racing**—off-road racing events held outdoors often across desert and/or mountainous terrain.

**Crossover Bike**— refers to a dual purpose motorcycle; can be a combination of sport bike and touring bike (sport-tourer) or a combination on-road (sport) off-road (dirt) bike.

**Crotch rocket**— racing bike or street-model racing or sports bike, many capable of reaching speeds up to 150–200 miles per hour.

**Crotch Rocketeer**— a sport bike (crotch rocket) rider.

**Cruiser**— motorcycle made for highway trips, usually equipped with windshield, saddlebags, and other amenities to make highway travel more comfortable.

**Darksiders**— motorcyclists who replace the rear motorcycle tire with an automobile tire.

**Daytona Bike Week**— held annually at Daytona Beach, Florida.

**Dirt-bike rider**— motorcyclist who rides sport bikes designed for off-road riding.

**DOT**— Department of Transportation. Stamped on back of helmet, it signifies the helmet passes safety tests established by the Department of Transportation.

**the Dragon**—a 14-mile stretch of U.S. Hwy 129 that begins at the "Fugitive Bridge" in North Carolina (the bridge off which Harrison Ford jumped in the movie *The Fugitive*) and ends across the Tennessee state line at the Tabcat Creek Bridge.

**Dual-Purpose Bike**—a crossover motorcycle. Usually refers to on-road sport bike that doubles as an off-road dirt bike.

**Dykes on Bikes**—slang term for motorcycle organization Women's Motorcycle Contingent for lesbian riders.

**Endo**—stunt that involves riding a motorcycle forward and applying the front bake abruptly which results in the rear tire coming off the ground in order to make the bike "stand" on the front wheel (also called a nosie or a stoppie).

**Enduro racing**—a form of off-road motorcycle racing that primarily focuses on the endurance of the racers and their equipment.

**Fairing**—fiberglass bodywork designed to deflect air and increase performance, protect the rider, and add to the aesthetics of the motorcycle.

**Flame**—inflammatory remarks posted on a website.

**Flamer**—person who routinely posts inflammatory remarks on websites.

**Floorboards**—instead of foot pegs many cruisers and touring bikes have large flat surfaces for the rider to rest his feet on while riding.

**Hardcore Biker**—motorcycle rider who is committed to the "lifestyle" and is often a member of a recognized motorcycle club (see **biker**).

**Headers**—straight pipes, or exhaust pipes with no muffler or baffles.

**Highway Bars**—sometimes referred to as crash bars, these bars attach to the motorcycle to protect the bike if it is dropped and, in case of an accident, they might help keep the bike from falling on and trapping the rider's legs.

**HOG**—refers to any cruiser or touring type motorcycle. Also, HOG is the abbreviation for a formal organization, the Harley Owners' Group.

**The Iron Butt Association (IBA)**—organization that recognizes and honors riders who complete a 1,000-mile cross-country ride within 24 hours.

**Jug Huggers**—a type of after-market exhaust pipes that make the motorcycle louder.

**Kraut bikes**—slang term for German motorcycles (e.g., BMW), but is sometimes used to describe other European motorcycles such as Ducatis and Moto Guzzis (Italian).

**Laconia Motorcycle Week**—one of the oldest motorcycle rallies in the U.S., held annually in Laconia, NH.

**Leather Lover**—female motorcycle "groupie" who likes to hang around bike shows, motorcycle rallies, and other places inhabited by bikers and motorcyclists.

**Leathers**—refers to any/all of the leather riding gear worn by motorcyclists (i.e., jackets, chaps, gloves, etc.).

**Mamas**—women in the one-percenter subculture who are considered to be the property of the club and, in exchange for shelter, protection, and transportation, are expected to serve any and all members' needs, sexual and otherwise.

**Metric**—usually used to describe Japanese motorcycles (e.g., Honda, Yamaha, Kawasaki, Suzuki, etc.), but can refer to any non–American-made bike (BMW, Ducati, Moto Guzzi, etc.) from countries that use the metric system and, consequently, require metric tools for adjustments and repairs.

**Military Veterans' Motorcycle Organizations**—organizations for motorcyclists who have served in the military.

**Mods**—any modifications made to the stock motorcycle (e.g., windshield, saddlebags, pipes, etc.).

**Motocross**—motorcycles racing on a closed, off-road, outdoor circuit.

**Motorcycle Show**—a sponsored contest where motorcycles are separated into different categories to compete for best appearance, most innovative modifications, or other criteria. Usually, trophies and/or prize money is awarded to winners. Some shows have official judges while others allow attendees at the show to "vote" on winners.

**Motorcycle enthusiast**—person who loves and rides motorcycles but is not committed to the biker lifestyle and is not affiliated with any motorcycle club or gang (see **motorcyclist**).

**Motorcycle Riders Foundation**—motorcycle organization that lobbies for motorcyclists' rights.

**Motorcycle Safety Foundation (MSF)**—motorcycle organization that promotes motorcycle safety and sponsors motorcycle training and safety courses.

**Motorcyclist**—person who rides a motorcycle but is not committed to the biker lifestyle and is not affiliated with a motorcycle club or gang (includes various subcategories. See also **Rolex riders, Rubs, motorcycle enthusiast, crotch rocketeer, stunter, racer, dirt-bike rider** and **off-road rider**).

**Motor Maids**—chartered by the American Motorcycling Association in 1940 and offers membership to women in the United States and Canada who own and ride their own motorcycles.

**Neo-Biker**—motorcycle rider who emulates the biker lifestyle but is not committed to it and is not affiliated with any recognized motorcycle clubs.

**Newbie**—somebody who has owned/ridden a motorcycle for a short period of time, usually less than a year.

**Nosie**—stunt that involves riding a motorcycle forward and applying the front bake abruptly which results in the rear tire coming off the ground in order to make the bike "stand" on the front wheel (also called an endo or a stoppie).

**OEM**— Original Equipment Manufacturer. Motorcycle owners often modify their bikes with both OEM and non–OEM after-market parts.

**Off-road rider**— motorcyclist who rides sport bikes designed for off-road riding.

**Old Lady**— in the one-percenter subculture, a woman who "belongs" exclusively to one of the club members (her "old man").

**One-Percenters**— after a 1947 fight between two rival motorcycle gangs at a rally in Hollister, California, the American Motorcyclist Association declared that 99 percent of motorcyclists were law-abiding citizens and that only one percent were outlaws. From that time on, hardcore bikers, especially members of gangs like the Hell's Angels, Bandidos, Outlaws, and Pagans, began referring to themselves as "one-percenters." Many of the so-called one-percenters embrace the outlaw moniker and image, while others contend that they are not "outlaws," but are simply committed to riding motorcycles as a brotherhood and lifestyle as opposed to just a weekend activity.

**Pilgrimage**— refers to the almost compulsory trip to Bike Week in Sturgis, South Dakota, this is more broadly defined as "a journey to a sacred place or shrine; any long journey or search, especially one of exalted purpose or moral significance" (*American Heritage Dictionary of the English Language*, Boston: Houghton Mifflin, 2009).

**Pillion**— the passenger seat on a motorcycle.

**Poker run**— usually involves a scenic ride of 75 to 100 or more miles where participants make five designated stops to pick up playing cards that comprise a poker hand at the end of the run. A cash prizes is usually awarded to the highest hand, and sometimes to the lowest hand. In some states, poker runs are illegal, so they are referred to as "joker runs" or "fun runs" and prizes are awarded in lieu of cash.

**Poser**— derogatory term used by hardcore bikers and one-percenters to refer to all other motorcyclists. More accurately refers to someone who dresses like a biker or motorcyclist but does not actually ride (see **wannabe**).

**Racer**— motorcycle rider who races motorcycles in organized amateur or professional races.

**Rally**— event where bikers and motorcyclists meet and usually includes poker runs, bike shows, bike washes, concerts, and other entertainment geared to the motorcycle subculture.

**Rice Burners**— Japanese motorcycles.

**Risers**— modification to handlebars that raises them higher than the stock setting but much lower than **ape hangers**.

**Road racing**— motorcycle races held on asphalt tracks.

**Road Rash**— the bruises, scrapes, and burns that comes from sliding across the pavement in a motorcycle accident.

**Rolex Riders**—middle- and upper-middle-class riders whose equipment and amenities far out-class their riding skills and abilities (see also **RUBS**).

**ROT Rally**—Republic of Texas motorcycle rally held annually in Austin the week after Memorial Day.

**RUBS**—Rich Urban Bikers (see also **Rolex Riders**).

**Scoot**—short for "scooter," an affectionate reference to a motorcycle used by riders of large cruiser and touring bikes.

**Sheep**—young women brought in by new initiates to one-percenter clubs as a "gift to the club."

**Sport bike**—high-powered, high-performance motorcycle. Often referred to as a **crotch rocket**.

**Stealers**—motorcycle dealers.

**Stoppie**—stunt that involves riding a motorcycle forward and applying the front bake abruptly which results in the rear tire coming off the ground in order to make the bike "stand" on the front wheel (see also **endo** or **nosie**).

**Straight pipes**—motorcycle exhausts with no muffler or baffles. Also known as **headers**.

**Stunter**—sport-bike rider who performs tricks or stunts on a sport bike (sometimes pronounced "stunta").

**Sturgis**—a small town in South Dakota with a population of approximately 8,000 that hosts approximately a million motorcyclists and bikers during the second week of August each year.

**Supercross**—indoor motocross that usually takes place in athletic stadiums and/or indoor arenas.

**Super Cruiser** or **Touring Bike**—ultimate highway motorcycle with windshield, farings, dashboard, radio, saddlebags, backrests, etc. (e.g., Honda Goldwing or Harley-Davidson Dyna Glyde or Ultra Classic).

**Sweetbutt**—young women in the one-percenter subculture who provide regular sexual service to one or a few club members while providing a source of income to both him and the club—usually through topless dancing, prostitution, and/or drugs.

**Tats**—short for "tattoos."

**Technomedia**—newer and more personalized information technologies (e.g., personal computers, CD-ROMs, fax machines, video games, handheld databanks, cell phones, the Internet, fiber-optic communications, and interactive television).

**Touring Bike**—see **Super Cruiser**.

**Trike**—three-wheeled touring bike that usually started out as a touring motorcycle and was converted with a kit. These motorcycles often include many of the amenities of a small car and cost upwards of $35,000.

**Troll**—person (often a non-rider) who "hangs around" motorcycle websites sometimes pretending to be a rider or otherwise joining forums and chat rooms usually reserved for motorcyclists.

**Twisties**—roads with lots of twists and turns that allow motorcyclists to test their riding skills along with the performance and handling of their motorcycles.

**Two-up**—two people riding on a motorcycle (rider and passenger).

**Two-uppers**—people who ride pillion on the backs of motorcycles.

**V-Twin**—the motor configuration of twin cylinders in a V-shape made popular by Harley-Davidson and copied by most manufacturers of cruiser-style motorcycles.

**Wannabe**—derogatory term used by hardcore bikers and one-percenters to refer to all other motorcyclists. More accurately refers to someone who dresses like a biker or motorcyclist but does not actually ride (also called a poser).

**Weekend Warriors**—people who drive their automobiles, SUVs, or trucks in most of their daily activities, and ride their motorcycles on weekends when the weather is nice. See also **Rolex Riders, RUBS, Posers/Wannabes.**

**Wheelie**—popping the clutch on a motorcycle and lifting the front wheel off the ground while accelerating in order to ride the motorcycle on the back wheel only.

**Women in the Wind (WITW)**—motorcycle organization for women.

**Women's Motorcycle Contingent**—organization for lesbian motorcyclists. Often referred to as Dykes on Bikes.

**Women on Wheels (WOW)**—women's motorcycle organization.

**Wrench**—somebody with mechanical ability who loves to work on motorcycles.

# Appendix: Motorcycle Subculture Interview Questions

1. When did you first start riding?
2. How long have you been riding?
3. What type of bike(s) do you ride?
4. Do you feel a sense of loyalty to that (or any) brand of bike?
5. Do you own/wear any apparel (clothing/caps/etc.) that promotes a particular brand of motorcycle?
6. Have you owned/ridden other types of motorcycles?
7. How do other brands of motorcycles compare to the one you own/ride?
8. Do you ever ride with people who ride brands of motorcycles different from yours?
9. Do you have a motorcycle endorsement on your license?
10. Do you have motorcycle insurance?
11. Is your motorcycle your primary means of transportation? If not, what is?
12. How often/how many miles do you ride per week? Month? Year?
13. Do you work on your own bike? If not, do you take it to a dealer or an individually owned shop?
14. Have you taken an MSF safety course? If so, when?
15. Do you wear a helmet when you ride? If so, what type?
16. Do you wear any other type of protective gear? If so, what type?
17. Does your spouse/significant other ride? If so, two-up? Or does he/she ride his/her own bike?
18. Do you have any children? If so, do they ride? With you? By themselves?
19. Do you belong to any motorcycle organizations? If so, which one(s)?

20. Do you attend motorcycle rallies, bike shows, etc.? If so, which ones? How often?

21. Have you ever been to Sturgis? Daytona? Laconia? Fayetteville? If so, how many times?

22. Do you ever go to "biker bars"?

23. Do you ever ride after you've been drinking?

24. Do you prefer to ride alone, with another person, or in a group?

25. What's your favorite "biker"/motorcycle movie(s)? Television show(s)?

26. Do you think the media portrays bikers/motorcyclists accurately?

27. What is your primary motivation for riding/why do you ride?

28. How would you identify yourself? Biker? Rider? Motorcyclist? Motorcycle enthusiast?

29. What do you do for a living?

30. How do people at your job view your motorcycle riding?

31. Do any of your fellow employees ride? If so, do you ride with them?

32. What is your primary concern/worry when riding?

33. Do you think people respond differently when you are on your bike or wearing motorcycle attire than they do when you are driving your car or not wearing motorcycle apparel? If so, in what ways?

34. Do you think you will ever quit riding motorcycles? If so, when?

35. Do you have any "favorite/worst" motorcycle experience you'd like to share?

Ride safe. (It always bothers me to say this, because I know it should be "safely," but almost all motorcyclists end every conversation with the admonition: "Ride safe!" When in Rome...)

# Chapter Notes

## Introduction

1. After widespread media attention focused on a fight between two rival motorcycle gangs at the 1947 rally in Hollister, California, the president of the American Motorcyclist Association (AMA) allegedly declared that 99 percent of motorcyclists were law-abiding citizens and that only one percent were outlaws. From that time on, hardcore bikers, especially members of patched motorcycle clubs like the Hell's Angels, Mongols, Bandidos, Outlaws, Pagans, and others, began referring to themselves as "one-percenters." Many of the so-called one-percenters embrace the outlaw moniker and image and wear a diamond-shaped patch with "1%er" on it, while others contend that they are not "outlaws," but are simply committed to riding motorcycles as a "brotherhood" and lifestyle as opposed to just a weekend activity. One-percenters are described in more detail in chapter 1.

2. Sociologists, demographers and other social scientists generally define Baby Boomers as the largest single age cohort in the United States (approximately 77 million Americans) and include those born after World War II, roughly between the years 1945 and 1964.

## Chapter 1

1. Because one motorcycle club named itself the Outlaws, other one-percenter clubs and most law enforcement officials replaced that descriptive term with one-percenters to avoid confusion.

2. Harley-Davidson enjoys an almost cult-like following based largely on the image created by its early association with the Hell's Angels and other outlaw biker clubs. Yet, the founder of the Hell's Angels wrote: "It's always been important for Hell's Angels to ride American-made machines. In terms of pure workmanship, personally I don't like Harleys. I ride them because I'm in the club, and that's the image…. We really missed the boat not switching over to the Japanese models when they began building bigger bikes" (Barger, 2005: 53).

3. Various articles and books disagree on whether there are 4, 5, 6, or even more one-percenter motorcycle clubs. Since none of these clubs or riders are included in this research, there is no need to pursue the issue here.

4. One-percenter clubs' patches usually consist of three distinct parts: a top rocker that bears the name of the club, a large logo or symbol representing the club and its colors often accompanied by the letters MC (motorcycle club), and a bottom rocker designating a territory controlled by that club (usually a city or a state). Only "full-patched" club members are allowed to wear all three parts of the patch. Sometimes affiliates, prospects, or other "friends" of the club may be allowed to wear the club name and perhaps even the club logo.

5. In order to become a "recognized" motorcycle club an organization usually must appear before a "council" comprised of members from other "recognized" clubs (usually the

"big four" who give "permission" for the new club to wear their colors). Trouble often erupts if a "non-recognized" club wears colors, especially with a bottom rocker claiming "turf" in an area where a "recognized" club operates. Importantly, one-percenter clubs are not officially "recognized" by the American Motorcycle Association or any other mainstream motorcycle organization (see chapter 4).

6. The motorcyclist subculture also includes numerous blue-collar workers—plumbers, construction workers, truck drivers, and others—some of whom are best described as motorcycle enthusiasts. Although a relevant variable, these categories are not based on social class. Rather, they serve to make the distinction between riders committed to the biker lifestyle, whether affiliated with motorcycle clubs or not, and the much larger number of people who ride motorcycles for fun and recreation or perhaps to commute to and from work to save money on transportation costs.

## Chapter 2

1. In the course of riding, I have met motorcyclists from Australia, Canada, England, Wales, France, Germany, Italy, Poland, Guam, Jamaica, India, Russia, and several of the Slavic states. Since this book is about the motorcyclist subculture in the United States, descriptions and analyses are based on observations and interviews with American bikers and generalizations about the motorcyclist subculture only apply to the United States.

2. The Hawthorne effect was discovered when Western Electric conducted a series of experiments at its Hawthorne plant. Attempting to determine if quality of lighting influenced worker output, what they discovered was that simply observing workers influenced their output. Hence, every researcher must be aware that simply studying people's behavior may influence their behavior.

3. Following standard institutional protocol, approval for this research was obtained from the Institutional Review Board (IRB) at the university where I teach.

4. My wife is not a sociologist and has had no formal training in qualitative research methods but, over a period of approximately 30 years of helping me conduct participant observation and ethnographic interviews, has developed remarkable observational and interviewing skills. My daughter completed a minor in sociology and has completed coursework in both quantitative and qualitative research methods. She has over 10 years of experience in conducting ethnographic interviews, and is currently completing a master's degree in sociology.

5. The author is a member of several online message boards for motorcycle riders with access to post entries, respond to other posts, and conduct and/or participate in online polls with other members of those boards. Numerous other boards allow "guests" to access and read posts, but not respond, and the author visited many of them on several occasions. Where data from online polls or forum posts are used, they are duly noted.

## Chapter 3

1. Sociologists and anthropologists use the term *values* to refer to shared ideas about what is desirable within a particular culture or subculture.

2. Bikers and motorcyclists usually refer to cars as "cages" and automobile drivers as "cagers."

3. "Me and Bobby McGee" was written by Kris Kristofferson and Fred Foster and originally performed by Roger Miller in 1969. The version probably best known is that of Janis Joplin who topped the U.S. singles chart with the song in 1971.

4. Almost half of the motorcyclists (92) interviewed for this research indicated that they had named their motorcycle. Men most often used women's names, although some used macho sounding names like "the Beast," while women tended to use descriptive names such as "blue angel" or "white lightning," often linked to the color of the bike.

# Chapter 4

1. One study showed that for every 1 motorcycle death on a cruiser or touring bike there are 4 deaths on sporting/performance bikes (Insurance Institute for Highway Safety, 2009).

# Chapter 5

1. Some of the content of this chapter first appeared in Thompson, William E. 2012. "'Don't Call Me Biker Chick': Women Redefining Deviant Identity." *Deviant Behavior* 33 (1): 1–14.

2. Only 3 percent of motorcycle drivers killed in 2009 crashes were women, while 91 percent of passengers who died were women (Insurance Institute for Highway Safety, 2009).

3. Although women work in motorcycle dealerships processing sales agreements, titles, and arranging insurance, and perhaps in some regions of the country as sales people, I have personally only encountered one female motorcycle salesperson and she was the wife of the owner of a relatively small dealership.

4. This is not meant to imply that women do not ride Harley-Davidsons or large, powerful motorcycles. Although it is somewhat unusual, I have seen numerous women riding HD Road Kings and Electra Glides as well as other large cruisers and touring bikes.

5. Shortly after this response was posted, the poll was removed from the forum by the site administrator since profanity is forbidden. The poll had been up for over three days by this time, however, and most posted threads run their course within 2–3 days with those who are interested usually responding within the first 24 hours.

# Chapter 6

1. Vendors at rallies often capitalize on this stratification between those who ride their bikes and those who trailer them by selling patches or pins that declare, "I Rode Mine!" as well as patches, t-shirts and bumper stickers that read, "I Rode My Bike to a Trailer Rally," or "Nice Trailer, Pussy!"

2. Maneuvering a large, high-powered motorcycle is much more difficult at slow speeds than high speeds. Consequently, skill competitions often include sharp turns, temporary stops, and other difficult maneuvers where riders are not allowed to exceed certain speeds or put their feet on the ground. At one rally, I witnessed a two-up obstacle course where blindfolded riders were not allowed to exceed 15 miles per hour as they maneuvered between traffic cones while being verbally guided by their passenger. Several bikes and riders ended up on the ground, but participants and the audience seemed to enjoy the competition. A $500, $300, and $100 for the first three finishers did not seem to dampen the enthusiasm any.

3. Over the years, I have learned to be very skeptical of crowd estimates at motorcycle rallies. Most of the events are held over several days and although certain events (such as rides, contests, poker runs, and concerts) may require registration or ticket purchase, most are open to anybody and everybody with no accurate way of determining exactly how many people are in attendance. In general, both rally sponsors and the media tend to inflate the numbers.

4. Riders interviewed in this study came from almost all of the lower 48 states (there were none from Alaska or Hawaii, and very few from the New England states). There were two from Canada, and one from Australia. The majority of them came from the South and Southwest with 101 (45.1 percent) coming from five states: Texas, Oklahoma, Arkansas, Louisiana, and Missouri.

5. Despite the fact that parking spaces at rallies, especially on the "main drag," are rare and highly valued, I am almost always amazed at the civility and courtesy that riders usually show in leaving and entering parking spaces. If a rider is clearly waiting on a space to be vacated, other riders lined up behind him/her usually wait patiently and do not honk or otherwise demonstrate impatience or anger. When pulling in and out of what are sometimes

very tight spaces, riders are very careful not to touch or bump another bike or even park too close to another motorcycle if it might infringe upon another rider's or motorcycle's "personal space."

6. There are a number of famous/infamous biker bars in and around Sturgis, but one, The Full Throttle Saloon, has risen to almost cult-like status after being featured in a reality television series. Subsequently, attendees at the rally make a point to visit the saloon and pose for pictures with the owner, his girlfriend, and other employees who enjoy celebrity-like status as a result of the TV series.

## Chapter 7

1. The *Great Escape* is not necessarily known as a "motorcycle movie," but Steve McQueen's (a motorcycle enthusiast in real life) dash for freedom from a German POW camp on a motorcycle is probably the most famous and most remembered scene in the movie.

2. Several popular expressions abound in the West and especially in Texas, used by "genuine" or "old-time" cowboys to describe "new cowboys" who manipulate all the appropriate symbols but are seen by "real" cowboys as not being legitimate. This is akin to terms used by urban gang members to describe those on the fringes of the gang as "wannabes" or "posers." A popular patch among bikers with the words "15,000 dollars and 15,000 miles doesn't make you a biker" expresses the same sentiment.

## Chapter 8

1. Sagal won a Golden Globe Award in 2011 for her role in *Sons of Anarchy*.

## Chapter 9

1. In the first edition of our introductory sociology book, *Society in Focus*, cultural anthropologist Joseph Hickey and I coined the term *technomedia* to refer to newer and more personalized information technologies (e.g., personal computers, CD-ROMs, fax machines, videogames, handheld databanks, cell phones, the Internet, fiber-optic communications, and interactive television).

2. According to the U.S. Bureau of the Census, the median home value in 1960 was $11,900 and in 1970 was $17,000 (source: U.S. Census Bureau, Housing and Household Economic Statistics Division, last revised October 31, 2011).

3. Many of the so-called "foreign-made" motorcycles are actually manufactured in the United States and many of the parts for "American-made" bikes are manufactured or assembled in other countries.

4. The *American Heritage Dictionary* (2009: 857) defines "motorcycle" as "a vehicle with two wheels in tandem, propelled by an internal-combustion engine, and sometimes having a side car with a third wheel."

## Chapter 10

1. Once when pulling into a restaurant parking lot for lunch, I pulled up next to a parked car with the driver-side window down to ask directions. When the woman sitting at the wheel turned and saw me, a look of panic spread over her face and she quickly rolled up her window, started the car, and sped off.

# Bibliography

Adams, Carl. 2008. *The Essential Guide to Dual Sport Motorcycling: Everything You Need to Buy, Ride, and Enjoy the World's Most Versatile Motorcycles.* Conway, NH: Whitehorse Press.

Adler, Patricia A., and Peter Adler. 1987. *Membership Roles in Field Research.* Newbury Park, CA: Sage.

Alford, Steven E., and Suzanne Ferriss. 2007. *Motorcycle.* London: Reaktion Books.

*American Heritage Dictionary of the English Language.* 2009. Boston: Houghton Mifflin.

American Motorcyclists Association. 2011. *<www.ama-cycle.org/>*

Anderson-Facile, Doreen Mae. 2003. "Dueling Identities: The Christian Biker." Unpublished doctoral dissertation, University of California, Riverside.

ASA. 2001. *Code of Ethics.* Washington, DC: American Sociological Association.

Austin, D. Mark. 2009. "Ritual and Boundary Distinction in a Recreational Community: A Case Study of Motorcycle Rallies and Riders." *Qualitative Sociology Review* V (August): 70–93.

Austin, D. Mark, and Patricia Gagne. 2008. "Community in a Mobile Subculture: The World of the Touring Motorcyclist." *Studies in Symbolic Interaction* 30: 411–437.

Babbie, Earl. 2013. *The Practice of Social Research* (13th ed.). Florence, KY: Cengage Learning.

Babchak, Jim. 2010. "Motor Maids." *American Iron Magazine,* January: 24.

Barbieri, Jay. 2007. *Bikers Handbook: Becoming Part of the Motorcycle Culture.* Minneapolis: MBI Publishing.

Barger, Sonny. 2005. *Freedom: Credos from the Road.* New York: HarperCollins.

Barger, Sonny, Keith Zimmerman, and Kent Zimmerman. 2001. *Hell's Angel: The Life and Times of Sonny Barger and the Hell's Angels Motorcycle Gang.* New York: HarperCollins.

Barker, Thomas. 2007. *Biker Gangs and Organized Crime.* Albany: LexisNexis/Anderson.

Barnes, Mark. 2011. "Mental Motorcycling: Why Bad Is Good." *Motorcycle Consumer News* 42 (November): 27.

Becker, Ernest. 1997. *The Denial of Death.* New York: Free Press.

Berg, Bruce L. 2009. *Qualitative Research Methods for the Social Sciences* (7th ed.). Boston: Allyn & Bacon.

Berger, Peter. 1963. *Invitation to Sociology: A Humanistic Perspective.* New York: Anchor Books.

Berra, Yogi, and Dave Kaplan. 2008. *You Can Observe a Lot by Watching: What I've Learned About Teamwork from the Yankees and Life.* Hoboken, NJ: Wiley.

Blumer, Herbert. 1969. *Symbolic Interactionism: Perspective and Method*. Englewood
Cliffs, NJ: Prentice-Hall.
Boslaugh, Sarah. 2006. "Getting Past the Stereotypes: Women and Motorcycles in Recent
Lesbian Novels." *International Journal of Motorcycle Studies* (March): 1–7.
Box, Terry. 2007. "Biker Chic." *Dallas Morning News*, June 24: 1D; 6D.
Bridges, A. 2006. "Study: Body Art Going Mainstream." *Dallas Morning News*, June 11:
12A.
Brown, Roland. 2002. *Classic Motorcycles: The Complete Book of Motorcycles and Their
Riders*. London: Anness Publishing.
Bryant, Clifton D. 1990. *Deviant Behavior: Readings in the Sociology of Norm Violations*.
New York: Hemisphere Publishing.
Burton, Hal. 1954. "Most Unpopular Men on the Road." *Saturday Evening Post* (25 Sep-
tember): 33.
Campbell, Richard, Christopher R. Martin, and Bettina G. Fabos. 2009. *Media and Cul-
ture: An Introduction to Mass Communication* (7th ed.). New York: St. Martin's Press.
Chrome Divas. 2010. <*www.chromedivas.com*>
Cockerham, William C. 2006. *Society of Risk-Takers: Living Life on the Edge*. New York:
Worth.
Coffey, Mary K., and Jeremy S. Packer. "The Art of Motorcycle (Image) Maintenance."
*International Journal of Motorcycle Studies* 3 (July): 1–21 (online).
Colson, John. 2005. "From Black Rats to Rolex Riders." *The Aspen Times*, Sunday, July
17.
Diamond, Jed. 1998. *Male Menopause* (2nd ed). Naperville, IL: Sourcebooks.
_____. 2010. *Mr. Mean: Saving Your Relationship from the Irritable Male Syndrome*.
Reston, VA: Vox.
Durkheim, Emile. [1915] 1965. *The Elementary Forms of Religious Life*. New York: Free
Press.
Dykes on Bikes. 2010. <*http://www.dykesonbikes.org*>
Eitzen, D. Stanley, and George H. Sage. 2011. *Sociology of North American Sport* (9th
ed.). Boulder, CO: Paradigm.
FTS. 2011. *Full-Throttle Saloon*. <*http://www.fullthrottlesaloon.com/*>
Goffman, Erving. 1959. *The Presentation of Self in Everyday Life*. Garden City, NY:
Anchor/Doubleday.
_____. 1963. *Stigma: Notes on the Management of Spoiled Identity*. Englewood Cliffs, NJ:
Prentice-Hall.
_____. 1967. *Behavior in Public Places: Notes on the Social Organization of Gatherings*.
New York: Free Press.
Goode, Erich, and D. Angus Vail (eds.). 2008. *Extreme Deviance*. Los Angeles: Pine Forge
Press.
Gramling, Robert, and Craig Forsyth. 1987. "Exploiting Stigma." *Sociological Forum* 2:
401–415.
Guisto, Betsy. 1997. "Mi Vida Loca: An Insider Ethnography of Outlaw Bikers in the
Houston Area." Unpublished Ph.D. dissertation, University of Houston.
Hammersley, Martyn. 2004. "Teaching Qualitative Method: Craft, Profession or Brico-
lage?" In Clive Seale, Giampietro Gobo, Jaber F. Gubrium and David Silverman
(eds.), *Qualitative Research Practice*, pp. 549–560. London: Sage.
Harman, Lesley D. 1990. "Acceptable Deviance as Social Control: The Cases of Fashion
and Slang." In Clifton D. Bryant, *Deviant Behavior: Readings in the Sociology of Norm
Violations*, pp. 62–76. New York: Hemisphere Publishing.
Hathaway, Barry. 2011. "Cannonball!" *Cycle World* 50 (March): 42–48.
Hauffe, Thomas. 1998. *Design: A Concise History*. London: Lawrence King.

Hayes, Bill. 2010. *American Biker: The History, the Clubs, the Lifestyle, the Truth.* Birmingham, MI: Flash Productions.

Henshaw, Peter. 2006. *The Encyclopedia of the Motorcycle.* Edison, NJ: Chartwell Books.

Herman, Nancy J., and Charlene E. Miall. 1990. "The Positive Consequences of Stigma: Two Case Studies in Mental and Physical Disability." *Qualitative Sociology* 13 (3): 251–269.

Hopper, Columbus B., and Johnny Moore. 1990. "Women in Outlaw Motorcycle Gangs." *Journal of Contemporary Ethnography* 18 (4): 363–387.

Hughes, Everett C., and Helen Hughes MacGill. 1952. *Where People Meet: Racial and Ethnic Frontiers.* Glencoe, IL: Free Press.

Hurst, Charles E. 2010. *Social Inequality: Forms, Causes, and Consequences* (7th ed.). Boston: Pearson/Prentice-Hall.

IBA. 2010. <*http://www.ironbutt.com*>

Ilyasova, K. Alex. 2006. "Dykes on Bikes and the Regulation of Vulgarity." *International Journal of Motorcycle Studies* (November): 1–10.

Insurance Institute for Highway Safety. 2009. "Research: Motorcycles." <*http://www.iihs.org/research/qanda/motorcycles.html*>

Jacobsen, Jeff. 2011. "Letter to the Editor." *Motorcycle Consumer News* 42 (February): 4.

Katz, Jack. 1996. *Seductions of Crime: Moral and Sensual Attractions of Doing Evil* (3rd ed). New York: Basic Books.

Kerr, Glynn. 2011. "Uniforms." *Motorcycle Consumer News* 42 (September): 38–39.

Knol. 2010. *The U.S. Motorcycle Market.* <*http://knol.google.com/k/the-u-s-motorcycle-market#*>

Kresnak, Bill. 2008. *Motorcycling for Dummies.* Indianapolis: Wiley.

Kushner, Harold S. 2009. *Conquering Fear: Living Boldly in an Uncertain World.* New York: Anchor Books.

Laurendau, Jason, and E.G. Van Brunschot. 2006. "Policing the Edge: Risk and Social Control in Skydiving." *Deviant Behavior* 27 (March-April): 173–201.

Lemert, Edwin M. 1951. *Social Pathology: A Systematic Approach to the Theory of Sociopathic Behavior.* New York: McGraw-Hill.

_____. 1967. *Human Deviance, Social Problems and Social Control.* Englewood Cliffs, NJ: Prentice-Hall.

Lieback, Ron. 2010. "Reality TV: 'American Chopper' Returns." *Ultimate Motorcycling.* April 19. <*http://www.ultimatemotorcycling.com/Reality_TV_Show_American_Chopper_Returns*>

Ling, Stephen. 2005. *Edgework: The Sociology of Risk-Taking.* New York: Routledge Taylor and Francis.

Linton, Ralph. 1936. *The Study of Man.* New York: Appleton-Century-Crofts.

Madson, Bart. 2011. "Motorcycle Sales Down 15.8% in 2010." January 20. <*http://www.motorcycle-usa.com*>

Martin, Diane M., John W. Schouten, and James H. McAlexander. 2006. "Claiming the Throttle: Multiple Femininities in a Hyper-Masculine Subculture." *Consumption, Markets and Culture* 9 (September): 171–205.

Mead, George Herbert. 1934. *Mind, Self, and Society.* Chicago: University of Chicago Press.

Miller, Walter B. 1958. "Lower Class Culture as a Generating Milieu for Gang Delinquency." *Journal of Social Issues* 14: 5–19.

Montgomery, Randal. 1976. "The Outlaw Motorcycle Subculture I." *Canadian Journal of Criminology* 18: 332–342.

_____. 1977. "The Outlaw Motorcycle Subculture II." *Canadian Journal of Criminology* 19: 356–361.

Motorcycle Industry Council. 2007. "Motorcycle and Scooter Sales Climb for 14th Consecutive Year." February 16. Media release, Irvine, CA.
_____. 2009. *2008 Statistical Annual*. Motorcycle Industry Council, Irvine, CA.
Motor Maids. <*http://www.motormaids.org*>
MRF. 2010. <*http://www.MRF.org*>
MSF. 2010. <*http://www.MSF-usa.org*>
Natalier, Kristin. 2001. "Motorcyclists' Interpretations of Risk and Hazard." *Journal of Sociology* 37 (March): 65–80.
National Safety Council. 2007. "Baby Boomers Drive Motorcycle Sales." *Traffic Safety* 7 (August): 1.
Neurendorf. Kimberly A. 2002. *The Content Analysis Guidebook*. Thousand Oaks, CA: Sage.
Nichols, Dave. 2011. "Get Your Motor Running." *AARP, the Magazine* 54 (July/August): 53–58.
Noyce, Wilfrid. 1959. *The Springs of Adventure*. Bedford Heights, OH: World Publishing.
NTSA. 1995. *Traffic Safety Facts 1995*. U.S. Department of Transportation.
Packer, Jeremy, and Mary K. Coffey. 2004. "Hogging the Road: Cultural Governance and the Citizen Cyclist." *Cultural Studies* 18 (September): 641–674.
Patriot Guard. 2011. <*www.patriotguard.org/*>
People. 2010. "Exclusive: Sandra Bullock Has Filed for Divorce." April 28. <*http://www.people.com/people/package/article/0,,20364464_20364640,00.html*>
Perlman, Allison. 2007. "The Brief Ride of the Biker Movie." *International Journal of Motorcycle Studies* 3 (March): 1–22 (online).
Person, Suzanna. 1996. "'Rolex' Riders Discover the Joys of Biker Bliss." *Jacksonville Business Journal* (June 24).
Pierson, Melissa Holbrook. 1998a. *The Perfect Vehicle: What It is About Motorcycles*. New York: W.W. Norton.
_____. 1998b. "ID Biker." In *Motorcycle Mania: The Biker Book*, pp. 62–66. New York: The Solomon R. Guggenheim Foundation and Universe Press.
Pirsig, Robert M. 1974. *Zen and the Art of Motorcycle Maintenance: An Inquiry into Values*. New York: Bantam Books.
Preston, David. 2011. *Motorcycle Heart, Theory, and Practice* (Kindle Ed.). Amazon Digital Services.
Queen, William. 2007. *Under and Alone: The True Story of the Undercover Agent Who Infiltrated America's Most Violent Outlaw Motorcycle Gang*. New York: Ballantine Books.
Quinn, James F. 1987. "Sex Roles and Hedonism Among Members of 'Outlaw' Motorcycle Clubs." *Deviant Behavior* 8 (January): 47–63.
_____. 2001. "Angels, Bandidos, Outlaws, and Pagans: The Evolution of Organized Crime Among the Big Four 1% Motorcycle Clubs." *Deviant Behavior* 22 (July-August): 379–399.
_____, and D. Shane Koch. 2003. "The Nature of Criminality Within One-Percent Motorcycle Clubs." *Deviant Behavior* 24 (May): 281–305.
Rau, Fred. 2007. "Motorcycle Advertising Part One: Wildly Successful Ad Campaign of the Sixties." *Motorcycle.com*, June 11.
_____. 2008. "Motorcycle Advertising Part Two: The Best and Worst Bike Ads." *Motorcycle.com*, February 8.
_____. 2010a. "Bikers and Motorcyclists." *Motorcycle Consumer News* 41 (March): 47.
_____. 2010b. "What Is a Motorcycle?" *Motorcycle Consumer News* 41 (December): 47.
_____. 2011. "Motorcycle Snobbery." *Motorcycle Consumer News* 42 (February): 47.

Rooney, Frank. 1951. "The Cyclists' Raid." *Harper's Magazine*, January: 34–44.

Roster, Catherine A. 2007. "'Girl Power' and Participation in Macho Recreation: The Case of Female Harley Riders." *Leisure Sciences* 29: 443–461.

R.O.T. Rally. 2011. <*http://www.rotbikeweekrally.com/*>

St. Clair, Charlie, and Jennifer Anderson. 2008. *Images of America: Laconia Motorcycle Week*. Charleston, SC: Arcadia.

Saladini, Albert, and Pascal Szymezak. 1997. *Harley-Davidson: History, Meetings, New Models, Custom Bikes*. New York: Barnes and Noble.

Sato, Ikuyu. 1998. *Kamikaze Biker: Parody and Anomy in Affluent Japan*. Chicago: University of Chicago Press.

Schouten, John W., and James H. McAlexander. 1995. "Subcultures of Consumption: An Ethnography of the New Bikers." *Journal of Consumer Research* 22 (June): 43–61.

Schultheis, Emily. 2011. "Motorcycles the Ride of Choice for Some Republicans." *Politico*, July 19. <*http://www.politico.com/news/stories/0711/59395.html*>

Schur, Edwin. 1971. *Labeling Deviant Behavior*. New York: HarperCollins.

Semack, Greg. "What Happened to My Motorcycle Movie?" *International Journal of Motorcycle Studies* 1 (November): 1–2 (online).

Sheehy, Gail. 1976. *Passages: Predictable Crises of Adult Life*. New York: Bantam.

_____. 1993. *The Silent Passage: Menopause*. New York: Pocket Books.

Shibutani, Tamotsu. 1955. "Reference Groups as Perspectives." *American Journal of Sociology* 60: 562–569.

Simmons, J.L. 1969. *Deviants*. Berkeley, CA: The Glendessary Press.

Smith, Jordan. 2006. "The 'One-Percenters.'" *The Austin Chronicle*, May 19. <*austinchronicle.com*>

Spradley, James P. 1979. *The Ethnographic Interview*. New York: Holt, Rinehart and Winston.

_____. 1980. *Participant Observation*. New York: Holt, Rinehart and Winston.

Thomas, William I. 1931. *The Unadjusted Girl*. Boston: Little, Brown.

Thompson, Hunter S. 1967. *Hell's Angels: A Strange and Terrible Saga*. New York: Random House.

Thompson, Steven L. 2008. *Bodies in Motion: Evolution and Experience in Motorcycling*. Duluth: Aero Design and Mfg.

Thompson, William E. 2009. "Pseudo-deviance and the 'New Biker' Subculture: Hogs, Blogs, Leathers, and Lattes." *Deviant Behavior* 30 (January): 89–114.

_____. 2012. "'Don't Call Me Biker Chick': Women Redefining Deviant Identity." *Deviant Behavior* 33 (1): 1–14.

_____, and Jackie L. Harred. 1992. "Topless Dancers: Managing Stigma in a Deviant Occupation." *Deviant Behavior* 13 (3): 291–311.

_____, Jack L. Harred, and Barbara E. Burks. 2003. "Managing Stigma of Topless Dancing: A Decade Later." *Deviant Behavior* 24: 551–570.

_____, and Jack E. Bynum. 2010. *Juvenile Delinquency: A Sociological Approach* (8th ed.). Boston: Allyn and Bacon.

_____, and Joseph V. Hickey. 2011. *Society in Focus: An Introduction to Sociology* (7th ed.). Boston: Allyn & Bacon.

Veno, Arthur, and Edward Winterhalder. 2009. *Biker Chicks: The Magnetic Attraction of Women to Bad Boys and Motorbikes*. Sydney: Allen & Unwen.

Walker, Carson. 2006. "Hells Angels Bikers Indicted." *Rapid City Journal*, August 9: 1A.

Wasef, Basem. 2008. "John McCain to Appear at Sturgis Rally." *About.com, Motorcycles*. August 4. <*http://motorcycles.about.com/b/2008/08/04/john-mccain-to-appear-at-sturgis-rally.htm*>

_____. 2011. "Are Motorcycles Merely Props for Politicians?" *About.com, Motorcycles.* August 4 <*http://motorcycles.about.com/b/2011/08/04/are-motorcycles-merely-props-for-politicians.htm*>

Watson, J. Mark. 1980. "Outlaw Motorcyclists: An Outgrowth of Lower Class Cultural Concerns." *Deviant Behavior* 2: 71–76.

Webb, Eugene J., Donald T. Campbell, Richard D. Schwartz, and Lee Sechrest. 1966. *Unobtrusive Measures: Nonreactive Research in the Social Sciences.* Chicago: Rand McNally.

Willett, Julie. 2009. "Behaving Like Brando: Transgressing Race and Gender in *The Wild One.*" *International Journal of Motorcycle Studies* 5 (Spring): 1–8.

Williams, Lena. 1998. "Do Real Women Ride Motorcycles? 440,000 Say Yes." *New York Times*, May 11: C1.

Woodard, Ryan. 2009. "Law Officer Shot Hell's Angels Member in Sturgis, Police Say." *Rapid City Journal*, August 26: 1A.

Women on Wheels. 2010. <*http://womenonwheels.org*>

Womenriders. 2010. <*http://motorcycles.about.com/cs/womenriders*>

# Index

Numbers in **_bold italics_** indicate pages with photographs.